The Architect in Practice

Also by Arthur J. Willis

AN EXAMPLE IN QUANTITY SURVEYING
GENEALOGY FOR BEGINNERS
INTRODUCING GENEALOGY

———————

By Arthur J. Willis and Christopher J. Willis

SPECIFICATION WRITING FOR ARCHITECTS AND SURVEYORS
ELEMENTS OF QUANTITY SURVEYING
MORE ADVANCED QUANTITY SURVEYING
PRACTICE AND PROCEDURE FOR THE QUANTITY SURVEYOR

The

ARCHITECT
IN
PRACTICE

by

ARTHUR J. WILLIS, F.R.I.C.S., HON.F.I.Q.S.

and

W. N. B. GEORGE, B.Arch., A.R.I.B.A., A.M.T.P.I.

in collaboration with
CHRISTOPHER J. WILLIS, F.R.I.C.S.

FOURTH EDITION
Revised

LONDON
CROSBY LOCKWOOD & SON, LTD.
26 OLD BROMPTON ROAD, S.W.7

© 4th edition Arthur J. Willis
and W. N. B. George, 1970
First published 1952
Second edition 1956
Third edition 1964
Fourth edition March 1970
SBN 258 96507 X

Printed in Great Britain by Richard Clay (The Chaucer Press), Ltd.
Bungay, Suffolk

THE INSPIRATION

From a pseudonymous letter of a quantity surveyor to *The Builder*, 9th March, 1951 :

" I have a great admiration for an architect who does his job well, because he has one of the most difficult jobs in the world. He must be an artist, but at the same time in his administration of a building contract be a business man, and in interpreting it even something of a lawyer."

THE DEDICATION

TO THE ARCHITECTURAL PROFESSION

in the hope that the book may encourage that co-operation of which its joint authorship is a symbol.

By different methods different men excel ;
But where is he who can do all things well ?
CHARLES CHURCHILL

PREFACE

THE need for a new edition has given the opportunity for making substantial revisions and additions. There have been changes in the controls to which we have to submit, such as the introduction of national Building Regulations in place of local bye-laws, the Town and Country Planning Act of 1968 and the Land Commission Act of 1967. A Building Control Act came and has been suspended for the present. The War Damage Commission has disappeared and changes in the names of Government Departments continue!

A major change in drawing practice comes with the change over to the metric system. The introduction of metric components is not far off, but after many months of discussion there seems to be no final answer to what one would think a minor point, how the decimal point shall be expressed. At first we understood that the familiar mid-line decimal point was " out " and that the alternatives were a full stop on the line or a comma. The full stop seemed to be chiefly favoured, but the comma was retained by some. Now comes B.S. 1192 *Building Drawing Practice (Metric Units)*, which reverts to the mid-line decimal point. A stop on the line is, however, admissible when using a typewriter. Perhaps entry into the Common Market will eventually provide another solution!

A. J. W.
W. N. B. G.

ACKNOWLEDGMENTS

WE value very much the help of Mr. Robert Cumming, barrister-at-law, on the two law chapters, and of Mr. R. J. Ash, Dip. Arch., A.R.I.B.A., who has contributed usefully to the Public Service chapter.

We are very grateful to the Royal Institute of British Architects and Royal Institution of Chartered Surveyors for permission to reproduce their standard forms in Appendix I, also to the National Joint Consultative Council of Architects, Quantity Surveyors and Builders, for permission to reproduce tender documents from the *Code of Procedure for Selective Tendering* in the same Appendix, as well as the Table of Consultative Machinery in the back pocket.

PREFACE TO THE FIRST EDITION

(With apologies to the shade of Plato and to his still living *Republic*)

Socrates : But the architects in this state of ours, shall we call them artists, or are they rather men of business ?

Glaucon : Artists undoubtedly they must be.

Socrates : And must they not also be efficient in business ?

Glaucon : Do you mean in the management of their own affairs or those of others ?

Socrates : In both, I think, but especially in those of others.

Glaucon : Why so ? The sculptor, the painter or the craftsmen in gold and silver : are they not artists ?

Socrates : Of course.

Glaucon : But they are only concerned to manage their own affairs. They buy for themselves their stone or paint or other materials, and arrange their work as they will. They may, of course, employ and pay workmen to help them, but if the workman makes mistakes only the artist suffers.

Socrates : I agree. But is there not this difference in the case of architects ? The sculptor and painter and others we have mentioned must themselves with their own hands fashion the works of art to which they give their names. The architect, even with his assistants, cannot be expected to work and lay all the stones of the buildings himself. If so, the Parthenon would indeed be still no higher than your shoulder. A contractor must be employed who will in turn employ gangs of workmen.

Glaucon : What then will be the architect's duties ?

Socrates : He will be employed by the man who wants to erect a building to prepare a design and to supervise the erection of the building. He will see that the contractor carries out his work properly, and say what payments are due to him.

Glaucon : I am beginning to see now why the architect must be skilled in managing the affairs of others. They are certainly very important duties we have given him, and particularly difficult, I think, for an artist.

Socrates : Shall we then see if we can help him in this business in which he has engaged himself? We shall have to enquire what rules the Guardians of our state may have laid down about buildings, and how that justice can be applied which we have been discussing and trying to define.

Glaucon : But shall we not need a lawyer to help us in this? For we were just saying that every man in our state must do that for which he is best fitted, and not try to undertake the work of others.

Socrates : Yes, we shall. I know the men who will certainly help us.* Then, too, we shall have to study the relations of architect and builder to their employer and to each other. We shall have to think of all the architect has to do apart from his designing, the difficulties he may meet, and how he can do this work best.

Glaucon : We seem to have set ourselves a formidable task.

Socrates : Let us, anyhow, try our best, and I think we shall not fail.

* *Mr. D. Grant, D.S.O., and Mr. D. Kemp, barristers-at-law, to whom our most grateful thanks for their invaluable help on Chapters XVI and XVII.*

CONTENTS

ABBREVIATIONS USED

R.I.B.A.	Royal Institute of British Architects
R.I.C.S.	Royal Institution of Chartered Surveyors
N.F.B.T.E.	National Federation of Building Trades Employers
M.P.B. & W.	Ministry of Public Building and Works
H.M.S.O.	Her Majesty's Stationery Office
B.S.I.	British Standards Institution
A.R.C.U.K.	Architects' Registration Council of the United Kingdom
N.J.C.C.	National Joint Consultative Committee of Architects, Quantity Surveyors and Builders
G.L.C.	Greater London Council

It should be emphasised that the reader must have regard to the date of publication, the last date given on the back of the title page. He must remember, too, that probably some three months elapsed between passing of final proof and publication. Every effort will be made to keep the book up to date, by supplements if necessary.

INTRODUCTION

ABILITY to design and skill in draughtsmanship will not alone make an architect. The purpose of this book is to present to architectural students, and perhaps the less experienced practitioners, some indication of the practice and procedure with which they must be acquainted if they are to follow their profession with success. They must find clients to employ them, they must be able to manage an office and be responsible for a good deal of administrative work in connection with building contracts, and they must know something of finance, law, the general structure of the Building Industry and the organisation and requirements of those authorities who exercise so much control over their day-to-day work. Let the reader therefore leave his drawing-table, forget his tee-square, his set-square and scales, take off his smock and settle down to his desk (or arm-chair) to study an aspect of his work which he may find requires some self-discipline but is nevertheless essential to make him an efficient architect.

The chapters have been arranged in the sequence which the progress of a building contract makes natural. After opening with the architect's relations with his client, they deal with the various preliminary stages of work leading up to the building contract, the progress and winding up of the contract, and conclude with such general matters as law, office organisation, &c. In appendices are given typical forms, letters, &c., which are, of course, only suggestions, and a list of some books relative to the subject which the architect may find useful.

The architect's work is here looked at mainly from the angle of the private practitioner dealing with the R.I.B.A. form of contract, though a chapter is included on the particular aspect of the architect in public service and some notes on the Government form of contract appear in the chapter on building contracts. As, in present circumstances, the architect in private practice is quite often commissioned to act for public authorities, he must be able to adapt himself to the differing conditions which this type of work involves.

Substantial parts of certain chapters, which are of equal

application both to architects and quantity surveyors, have been taken with slight adaptation from *Practice and Procedure for the Quantity Surveyor* by Arthur J. Willis, one of the joint authors of this book. There seemed no object in re-writing or paraphrasing something already expressed in what the author felt was the best form. The chapters concerned are those entitled " Cost Control ", " Finance ", " Partnership ", " The Structure of the Building Industry ", as well as parts of the two chapters on Law and some other extracts.

There is some overlapping in the subject-matter of chapters, but such repetition as has occurred has been purposely left to ensure completeness in the subject being dealt with.

There is a certain amount of technical knowledge which the student must acquire apart from Design and Building Construction. Such subjects as Specifications, Town Planning, Arbitrations, Dilapidations and Contracts are all worthy of individual study, and the student must not rely on a smattering of knowledge picked up in a text book on " Practice ". These subjects have, therefore, been treated mainly from the procedure angle and not with any idea of imparting detailed technical knowledge. Each has its own text books, and a list of some recommended appears in Appendix II.

In a book on practice there is necessarily a good deal of reference to rules, law, publications, &c. current at the time of its preparation. The reader will realise that these are periodically revised by the authorities responsible for them. Such references in the book should be looked on only as a guide and subject to verification.*

* See note on page 314.

THE ARCHITECT AND HIS CLIENT

The Architect.—Architecture is undoubtedly one of the more enjoyable professions. It offers a wealth of interest in a variety of fields which few other professions can match, and provides an emotional satisfaction which only the other arts can stimulate. It exacts a high price for this enjoyment, however, and in order to derive the fullest pleasure from it, the architect must devote himself completely to its study and practice. The more proficient he can become and the greater the mastery that he can acquire the more complete will be his enjoyment. At the same time he has a very real responsibility towards his fellow men, for the buildings and environments which he creates may well have a profound effect on their lives and those of their children.

As the name implies,* the architect should be the master-builder—the leader of the team which constitutes the Building Industry. He is qualified to design and supervise the erection of buildings, and must possess both theoretical and practical knowledge. His work is a science as well as an art, for he must produce a structure as well as create form, and must combine æsthetic effect with practical considerations. He must visualise the interior as well as the exterior of the building, and must ensure that the accommodation is properly related to the requirements of owners or occupiers, and that the form and construction are appropriate to the function of the building and its setting.

Like the playwright, he is dependent on other people to interpret his designs, and his supervision during the erection of a building is as important to its ultimate success as are the directions given by the producer and stage manager for a play.

He must have a good and practical knowledge of the building and allied trades, and must have at least a working knowledge of the more specialised aspects of building, such as the mechanical and electrical engineering services, &c. Finally, he must always endeavour to be creative, and cannot ever afford to rest on his laurels!

---

* The word " architect " is derived from the Greek root " *arch-* " meaning " chief " and the word " *tekton* " meaning " carpenter " or " builder ".

Qualifications.—Under the Architects' Registration Acts 1931–38 every person who carries on a business under any name, style or title containing the word "architect", must be registered. Failure to register may result in a fine, on summary conviction, of a sum not exceeding £50, and a further fine not exceeding £10 for every day on which the offence continues after conviction.

The Architects' Registration Council of the United Kingdom controls the register of architects, and qualification for registration may be in any of the following ways :—

1. By being a member of the Royal Academy or the Royal Scottish Academy.
2. By passing an examination in architecture which is for the time being recognised by the Council.
3. By possessing such other qualification as may be prescribed by the Council in Regulations approved by the Privy Council.

The architectural bodies represented on the Council are the Royal Institute of British Architects, the Incorporated Association of Architects and Surveyors, the Faculty of Architects and Surveyors, the Architectural Association (London) and the Association of Building Technicians. There are also representatives of " unattached " architects.

A registered architect who is convicted of a criminal offence or who is guilty of disgraceful conduct in his practice as an architect may, after an inquiry by the Discipline Committee of the Council, have his name removed from the register. An annual report is published by the Council in which such cases are recorded.

The offices of the Council are at 78, Hallam Street, London, W.1, and a copy of the Council's Regulations may be obtained on application to the Registrar.

Amongst the examinations which are recognised by the Architects' Registration Council as a qualification for registration, are the Final and Special Final Examinations of the Royal Institute of British Architects and the Final Examinations at certain Schools of Architecture at which the Degree of Bachelor of Architecture or the Diploma in Architecture is awarded.

Professional Activities.—The architect must adhere to a strict Code of Professional Conduct,* which is designed to uphold the dignity and integrity of the profession. It precludes an architect from touting or advertising for work, prohibits him from assuming or accepting any position in which his interest may be in conflict with his professional duty, limits his activities as a company director to such businesses as have no direct connection with the Building Industry and governs the remuneration which he may receive for his professional services. It should be noted that, under the R.I.B.A. Code of Professional Conduct, an architect's professional affixes may not appear on the notepaper of any Company of which he is a director.

An architect must not attempt to supplant another architect nor compete with him by reducing his fee or offering any other inducement to the client, and if he is approached to proceed with any work on which another architect had previously been employed, he must notify the fact to that architect.

He may only participate in architectural competitions which comply with the regulations of his Institute governing the conduct of such competitions, and must himself comply with such regulations in so far as they relate to the limitations placed on architects acting as assessors.

He must apply the conditions of contract with absolute fairness between the employer and contractor.

The remuneration which an architect is entitled to receive for his services is dealt with in Chapters 15 and 16† but it is relevant to mention here that he is debarred from accepting any payment or discount other than his professional fee or salary.

The Client.—The architect must have a client before he can start practice. Unlike the painter, the author or the poet, he is not at liberty to choose his own subject. He may, of course, be his own client, as, for instance, when he designs his own house ; but otherwise he is dependent on a commission from somebody else. This applies whether the architect practises privately or is a salaried official, when his client will be the Council, Committee or Company which he serves.

The architect's client may sometimes be a personal friend or

---

* *Code of Professional Conduct :* A.R.C.U.K.
† Pages 159 and 166.

acquaintance, but more generally he is a complete stranger. His relations with his client are therefore of the utmost importance, as, not only must he attempt to embark on a process of design (which is a personal thing), but he must also interpret his client's wishes and provide him with the article that he wants.

He acts as his client's agent in spending sums of money which may be substantial, and upon his skill and efficiency may depend the amount of the bill which his client will eventually have to meet. It is essential, therefore, that client and architect should feel complete confidence in each other, particularly as the architect has also certain responsibilities towards the builder. The old adage that a good building requires a good client as well as a good architect remains perfectly true to-day.

Now, how does the client choose his architect and how does the architect meet his client, if he is not allowed to advertise? It may be in one of several ways. Possibly the client has seen a building or photographs of a building which he likes, and goes out of his way to find out the name of the architect. Possibly the architect is recommended by a mutual acquaintance. Perhaps he has specialised in a particular category of building and established a reputation in a particular field of design. Or he may meet his future client through social contacts. And, finally, it may be through success in an open competition for a particular building or project.

Taking Instructions from the Client.—The legal implications of an architect's appointment are dealt with in Chapter 16,* so, assuming that his appointment has been confirmed, let us pass on to the next stage—that of " taking instructions ".

The client may know in detail what he wants and may have drawn up a specific programme for a particular site before approaching the architect. Alternatively, he may require the architect to advise him on the choice of a site and to assist him in the preparation of a schedule of accommodation. In either case the architect must use his judgment and experience in advising his client, and must not hesitate to let him know if he thinks that the site chosen is unsuitable or that the accommodation suggested is either inadequate or extravagant.

In giving his advice the architect must not be dogmatic, nor

* Page 162.

must he presume to make decisions for his client—rather must he analyse the " pros " and " cons " and put them to his client clearly, so that he can make his own decisions, fully appreciating their implications.

The early stages in drawing up the programme are of the utmost importance, but the architect must be careful not to go into too much detail too soon, and must avoid the danger of allowing any preconceived ideas to restrict the natural development of the scheme. It is seldom that a satisfactory solution can be found without the fullest study and without a systematic process of evolution.

It is the responsibility of the architect to take his client along with him in the development of the design and to keep him informed at each stage of its evolution. This can probably best be done by personal discussion in the first instance and by confirmation in writing later. It will be found to be mutually advantageous to keep a written record of all stages of the development of the scheme, and to retain the earliest sketch-plans— even though they only be scribbles—in some sort of chronological order.

Finance.—In the case of public authorities finance for building work will be provided by a vote of the controlling authority, who in their turn may have from Government sources an allocation of money or authority to raise a loan to cover a programme of such work. A Government Department will in its turn have a bulk allocation approved by the Treasury, from which it can make its grants or give authority for loan. It will be important throughout the contract to watch that the amount authorised is not exceeded and, if there is a prospect of excess, for an application to be made for a supplementary vote to cover it.

A private client may consult his architect on the subject of financing building work. In this case it will probably be necessary for the architect to prepare a " feasibility study " in order to assess the amount of accommodation which can be provided and to obtain some indication of the return on capital which may be received, either in the way of rent or by appreciation in the value of the developed site. The assessment of rent and the valuation of the developed site are both in the realms of specialist experience, and the architect, without the necessary expertise himself, will be well advised to consult an estate agent or valuer in this connection.

The finance may be raised by the client by obtaining a mortgage from a Building Society, borrowing from a Bank, Insurance Company or other financing organisation, or he may float a company for some special enterprise. This, again, requires specialist advice which is outside the scope of this book.

It must be remembered that maintenance and running costs have an important bearing when considering the amount of first cost. Not only must buildings be kept in repair and good decorative condition but the running cost of mechanical installations may vary considerably according to the type adopted. It may be worth meeting a higher initial cost to save expensive periodical outlay. A simple example is the use of aluminium or plastic rainwater goods in housing, which, though they may cost a little more, save constant repainting. This subject should be considered in broad terms when discussing first cost.

The Programme.—It is important to draw up a full and clear programme with the client before beginning a serious study of the proposed building. This will save time in the end, and will be more economical for both the architect and the client and help to avoid troublesome misunderstandings.

It will usually be necessary to obtain all the information required by discussion and methodical questioning, but, to quote Aristotle, " to succeed, you must first ask the right questions ". The client should be persuaded to devote time and care to this stage of the scheme. He should be asked to provide a " functional brief ", describing the way in which the building is to operate. This form of brief is essential for the more technical categories of building, where the architect must know not only the functions of each department and room but also a good deal about the organisation and administration.

Each programme will demand special study and will suggest particular points for discussion, but the following items will apply fairly generally, and are worth listing as a basis for such discussions :—

1. THE SITE

(a) Whether it has already been acquired, or whether further advice is to be given after inspection by the architect ;

(b) whether any restrictions or easements exist, or whether any conditions are attached to the freehold or leasehold (examination of deeds may be advisable);

(c) the availability of public services, or whether these will have to be provided privately;

(d) whether the site is complete, or will be extended at some future date : its present area and the area of the future acquisition.

2. ACCOMMODATION

(a) Areas and relation of principal rooms or units ;
(b) heights of rooms ;
(c) natural or artificial lighting and ventilation ;
(d) internal and external finishings ;
(e) population of building and numbers of either sex to be accommodated ;
(f) whether any sections of the building are to be used separately or at different times.

3. BUILDING PROGRAMME

(a) Date of completion ;
(b) whether the project has been discussed with the appropriate Sponsoring Authority ;
(c) whether the building is to be erected in one operation or by stages ;
(d) possible future extensions.

4. MECHANICAL AND ELECTRICAL ENGINEERING SERVICES

(a) Type of heating and fuel to be used : exposed or concealed form of heating ;
(b) lifts ;
(c) refrigeration ;
(d) air conditioning ;
(e) temperature and quantity of hot water ;
(f) type of lighting ;
(g) electric power requirements ;
(h) refuse disposal ;
(i) peak periods for services, and whether the building is to be in use by night ;
(j) any special provisions.

5. FINANCE

(a) Amount of money available ;
(b) whether the building is a speculation or is for a specific use ;
(c) employment of quantity surveyor, consultants and clerk of works ;
(d) professional fees.

Stages in Development of the Scheme.—The early stages in the development of the scheme are rather like the preparation of a plum pudding—the ingredients are collected, weighed and mixed together, and only after a period of cooking will the finished product emerge! The ingredients which the architect will handle are the site, the nature of the proposed building, the schedule of accommodation required and the cost. Each item must be carefully analysed and will have a major influence on the finished product, and the test of the architect's ability is the way in which he assimilates all these factors into the finished design.

During the process of analysis and synthesis many sketches may be prepared and rejected, until the basic scheme is evolved. The sketch-plans are then put into final form and presented to the client for approval, together with an approximate estimate of cost, arrived at from the cube or floor area, as described in Chapter 4,* or, in the case of alterations to an existing building, by applying spot prices to the items of work involved.

When the client has approved the sketch scheme and the approximate estimate of cost, he will instruct the architect to invite tenders for the work. It is important that this instruction should be confirmed in writing, because it implies the preparation of working drawings and a specification, and in all probability the appointment of a quantity surveyor to prepare bills of quantities, which, of course, makes the client liable for the payment of additional fees.†

The appointment of the quantity surveyor is usually made on the recommendation of the architect, unless the client happens to have a particular choice of his own, and this appointment should be confirmed with the client.

Working drawings are normally prepared to a scale of 1:100 or 1:50 to 1:10‡, but typical details and certain complex sections, which would not otherwise be clear, are drawn to a larger scale. In addition, a series of full-size details will be required covering items of joinery such as windows, doors and staircases, and any other items which the architect wishes to have constructed in a particular way. Schedules of windows, doors, ironmongery, internal finishings, &c., will also have to be prepared.

For the more complex buildings, such as hospitals, where special services must be accurately arranged to serve their function, it may be necessary to prepare elevations of each wall of a room in addition to floor and ceiling plans. These are usually drawn to a scale of 1:50 and may incorporate a schedule

---

* Pages 23 and 25.   † See pages 75 and 164.   ‡ See page 223.

of services and finishes on each sheet, so that the information is complete for each room on the one drawing.*

It is usually advisable to set up the detailed drawings at the same time as the 1 : 100 or key drawings are being drafted, so as to ensure that dimensions and any awkward constructional problems are fully studied. Unless this is done, one is liable to overlook details which may prove troublesome and expensive to rectify during the erection of the building. The more details that can be studied and supplied before the bills of quantities are prepared, the less likelihood there will be of " extras " on the contract sum becoming necessary.

The specification is the architect's responsibility, and he must instruct the quantity surveyor as to what materials are to be used, the composition of mortars, plaster, &c., and describe the manner in which the work is to be carried out, so that each item in the bills of quantities can be measured and clearly defined. It is becoming a common practice now, however, for the architect to supply the quantity surveyor with an outline specification only in which the materials are described and also any details of construction which are not accepted common practice. If the specification is required as a separate document, the detailed writing up describing the sequence of the work is then left to the quantity surveyor, and is best done after the bills of quantities have been prepared (see Chapter 10).†

Concurrently with the preparation of the working drawings, it is necessary to obtain certain statutory consents for the work. These are described in detail in Chapters 5 and 6, but it should be remembered in passing that it is wise to obtain these consents at an early stage, so that any specific requirements may be incorporated in the drawings and bills of quantities before tenders are invited.

Once the bills of quantities are ready, competitive tenders can be invited, and here again it is important to follow certain accepted rules in sending out the tender documents (see Chapter 11). The essence of good tendering is keen competition, and it is very necessary that all tenderers should be able to tender on the same basis. It is therefore essential to supply the fullest information to the firms competing. It is advisable not to disclose the names of the firms tendering, although this may be difficult, due to the fact that the contractors will have to obtain

* See Appendix 1, page 305.   † Page 96.

certain prices from builders' merchants, and several similar enquiries reaching the same merchant at the same time obviously enable him to " put two and two together ". Moreover, Builders' Federations have their private information service. When the tenders are received, analysed and checked, the architect will submit a report to his client and will put forward his recommendation for acceptance of a particular tender. This is usually the lowest tender submitted, but may not necessarily be so, if there are good reasons for recommending a higher one.*

The Architect's Duties.—The architect's duties, briefly, consist of the design of the building, the preparation of working drawings and contract documents, the arranging of the contract, the supervision of the work whilst in progress, the certifying of interim payments and the examination of final accounts (including their checking if no quantity surveyor is appointed).

Whilst the architect is required to supply the fullest possible information to the contractor, he is not expected to give constant superintendence during the erection of the building. He is only required to give such periodical supervision as may be necessary to ensure that the works are being executed in general accordance with the contract. Should constant superintendence be required, a clerk of works must be employed.

The architect has authority to give orders on behalf of the client, provided that the contract sum is not materially altered, but he must always advise his client if any variations become necessary which will materially alter the scheme.

Although the architect is appointed by the client to look after his interests, he has a very real responsibility towards the building contractor, and must act quite impartially and fairly between the building owner and the contractor. This is of the utmost importance, and should be made quite clear to the client in the event of any dispute between the two parties to the contract. To maintain this impartiality will require tact and strength of character and will provide the greatest test of the architect's integrity. It is only by such integrity that he can do his duty to both client and builder—and at the same time retain the respect of both.

* See page 119.

2

ARCHITECTURAL COMPETITIONS

Opportunities of Competitions.—It has been mentioned in the previous chapter that one of the ways in which a young architect may secure a new client is by winning an architectural competition. Many an architect has started his practice in this way, and some have established a reputation through success in a large or important competition. In normal times there will be no lack of opportunity to enter for architectural competitions if an architect really wishes to do so, because one or more covering a variety of building types can quite often be seen advertised in the technical press.

Types of Competition.—Depending on the particular requirements of the promoters, a competition will normally conform to one of several types. Competitions for an actual building project may be held in either one or two stages. In a single-stage competition competitors are required to submit fairly complete small-scale drawings sufficient to describe their design, but in a two-stage competition they are required in the first stage to submit simple line drawings only, indicating the broad basis of the scheme. From these entries a limited number are selected for the second stage, in which small-scale drawings will be submitted similar to those required for a single-stage competition. A variant of the two-stage competition is when the second stage consists of the competitors selected from the open first stage together with a limited number of competitors specifically invited to submit schemes at the second stage. Persons invited to submit entries at the second stage must be named in the conditions.

Another type of competition is an " Ideas Competition " set (as the Regulations referred to below put it) "as an exercise to elucidate certain aspects of architectural and planning problems ".

Competitions may also either be " open " or " limited ". Open competitions are those which any eligible architect may enter. Ideas competitions and the first stage of two-stage competitions are usually open. Single-stage competitions, however, if not open, may be limited to selected competitors.   These may be invited to compete on the grounds of their established reputation in design, or the promoters may wish to restrict entry to the competition to members of a particular institute, society or group, or to architects who practise in a particular locality.   In certain cases the promoters may invite architects to submit applications to compete, and then draw up a short selected list from the applicants.

Unless a competition is limited, an advertisement will be inserted in the lay or technical press by the promoters giving brief particulars of the object of the competition, together with details as to where the conditions may be obtained, the deposit (if any) which will be required, the name of the assessor or assessors, the last date for questions, the last date for submitting designs and the premiums offered.   In two-stage competitions no premiums are awarded at the first stage, but all competitors selected to proceed to the second stage receive an honorarium.

Regulations.—As the wish of the promoters will be to obtain the best design for the particular purpose they have in mind, they will want to attract the widest possible field of entrants. To do this they will have to offer suitable premiums and conduct the competition on recognised lines.   The R.I.B.A. has drawn up comprehensive regulations to govern the promotion and conduct of architectural competitions,* and its members are not permitted to enter for any competition which is not drawn up substantially in conformity with these regulations.   In practice it is seldom that the conditions of a competition do not comply with them.

The principal requirements are as follows :—

1. The appointment of an assessor or assessors who shall be approved by the President of the R.I.B.A., and to whom all the designs shall be submitted for judging.
2. Each competitor must be prepared to satisfy the assessor that he is the bona-fide author of the design submitted, and must forward a signed declaration to that effect with his scheme.
3. The promoter, assessor or the associates or employees of

* *Regulations for the Promotion and Conduct of Competitions:* R.I.B.A. Revised 1968.

either are debarred from competing. This ban also applies to students of a school of architecture, if there is a sole assessor who is a member of the regular teaching staff.

4. The premiums as advertised shall be paid in accordance with the assessor's award, and the author of the design placed first shall be employed to carry out the work, unless the assessor shall be satisfied that there is some valid objection to this, in which case the author of the design placed second shall be employed.

5. If no instructions are given to the author of the selected design to proceed with the work within two years from the date of the award, he shall be paid for his design in accordance with a prescribed scale of fees. Further regulations cover the fees to be paid in the event of only one part of the work being proceeded with.

6. The selected architect, having been instructed to carry out the work, shall be paid a fee in accordance with the R.I.B.A. Scale of Charges, and the premium already paid shall merge in this fee. When a competition is limited to a small number of selected architects, *each* competitor will be paid a specific fee for his design.

7. No design which is submitted shall bear any motto or distinguishing mark, but shall be numbered by the assessor in the order of receipt. (Paradoxically, however, this rule is varied for R.I.B.A. prizes and studentships, where competitors are usually instructed to attach a pseudonym to their drawings.)

8. Where a deposit is required for supplying the instructions and conditions, it must be returned by the promoters on receipt of a bona-fide design, or if the applicant returns the instructions before a prescribed date.

9. Designs shall be excluded from the competition on certain prescribed grounds, which will be stated in the conditions.

10. All competitors must be notified of the assessor's award.

The conditions of the competition should set out quite clearly, not only the nature of the project, details of the site and the limit of cost where this is applicable, but also full particulars as to the number, scale and method of finishing the drawings. The object of this will be to secure a degree of uniformity in presentation which will be perfectly fair to all the competitors, and it is therefore important to comply absolutely with such instructions.

Competitors will be required to submit with their designs a report describing the scheme and materials to be used and including an estimate of cost based on cubic measurement or some other equally suitable calculation. The R.I.B.A. regulations allow the assessor to permit or require perspective or axonometric drawings in line form or block models or photographs of block models, or explanatory diagrams in competitors' reports. These will, however, be specifically limited in scope and permitted only where appropriate, since the preparation of elaborate drawings and presentation material should be avoided in the interests of fair competition.

Questions.—Every competitor will usually be allowed to submit " questions " in order to clarify any matters in the conditions which may seem obscure, and a limiting date will be specified for the receipt of such questions. The assessor is required to give a clear answer to each question, and it is usual to circulate a complete list of all questions and answers to all competitors. He may then embody them into the conditions of the competition.

Results.—The R.I.B.A. conditions require that all accepted entries, with their reports, and the assessor's award, shall be publicly exhibited for not less than six days. Notice of the time and place must be publicly advertised as well as being sent to all competitors.

All drawings, except the winner's must be returned, carriage paid, to all competitors within fourteen days of the close of the exhibition.

Advantages and Disadvantages.—The competition system is not perfect by any means, and, indeed, its results have frequently aroused considerable controversy, but it is at least one way of giving opportunities to young or unknown architects to obtain commissions and provide a variety of designs for the promoters to consider.

The obvious disadvantage is that it is difficult for assessors to take a completely objective view of the designs submitted, and they are bound to be influenced to a certain extent by personal preferences in design or style, but most people will agree that the advantages outweigh the disadvantages. It is undoubtedly discouraging for a competitor to feel quite genuinely that a winning design is inferior to his own, or that a particular condition has been given a different interpretation from his own, but every competitor will find that " doing " a competition is a most stimulating and exciting experience and well worth while.

The results, on the whole, too, have been satisfactory and have produced many very good buildings.

3

SITE SURVEYS

Zoning Requirements.—The site chosen for a building or group of buildings may have a considerable influence on its design, general form of construction, cost and future maintenance, and warrants very careful consideration. Broad restrictions in the choice of sites were imposed under the Town & Country Planning Act, 1947, by which every Local Planning Authority was required to prepare an Outline Development Plan by 1951, determining the future use of all land in its locality.* By this the location of the main categories of buildings, their density, the provision of open spaces and other uses of land (for market-gardening, agriculture, &c.) were broadly zoned to ensure the best possible future development of the locality in the public interest.

The first problem of the prospective developer is to investigate the possibility of obtaining a site within this broad zoning. The final selection, however, will depend not only on his own particular requirements but also on those of the Planning Authority. Once a suitable geographical location has been selected, it will be necessary to carry out a detailed survey of the site to determine its particular characteristics, and the importance of doing this thoroughly cannot be over-emphasised, as failure to investigate in detail may ultimately involve the owner in unexpected expense or inconvenience.

The Town and Country Planning Act, 1968,† established a new development plan system, but this will take some years to come into operation throughout the United Kingdom. The zoning shown on existing development plans will continue to apply until local authorities draw up new Structure Plans.

History of the Site.—After first ascertaining that the proposed development is " permitted " under the Development Plan, it would be wise to investigate the history of the site through official sources as well as by consulting local inhabitants

* See page 32.   † See page 36.

—particularly in the case of a rural site. For instance, an inno-cent-looking footpath may turn out to be a public or private " right of way " involving legal proceedings and considerable delay before its diversion can be secured. The history of adjacent sites should also be investigated to determine whether they enjoy any " easements " against the site under consideration. " Ease-ments " (rights acquired by prescription or under agreement) may relate to drains, sewers, passage of water, ancient lights, or even a right to draw water from a well on the site, and may give the adjoining owner privileges vis-à-vis his neighbour which will cause him considerable embarrassment in carrying out his pro-posed development.

The history of the site may also reveal that the land consists of " made-up ground " or has been undermined and is liable to subsidence, necessitating special precautions in the design of the foundations, and in these circumstances a report should be obtained from the Mineral Valuer before commencing any building operations. Whether the site is considered stable or not, trial holes should be sunk before building operations actually begin, in order to determine the nature of the subsoil, unless some other reliable evidence or local knowledge is avail-able. The Building Surveyor of the Local Authority will usually provide useful information in this connection. The owner should be advised at an early stage of the implications, for instance, of building on a clay subsoil which is subject to seasonal variations, or on a water-bearing subsoil which may involve piling operations.

General Considerations.—Other considerations which should be carefully studied are the aspect, orientation, shelter, over-shadowing from adjacent buildings, existence of utility services such as sewers, water, electricity and gas, means of access to the public highway and communications. In rural districts the suitability of the site for a sewage-disposal plant or the sinking of a well may also have to be considered. Finally, the topo-graphical and other features of the site have to be recorded— the levels, dimensions, bench-marks, if any, positions and types of trees, existing buildings both on and adjacent to the site, over-head cables, if any, and their poles, and any other physical features which will influence the design or siting of the proposed building.

In passing, it is worth mentioning that much useful information can be gleaned from Ordnance Survey maps, but that these are the copyright of the Crown and may not be copied or traced unless a licence is first obtained from H.M. Stationery Office. This licence costs 7/6 a year for hand tracings and 15/- a year for both hand tracings and mechanical reproductions; the fee is payable by each partner or by each separate office of a firm, whichever results in the higher fee.

Surveys of Existing Buildings.—When alterations or additions to existing buildings are contemplated, a careful survey must be made, both to show the exact position of the existing work in relation to the new and to determine its method of construction. Where an addition is being made it will be sufficient to survey only the part of the building immediately adjoining. Some suitable point on the existing building will probably be chosen as a temporary bench-mark (which may or may not be related to ordnance levels). The exact positions must then be determined of any plinths, cornices, string courses, openings, &c., on the elevations likely to interfere with the addition, and the level of the existing floors must be fixed as well as that of the adjoining ground. The thickness and construction of any walls to be cut through should also be determined; in old buildings such things as battened-out wall surfaces, stone hidden by stucco, &c., need investigation.

Disappointment over " extras " at a later stage will be avoided if the condition of repair of the existing premises affected is carefully studied. In timber floors any signs of dry rot or other trouble should be looked for. Old plaster surfaces must be examined: it will often be found more economical to decide at an early stage on complete replastering of a ceiling, a complete room or an elevation. When repair work of plaster is put in hand it seems nearly always to involve a more extensive area than was anticipated. Plaster will be found to be loose without a proper key and cannot be left: this particularly applies to lath-and-plaster ceilings. Not only is it often not possible to see defective plaster until the adjoining work is removed, but there is also damage resulting from disturbance of adjoining work or the general vibration caused by work in progress.

It may be necessary to employ a builder during the survey

to assist in the investigations by, for instance, taking up a few floor-boards to reveal the condition and form of the floor construction, or to open up a part of the foundations to show the type and size of footings, or even whether concrete foundations have been used at all. It is astonishing how many old buildings have been erected on the flimsiest of foundations, and this information may be vital if it is intended to place any additional load on the existing walls or to underpin the existing foundations.

The investigations should also be directed to the condition or absence of the various services—gas, water, electricity, hot-water supply, drainage, &c., as these may eventually require substantial alterations or complete renewal.

The condition of the roof, eaves, flashings, rainwater pipes and gutters, damp-proof course and any other features which prevent moisture from penetrating into the building deserve particular attention, as all the money spent on improving or re-decorating the property may be wasted if some fault in these is overlooked. It is probably true to say that damp is responsible for 95% of the defects which can develop in a building, and money spent on excluding or eliminating it will repay the owner many times over.

Where the work involves substantial alterations to the existing building a complete set of plans of the building must be made, with any elevations which are to be altered. The floor-to-floor heights must be recorded, with a note of where changes occur. Sections will probably only be set up for those parts where structural alterations are being made. If the architect has in mind the purpose of his survey, he will easily decide what is and what is not necessary. The purpose is to record information, not only to enable him to make drawings of the revisions, but also to make clear to a contractor tendering, whether with or without bills of quantities, what is the existing construction and how it is to be adapted.

Where alterations are extensive the contractor should be supplied with a survey drawing as well as the general drawings showing the alterations. Even if he has a bill of quantities, these are helpful in pricing. Further detail drawings could be made available on the premises at the time of tendering. If there is no bill of quantities, each tenderer *must* be supplied with a copy of all drawings.

Survey drawings should have each room or space given a serial

B

number for identification.   References by name, such as " Dining Room ", " Library ", &c., are not of much use in an empty house.   Where no separate survey drawing is provided, existing walls, &c., to be removed should be shown dotted on the plans of alterations, and the numbering be imposed according to the rooms existing (not to the revised plan).   Descriptions in a specification must be such that they can be understood by the tenderer standing in the existing building, and should therefore refer to rooms as existing.

Summary.—It may be helpful to give in summarised form the main information to be obtained when considering or inspecting a site or existing premises for a building project :—

BUILDING SITES

1. DEVELOPMENT

   (a) Permitted development and restrictions under the Local Development Plan or Action Area Plan ;
   (b) zoning, density, floor-space index, &c., as applicable ;
   (c) improvement lines.

2. HISTORY OF SITE

   (a) Rights of public and adjoining owners ;
   (b) boundaries and party walls or fences.

3. NATURE OF GROUND AND SUBSOIL

   (a) Trial holes or other evidence of nature of subsoil ;
   (b) precautions against subsidence, seasonal variations in subsoil, water table ;
   (c) safe bearing capacity of subsoil ;
   (d) report from Mineral Valuer or a geologist ;
   (e) liability to flooding.

4. CONDITION OF SITE

   (a) Levels and gradients ;
   (b) bench marks ;
   (c) shelter or exposure from surrounding ground ;
   (d) direction of prevailing wind ;
   (e) aspect and orientation ;
   (f) dimensions and area of site ;
   (g) existing trees and features ;
   (h) existing buildings on the site and on adjoining land ;
   (i) overhead cables and poles.

5. SERVICES

(a) Position, size and depth of public sewers;
(b) if no sewer, suitability and possible siting of septic tank and overflow outlet;
(c) utility services available, such as gas, water, electricity, &c., with names and addresses of Supply Undertakings;
(d) position and pressure of water-main;
(e) AC or DC electricity supply, voltage, capacity of any existing cables.
(f) position and size of gas-main;
(g) telephone service;
(h) possibility of sinking well.

6. COMMUNICATIONS

(a) Means of access;
(b) nature and proximity of public highway;
(c) rights of way across site.

EXISTING BUILDINGS (*in addition to the foregoing, so far as applicable*)

1. DRAWINGS

Plans, elevations and sections as applicable drawn to scale.

2. CONSTRUCTION

(a) Type and method of construction of foundations, walls, floors and roof;
(b) wall and floor thicknesses;
(c) battened-out wall surfaces or other hidden construction;
(d) stone and stucco finishes.

3. CONDITION OF STRUCTURE

(a) Signs of dry rot, beetle, &c., in timber;
(b) looseness of plaster surfaces;
(c) penetration of damp through roofs, flashings, gutters;
(d) damp-proof course to walls;
(e) settlement cracks;
(f) windows and doors, &c.

4. CONDITION OF SERVICES

(a) Gas, water, electricity, drains, wells, central heating, hot water;
(b) possibility of extending these services.

5. HISTORY OF BUILDING

(a) Age;
(b) purposes of its previous occupation;
(c) quality of previous maintenance work.

PRE-CONTRACT COST CONTROL

Whoever proposes to erect a building, whether an individual having a house built for himself, or a large Company, Corporation or Department of the Public Service, spending in six or seven figures, they must control their expenditure. In order to be able to finance the building they will either state how much they have to spend or they will ask how much the building will cost. In either case, a figure being arrived at, it is the duty of the building owner's professional advisers—architect, consultants and quantity surveyor—to do their best to suit the building to the client's pocket, both at the tender and final account stages.

Definitions.—The term *cost control* is here used to cover the whole service required to meet this end. In the first instance, an *approximate estimate* must be given based on the client's stated requirements. This will be conveyed to the client as his advisers' considered opinion from the information they have. Much has to be done to develop the scheme from that stage, and it is important that a careful watch should be kept to see that the progress of designing will not upset the estimate and the client's budget. In his design the architect will consider alternative solutions to the various aspects of his problem, and may require information from the quantity surveyor on *comparative costs* of alternative materials or construction. In recent years this stage has been developed in more detail, the specialised elaboration of this aspect being given the name of *cost planning*. This may be described as "a system of relating the design of buildings to their cost, so that, whilst taking full account of quality, utility and appearance, the cost is planned to be within the economic limit of expenditure".

To enable any form of cost planning to be undertaken there must be a *cost analysis* of the scheme, a splitting up of the approximate estimate into subdivisions, whether of the various trades and trade sections or of the constructional elements of the building, a combination of these or of some other classification. These sub-divisions are then available for comparison with other records.

It has been the traditional practice to divide the bill of quantities into trades, but in view of this development a system has been devised of dividing it according to constructional elements, there being separate bills under such headings as Floors, Roofs, Windows, &c. This type of bill is called an *elemental bill*, useful for cost analysis by elements, but not essential for that purpose, since the cost analysis can be prepared from the normal trade or sectional bills.

Approximate Estimate, Square Metre Basis.—The first requirement of the client, an approximate estimate before the scheme has been developed at all, is, perhaps, the most difficult part of cost control. There may be little in the way of drawings, but the architect must have converted the client's floor space requirements into some kind of outline plan. It has been found that the cost of buildings bears a relation (*more or less*) to their floor area (usually expressed in square metres) with the qualification that user, site conditions, construction and type of finish must also be considered. In other words, if a building is to be erected similar in these respects to one built, it should be possible to relate its price to that of the first one in proportion to the floor area, also bearing in mind fluctuation in cost of labour and materials which may have occurred in the interval. The more dissimilar the buildings are in their character, the more difficult comparison becomes. It is obvious, therefore, that in order to give an approximate estimate on this basis there must be records available as a guide.

The best records for the purpose are those which the architect or quantity surveyor has himself prepared from his own experience. He will remember something of the job and probably have drawings and priced bill of quantities to refresh his memory. It is obviously important, therefore, to keep cost records of every job. Difficulty, of course, faces the newly established practitioner who may have few or no records of his own. The technical press, when they report and illustrate new buildings, often provide not only overall costs according to floor area but also an analysis of such costs, a file of which will be useful. The quantity surveyor may be able to give figures from an information service of the R.I.C.S. which has analysed a large numbers of tenders. A friend in the profession who has done similar work may be ready to help. Otherwise, the architect will have to adapt such data as he has to the best of his ability. The figures in price books should be treated with great caution, as they can only be generalities.

The reference to user as affecting price means that buildings having the same use, e.g. schools, town halls, &c., have an obvious basic similarity which should enable costs within each category to be more comparable than those of buildings in different categories.

Site conditions are obviously an important factor. A steeply sloping site must make the cost of a building higher than it would be for the same building on a flat site. The nature of the sub-soil too may have a serious effect, e.g. if it necessitates piling.

Construction, of course, has an important influence. A single-storey garage of normal height will merit a different rate per square metre from that for one constructed for double-decker buses. Again, a requirement for, say, a 20 m clear span is a different matter from allowing stanchions at 5- or 7-m intervals. Further, an overall price per metre will be affected by the number of storeys. A two-storey building of the same plan area has the same roof and probably much the same foundations and drains as a single-storey on that area, but has double the floor area. On the other hand, the prices for high buildings are increased by the extra time in hoisting materials to the upper floors and the use of expensive plant, such as tower cranes.

The shape of a building on plan also has an important bearing on cost. A little experimental comparison of the length of enclosing walls for different shapes of the same floor area will show that a square plan is more economical than a long and narrow rectangle, and that such a rectangle is cheaper than an L-shaped plan.

Standard of finish naturally affects price. There will be the client who wants a block of offices with the simplest finish and there will be another to whom, perhaps, more lavish treatment has advertisement value: he may want expensive murals or sculpture.

To measure floor area, the usual practice is to take measurements of all usable floor space within external walls but over internal partitions, the areas of all floors being added together. Deduction is not made for stair or lift wells, &c. Detailed rules are laid down by various authorities which, of course, must be followed in their particular cases.*

Approximate Estimate, Cube Basis.—For very many years the basis of approximate estimates was the cube rather than the square. The idea behind this was probably that the cube reflects variations in the height of storeys, which a square unit does not. In fact, this qualification is not as marked as may at first appear. The difference per square metre for differing storey heights can always be estimated by comparing approximate quantities of the material items in each case.

If used, measurements of cubic contents for approximate estimates are taken, for length and width between the outer faces of external walls, and for height from the top of the concrete foundation to halfway up a pitched roof, or, in the case of flat roofs, to a height above the flat, which used to be two feet. As the cube basis has rather fallen into disuse, no recognised height has been adopted, but 0·75 m would be suitable. The full volume is taken for a mansard roof. Projections such as porches, dormers, roof lights, chimney stacks, &c., are added. Such projections may in some cases need to be priced at a different rate or separately assessed as a lump sum. A boiler chimney stack cannot be priced at the same rate per foot cube as the building. In the case of a raft foundation or a basement it is best to measure from the underside of the slab and bear in mind the circumstances when assessing the rate per foot cube. Large ducts should be added to the cube and again remembered in assessment.

Approximate Estimate, Unit Rate Basis.—Certain types of building lend themselves to estimates based on a price per place, seat, &c. Primary schools might work out at, say, £200 per place; churches, theatres, &c., could be rated at so much per seat; hospitals at so much per Department.† Such estimates

* See, for instance:
  for Housing   Ministry of Housing and Local Government Circular 48/57, (H.M.S.O.), page 9.
  for Schools   Department of Education and Science Building Bulletin No. 4 (H.M.S.O.), 2nd Edition, page 30.
  for Hospitals   Ministry of Health Hospital Building Notes No. 2 and others as required (H.M.S.O.).
† See Department of Education and Science Building Bulletin No. 4; Hospital Building Procedure Note No. 6, Cost Control. H.M.S.O.

must be very approximate and vary according to the type of construction and finish, but they might in the very earliest stages give a guide to a board or building committee as to whether their expenditure is likely to be £200,000 or £500,000. They must be understood to be subject to a subsequent proper estimate for the particular scheme.

Approximate Estimates, Alterations.—For work of alterations, such as the modernising of an old building, it is not practicable to use any of the above rules for estimating. The only way is to analyse the work, splitting it up into sections, such as structural repairs, new partitions, new sanitary fittings and their plumbing, redecoration, engineering services, &c. and to put a figure to each. The quantity surveyor would be able to assist by taking approximate measurements in some cases and pricing them.

Cost Planning.—An approximate estimate being established and reported to the client, the ideal of cost planning is to see not only that design is so controlled that the tender figure agrees with the estimate, but that (this is sometimes overlooked), if possible, it shows a saving through finding reasonable economy without detriment to the client's requirements.

One way recommended to do this is to prepare a cost analysis according to the elements of the building. This is prepared from data in records to split up the overall price per foot super, already arrived at in the approximate estimate, into separate rates for each element. Then, as each element is designed, approximate quantities are prepared and priced to check the rate against each. Differences are adjusted either in the design or by transferring the surplus or deficit to other elements. Those who find this nutshell hard to crack may refer to the prolific supply of articles and papers on the subject and textbooks recently available, particulars of which are given in Appendix 2. The subject cannot be mastered without study, experiment and practice, and its detail must be left as being outside the scope of this book.

It is noteworthy that the leading advocates of such cost planning have been officers of Public Authorities carrying out building work, for the most part of a particular type—schools, barracks,

&c.   Such Authorities have the advantage of a large staff on which to draw for research and a correspondingly large quantity of available data for analysis.   Since it has been more than once emphasised that cost data are mainly of value to the firm or Department who prepare them, such Authorities naturally start with an advantage.   What is suited to their problems may not suit everybody's.

An interesting variation on the above system of cost analysis is one which has been used by the Ministry of Public Building and Works.   In this, the square unit of floor area not being considered suitable for analysis of all elements, some are priced on a unit of their measurement, e.g. the general structure by the cube, internal partitions by an overall area, plumbing at so much per sanitary fitting, and so on.

The carrying out of this full cost planning necessarily needs ready and willing co-operation between architect and quantity surveyor.   Here, again, perhaps Public Authorities have an advantage in having the architect and quantity surveyor mostly in the same building and both subject to a common discipline. But this is no reason why the private architect and quantity surveyor should not work together in the same way.   Indeed, it is essential that they should do so—particularly now that, in addition to the brief, most projects, whether publicly or privately sponsored, are set a calculated cost limit within which the building must be designed.

Cost planning must be a part of the design process—initiated early on—and not simply applied as a means of reducing cost during the later stages of the working drawings.

Apart from a full system of cost planning the surveyor can be of use to the architect on the cost aspect by assisting with comparative costs for alternative systems of construction or finish. It may be a question of comparing different shapes of plan or different forms of internal partition or external cladding.   The particular problem must be examined and, in the case of materials, investigation made into their cost and methods of fixing, where these are not already known.

Approximate Quantities.—Until recent developments the main check on a first approximate estimate was made when the architect's scheme had been developed and probably drawings were available in pencil form. The surveyor could then take off approximate quantities, leaving out all the minor items and grouping items together where practicable. This, of course, is still a useful practice. Normal foundations would be measured per lineal metre, to include excavation, concrete and brickwork, a unit rate for which is fairly easily built up. Walls would include internal and external finish and windows be measured as extra over walls to include glass, paint, &c. With such a system an approximate bill of quantities can be prepared and priced.

The disadvantage of this system of cost control is that it comes too late. By the time the drawings have reached the required stage, many matters of principle have been settled, which cannot be altered without a major disturbance of the whole scheme. For this reason there was a tendency to avoid preparing approximate quantities, the tender stage being so near, and just to hope for the best. The test of the tender may still be sufficient if the client is determined on what he wants and the architect gives him that, in other words if the client says " I want so and so: find out what it will cost " and asks for the best evidence—a tender.

Approximate quantities prepared from the architect's sketch plans can, however, be used to invite competitive tenders, so that a contractor can be appointed at an early stage in the development of the working drawings. The notional tender would then form the basis for further negotiation of the contract sum with the contractor and would establish basic rates for the cost plan. On completion of the negotiations a final bill of quantities would be prepared and priced to provide the contract sum. On complex projects, such as hospitals, it is useful to apply this method to the appointment of the principal nominated sub-contractors as well, so that the construction team can collaborate with the design team in the cost planning, co-ordination of services, programming of site operations and pre-ordering of materials if necessary, before the work starts on the site. This provides the opportunity for all the members of the project team to get to know each other; to understand their respective areas of responsibility; to avoid any ambiguity of specification, and to work together as a team. As a result, when the project actually starts on the site, as many problems as possible will have been discussed and resolved and the work will be carried out more quickly and efficiently.

Reliability of Approximate Estimates.—It will be realised that whether the check of cost planning at the design stage is used or not, cost analysis of tenders is of value as a more reliable guide in future approximate estimates than an overall price per square unit of floor area or per cube unit.   But however carefully such estimates are prepared, there will often be considerations that one cannot anticipate two or three years before.   One must, of course, watch the tendency to fluctuation in the cost of labour and materials and make reasonable provision according to the prospect at the time of the estimate.   One cannot forecast future legislation nor exceptional swings in existing tendencies. The introduction of National Insurance and the Holidays with Pay Schemes caused major disturbances in costs, and such an increase as the Selective Employment Tax could not be anticipated before the announcement.   However, the architect should be alive to current developments which he will find referred to in the Journal of his Institute or the subscription service of a builders' Federation.   Any serious qualification of an estimate should be reported promptly and not left to contribute to an explanation of an unexpectedly high tender.

One thing may be found to affect estimates seriously where a series of contracts is planned on the same site.   There is a certain reluctance on the part of tenderers to submit a really competitive tender when there is a contractor already working on the site, which that contractor knows well.   The result is obvious.   If, therefore, a scheme so develops that these circumstances arise, the approximate estimate may need qualification.

The continuation of cost control after the tender stage is referred to in Chapter 14.*

* Page 153.

5

APPROVALS AND CONTROLS

The Purpose of Approvals and Controls.—The wide powers of control over building operations which are exercised by various public authorities are given to them for a number of reasons : to secure better standards of design and construction in building; to ensure the safety and health of the occupants ; to provide for the proper location of buildings and industry and the best use of the land; to preserve amenities and to allocate labour and materials available during a time of shortages according to the importance of the work by national as well as individual standards.

These controls have been established by various Acts of Parliament and are implemented by both Central and Local Government Authorities. The contravention or disregard of any of them will render the offender liable to prosecution and to the imposition in certain cases of severe penalties.

It is highly important, therefore, to make quite certain that all the relevant consents have been obtained before any building work is started : it is the architect's responsibility to make himself fully acquainted with all the statutory regulations governing such work and to advise his client accordingly. It should be remembered that ignorance of the law is no defence.

Planning Control.—Planning control was first introduced in a modest way under the Housing, Town Planning, Etc., Act, 1909, when the smaller Local Authorities were permitted, with the approval of the Local Government Board, to prepare town planning schemes " as respects any land which is in course of development or appears likely to be used for building purposes, with the general object of securing proper sanitary conditions, amenity and convenience in connection with the laying out and use of the land, and of any neighbouring lands ".

This legislation sufficed until immediately after the 1914–18

War when " The Housing, Town Planning, Etc. Act, 1919 " was passed, enabling groups of Local Authorities to form Joint Town Planning Committees for the preparation of schemes without first obtaining the approval of the Minister of Health, to whom the functions of the Local Government Board had been transferred. " The Housing (Additional Powers) Act 1919 " followed and enabled land to be purchased for garden city and town planning schemes.

" The Housing, Etc. Act, 1923 " extended the powers of the previous Act by enabling the Minister of Health to authorise the preparation of a planning scheme with the object of preserving the existing character and features of a locality with special architectural, historic or artistic interests.

It was not until 1925 that the first statute dealing solely with town planning came into force on the passing of " The Town Planning Act, 1925 ". This was re-enacted with amendments and extensions by the " Town and Country Planning Act, 1932 ", which for the first time brought country as well as urban development into planning schemes. It also, for the first time, referred to the regulating of the design and external appearance of buildings. It provided, too, for the prohibition of building operations in certain areas, if these were likely to injure the amenity of the locality or might be injurious to health by reason of the lack of roads, sewers, water supply or any public services, and the provision of these necessary services would be premature or likely to involve excessive expenditure of public money.

The 1932 Act was a great advance on previous planning legislation and consisted of fifty-eight sections and six schedules. It remained in operation until " The Town and Country Planning (Interim Development) Act, 1943 " was introduced to bring under planning control, also, land which was not subject to a scheme or resolution under the previous Act, and to secure more effective control of development pending the coming into operation of planning schemes.

The year 1943 was also notable for the passing of the " Minister of Town and Country Planning Act, 1943 ", by which for the first time a Minister was made solely responsible for Town and Country Planning, being " charged with the duty of securing consistency and continuity in the framing and execution of a national policy with respect to the use and development of land throughout England and Wales ". Previous to the passing of this Act the duty of administering Town and Country Planning legislation was vested in the Minister of Health (under the 1932 Act) and the Minister of Works and Planning (under the " Minister of Works and Planning Act, 1942 "). In 1951 the duties of the Minister were further extended to embrace Local Government and his designation was altered to " Minister of Local Government and Planning ". Later in the same year this was again changed to " Minister of Housing and Local Government ", and to-day this Ministry remains the central authority for planning matters.

A further Town and Country Planning Act was passed in 1944, its main purpose being to empower Local Authorities to purchase and develop land for planning purposes and to assess, by reference to 1939 prices, compensation payable in connection with the acquisition of land for public purposes and the rate of interest thereon. It also empowered the Minister, on the application of a local planning authority, to declare areas of extensive war damage as being subject to compulsory purchase.

The Town and Country Planning Act, 1947.—In 1947 a new planning system was set up by the passing of the " Town and Country Planning Act, 1947 ". With effect from the 1st July 1948 (the " appointed day ") planning powers were vested in County Councils and County Borough Councils only, although these authorities were empowered to delegate their development control functions to District Councils if they so required. In London, although the L.C.C. is the Planning Authority, it is bound to delegate to the Common Council of the City of London its functions in relation to applications for planning permission for land in the City of London. Under the Act every local Planning Authority was obliged to carry out a survey of its area and to prepare a Development Plan. All Development Plans were required to be submitted by the 1st July 1951 and were subject to review at five-yearly intervals.

The Act also provided for Exchequer grants to be available to Planning Authorities to purchase land and carry out development themselves. Other powers included the control of advertisements, the preservation of buildings of architectural or historic interest, the preservation of trees and the right to require (on payment of compensation) the removal or alteration of existing buildings or the stoppage of existing uses in the interests of the neighbourhood.

A further important provision was the vesting in the State of all development values in land after the " appointed day ". The Central Land Board was set up to administer this side of the Act and its principal functions were the determination and collection of the development charge payable in respect of the future development of any land which was not exempt under regulations, and also the acquisition of land, by agreement or compulsorily, and its disposal at a price, inclusive of the development charge, for the purpose of development, if the Minister was satisfied that this was expedient in the public interest. A private developer was able to apply to the Board to exercise its powers, if he was otherwise unable to acquire the land on reasonable terms and if his proposed development was of a type specified in an approved plan. The levying of a development charge in effect secured for the State the improvement value of property. It therefore prevented the purchase of agricultural land as an investment with the idea that in a few years' time it might increase in value for use as building land. Exception was made for owners of single building plots in certain circumstances, so that those who had already bought plots on which to build themselves a house should not suffer. Provision was also made under the Act for the payment of compensation out of a central fund of £300,000,000 to owners whose land may have depreciated in value as a result of the provisions of the Act.

The Act stipulated that development could not be undertaken without permission, nor until the development charge had been paid or some specific alternative arrangement for security agreed by the Central Land Board. However, in certain circumstances compensation was payable to the owner of the land if his proposals to develop were refused.

Under the Act, development was defined as " the carrying out of building, engineering, mining or other operations in, on, under or over the land or the making of any material change in the use of any buildings or other land ".* Certain operations were excluded, such as works of maintenance, improvement or alteration which might affect the interior of a building but would not materially alter the external appearance ; certain works of maintenance or improvement carried out by a local highway authority ; works of

* Section 12 of the Act.

repair or for inspection carried out by Local Authorities or statutory undertakers ; the use of land or buildings within the curtilage of a dwelling-house for any purpose incidental to the enjoyment of the dwelling-house as such ; the use of any land for agriculture or forestry and the use, for any of those purposes, of any building occupied, together with the land so used.

Provision was made in the Act for appeal to the Minister in certain cases against a Planning Authority's refusal, but it specified that this must be done in a prescribed manner and within twenty-eight days of the notice of refusal being received.

Failure to obtain planning permission or the contravention of any conditions under which permission may have been granted rendered the developer liable to being required to restore the land to its condition before development took place or the alteration of the development to comply with those conditions, and powers were given to the Planning Authority to enforce those requirements.

A further provision under the Act permits an applicant to apply to a local Planning Authority to determine his position if he is in any doubt as to whether his proposals constitute development as defined by this Act, or to inspect the register of all land in the area of the Local Planning Authority in order to ascertain the previous planning history of the land in question and so possibly establish what development may or may not be permitted.

The Town and Country Planning Act, 1951.—This Act corrected certain drafting errors of the 1947 Act, but did not disturb the main principles involved.

The Town and Country Planning Act, 1953.—This Act came into operation on the 20th May 1953. It re-enacted most of the provisions of the 1947 Act, but made certain changes in the financial provisions, the most important being that developers were relieved of the liability to pay development charges and the Government was released from the obligation of distributing the £300 million fund to those who had established claims on the 1st July 1951. Development commenced on and after 18th November 1952 was exempt from development charge, although the whole of any development commenced before that date remained liable to such charge. Where the charge had already been paid but development had not commenced, the amount of the charge was repayable.

The distribution of the £300 million set aside under the 1947 Act was cancelled, but provision was made under the new Act for the payment (subject to certain exceptions based on the principle of good neighbourliness) of compensation for loss of development value up to 100 per cent on claims admitted by the Central Land Board, as and when development of the land was prevented or severely restricted. Compensation for planning restrictions may not exceed the value of the claims ranking for payment from the fund (with accrued interest), and compensation for compulsory acquisition is based on the current value of the land for its existing use at the time of the acquisition, plus any unexpended part of the claim with accrued interest. The assignment of claims (subject to certain exceptions) requires the approval of the Central Land Board.

The Town and Country Planning Act, 1954.—This Act became effective on the 16th August 1959 and brought to an end the double code of compensation payable on the acquisition of land by private treaty and by a Compulsory Purchase Order which resulted from the 1947 and 1954 Acts. It substituted new principles which

(a) provided for compensation in the case of Compulsory Purchase Orders served after the 29th October 1958 to be assessed at the market value;

(b) enabled Local Authorities and public bodies to exercise greater freedom from Ministerial control in the acquisition, appropriation and disposal of land;

(c) provided further opportunity for challenging in the Courts certain orders made under the 1947 Act and certain decisions and directions of the Minister under the previous Acts;

(d) secured greater publicity for planning applications, particularly as these affected owners and agricultural tenants;

(e) made it obligatory for Local Authorities to purchase the interest in land of owner-occupiers which became detrimentally affected by Town Planning proposals;

(*f*) gave additional powers to Local Authorities to purchase land in advance of their immediate requirements.

The Town and Country Planning Act, 1962.—This Act substantially repeals the Acts of 1947, 1951, 1953, 1954 and 1959, and also Part II of the Caravan and Control of Development Act 1960, and collects the whole of these provisions into a single enactment.

The Town and Country Planning Act, 1963.—With certain exceptions, the provisions of this Act were operative from the 25th February 1963. They are mainly limited to the field of valuation and compensation. However, it does make an important amendment to the 1962 Act by qualifying the right to add 10% to the cubic capacity of a building, either on re-development or enlargement by introducing a condition restricting the increase in floor space for any use.

The Town and Country Planning Act, 1968.—The planning system set up by the 1947 Act had operated for twenty years, but it became necessary to make positive changes in the system as a result of experience and changing circumstances. The new Act which became law on 25th October 1968 applies to England and Wales, but legislation for Scotland will follow. However, the provisions of the Act have to be brought into force by Ministerial Order, and it will be necessary for architects to establish the up-to-date regulations which are in force for each project.

The Act has seven parts, of which Part I establishes a new development plan system. Planning authorities will be required now to submit Structure Plans for Ministerial approval. These will cover planning in a wider aspect than Development Plans under the 1947 Act, but will be less concerned with precise details of use for particular areas of land. Structure Plans will co-ordinate local planning with regional and national planning and policies. Local planning will include Action Area Plans, which are indicated in Structure Plans as areas where comprehensive development, redevelopment and improvement is envisaged within ten years. Local Planning Authorities must prepare local plans for Action Areas within the framework of policies approved in the Structure Plan for the area. These and other local plans will be adopted by local authorities and will not require ministerial approval. The Act gives local planning authorities the duty of obtaining adequate publicity for both Structure Plans and local plans during their preparation.

Part II of the Act makes provision for obtaining better enforcement of planning control. Under the 1962 Act unauthorised development could become established and immune from enforcement action after four years. The 1968 Act abolishes this " four-year rule " except for breaches involving development or the change of use to a single dwelling house. There is a new provision empowering planning authorities to serve a " stop notice " requiring the immediate stopping of operations which are the subject of an enforcement notice.

Planning appeal procedure is altered under Part III of the Act, in which the Minister is enabled to delegate to selected inspectors the responsibility for deciding certain cases. In exceptional cases involving wider national issues the Minister can call in for his own decision an appeal which would be delegated by these provisions. It is expected that the new procedure will shorten the time which has been taken in deciding planning appeals hitherto. Local planning authorities may also delegate certain planning decisions to their officers under provisions in Part VI of the Act.

The Act provides that a time limit is to be included in all future planning permissions. Where outline planning permission is given, application for permission in detail must be made within two years of detailed planning permission or within five years from the original application.

Planning Permission.—Application for planning permission throughout the United Kingdom, where this is necessary, must be made to the Local Authority in the form laid down by the " Town and Country Planning (Making of Applications) Regulations ".* In most cases a single form is available from Local Authorities to cover an application for planning permission and approval under building regulations, and this normally has to be completed in triplicate with three copies of the appropriate drawings and returned to the Local Authority. The drawings required are a block plan drawn to a scale sufficient to show the

* S.I. 1948, No. 711.

location of the site, and small-scale plans and elevations of the proposed buildings, but not necessarily working drawings unless these are specifically asked for by the Local Authority. The Local Authority will forward one set of the documents to the Local Planning Authority.

The Act requires that Local Authorities should send a notice of acknowledgement to every applicant for planning permission (in a prescribed form) and must notify him, within two months, of its decision in writing. This period may be extended, if necessary, by mutual agreement in writing. If permission is refused or granted subject to conditions, the Planning Authority is required to give its reason for such action in writing. Failure of the Planning Authority to notify an applicant of its decision within the prescribed period constitutes a refusal of permission, and the applicant may, if he wishes, make an appeal to the Minister.

The Town and Country Planning Act 1968 contains new provisions in connection with planning appeal procedure and time limits for planning permission.*

The Land Commission Act, 1967.—This Act provides for the assessment and collection of a betterment levy on any additional value attached to land by the prospect of its development. It differs from the system of " development charges " under the 1947 Act. The person responsible for the development is called the " developing owner " in the Act, and he is obliged to notify the Land Commission of his intention to start. The Act defines what operations on site constitute " starting ". Notification must be made on Form BL2 obtainable from regional offices of the Land Commission at least six weeks before start of development unless detailed planning permission has been obtained. Notification, however, may not be made more than one year before starting. The Act lists certain types of minor developments, such as the normal extension or conversion of a house, which are not liable to levy.

Industrial Development Certificate.—Provisions to ensure the proper distribution and location of industry throughout the country were contained in Section 38 of the Town and Country Planning Act, 1962. These provisions do not apply to existing

* See page 37.

factories, but any firm wishing to extend its present buildings above a certain limit or to erect new buildings elsewhere is obliged to inform the Board of Trade and obtain a certificate that the proposed development can be carried out consistently with the proper distribution of industry. This certificate must be forwarded with the application for planning permission.

Section 39 of the Act makes provision for certain classes of development to be exempt from the need to obtain a Board of Trade certificate. It is not necessary to obtain a certificate if the industrial floor space to be created by the development in question, together with any other industrial floor space created or to be created by any related development (i.e. development in the same buildings or group of buildings which has been carried out or approved on or after the 1st April 1960) does not exceed 5000 square feet. In considering related development, if an industrial development certificate had already been granted, the area so authorised may be excluded. Similarly, any floor area existing in a related development (or for which planning permission had been granted) before the issue of the industrial development certificate may be excluded.

The Board of Trade may also direct that an industrial development certificate is not required in respect of the erection of certain classes of industrial building in any areas prescribed by or under Regulations, or in respect of a change of use of a building in such an area which might become an industrial building of such class.

Applications for certificates must be made on Form IDC/1 and forwarded to the appropriate Regional Controller of the Board of Trade.

Section 40 of the Act provides that where an application is made to a Planning Authority for planning permission for an industrial development without first obtaining a Board of Trade Certificate, the Planning Authority must consider whether they would have refused permission even if a certificate had been issued, and if they would have refused permission they must serve on the Applicant a notice to that effect. The Applicant may then appeal to the Minister under Section 23 of the Act.

Office Development Permit.—The Control of Office and Industrial Development Act, 1965, requires the issue of an office-development permit for erection or extension of office buildings in Greater London and certain more densely populated areas in the Home Counties set out in the Schedule to the Act or extended by Order. Change of user from other uses to office use requires a similar permit. A floor area not exceeding 3000 square feet, including any related development which is part of the same project, is exempt.

The same Act gives the Board of Trade powers to vary the exemption limit of 5000 square feet in regard to a certificate under the Town and Country Planning Act, 1962, as well as the above-mentioned limit of 3000 square feet for an office development permit. Application for an office development permit must be made on Form OD/1 and forwarded to the appropriate Regional Controller of the Board of Trade.

Building Bye-Laws.—Under the Public Health Act, 1936,* Local Authorities had power to make bye-laws, constituting a code of building regulations enforceable by them. They varied in detail over the whole country, and they did not uniformly take into account advances in knowledge and developments in building materials and constructional techniques as these arose. This was changed by the Public Health Act, 1961, when powers were taken to make national building regulations, which except within the administrative area of the former L.C.C. (now known as the Inner London Boroughs), would apply to the whole of England and Wales, replacing local building bye-laws. These powers, initially vested in the Minister of Housing and Local Government, were transferred to the Minister of Public Building and Works in 1964, and the first set of building regulations made under the Act and published in July 1964 came into force on 1st February 1966 as The Building Regulations, 1965.

Under the Building (Scotland) Act, 1959, powers to make building regulations in Scotland are vested in the Secretary of State for Scotland, and at present these are embodied in The Building Standards (Scotland) Regulations, 1963.†

While they cover the same ground with the same objectives as the building regulations that apply in England and Wales, the procedures for obtaining approvals (warrants) and relaxations

---

* Section 61.
† *The Building Standards (Scotland) Regulations 1963:* S.I. 1963 No. 1897 (S. 102).

differ substantially, and many of the specific constructional requirements vary quite considerably.

The following section refers only to practice and procedure in England and Wales under The Building Regulations, 1965, and readers are advised to refer to the Scottish regulations for practice and procedure in Scotland.

Building Regulations.*—The building regulations require that any person intending to erect a building or to carry out alterations to an existing building must apply for approval by depositing plans and particulars on an appropriate form in duplicate. The types and scales of drawings and the information which should be given on them is laid down in Schedule 2 of the Regulations.

Drawings must be made with " suitable and durable materials ", which may be taken to mean on linen, and it is necessary for the applicant or his authorised agent to sign every drawing or other document. The form on which this application must be made is obtainable from the offices of the local Authority and since the passing of the Town and Country Planning Act, 1947, the form has been combined with the application for planning consent.

If a change of use is contemplated or additional fittings are to be installed, even though no structural alterations are involved, it may be necessary to give notice to the Local Authority, but plans need not be deposited. The regulations indicate what work or buildings are exempt from compliance.

Section 10 of the Public Health Act, 1961, requires the Local Authority to give written notice of the approval or rejection of the application within five weeks from the date on which the plans are deposited. This period may be extended up to a maximum of two months, if necessary, by mutual agreement in writing.

Notice of rejection of the application must be given in writing and reasons for the decision stated. The rights of appeal must also be stated in the notice. It should be noted that the Local Authority only has powers to approve or reject the application, and cannot approve it conditionally. It will therefore save delay if a careful study of the regulations is made before the application is submitted to ensure that the proposals comply with them.

---

* *The Building Regulations 1965:* S.I. 1965 No. 1373, and *The Building (First Amendment) Regulations 1965:* S.I. 1965 No. 2184.

The procedure for depositing plans is clearly described in the Regulations, and should be closely followed, as it is itself a Regulation.

It is an offence to proceed with any work subject to compliance with the regulations without depositing the plans, even though the actual work may comply, and prosecution may follow. It is not essential, however, to defer the commencement of the work until the deposited plans have been approved, but if work is begun it would be wise to make quite sure that the work complied in all respects, otherwise the risk would be run of having to make alterations later on.

An appeal against rejection of an application for approval under the Building Regulations must be made within twenty-one days of the service of the notice, and must be made to the Justices " before the work is substantially commenced ". Under Section 64 (3) of the Act, the Justices must determine whether the plans are defective or the work would contravene any of the Building Regulations. Alternatively, an aggrieved person may, jointly with the Local Authority, refer the matter to the Minister. A further course would be for the owner to proceed with the work and then defend himself in Court, if proceedings were taken against him by the Local Authority (but unless he is very sure of his ground it would be most unwise to do so).

Apart from specific contravention of building requirements, an application for approval may be rejected on the grounds of impregnated sites, building over drains or sewers, unsatisfactory drainage, closet accommodation or water supply, inadequate natural lighting and ventilation for habitable rooms, lack of access for disposal of refuse, or short-lived materials. In the last case approval may be given for a temporary building for a limited period, after which the building must be removed, unless a further application for extension of the period is granted.

The Local Authority has the following powers for enforcing the bye-laws :—

(a) Taking legal proceedings before the Justices within six months of the offence, when the penalty on conviction may be a fine.

(b) Serving within twelve months a notice (under Section 65 of the 1936 Act) on the owner to pull down or remove the work or bring it into conformity with the bye-laws. If the owner fails to obey this notice or fails in an appeal, the Local Authority may itself carry out the work at the owner's expense.

(c) Applying to the High Court for an order requiring the removal or alteration of the work. This may be done at any time.

If any other person is aggrieved by work carried out by someone else which does not comply with the bye-laws, he may take legal proceedings against the owner.

New streets are governed by bye-laws under the Public Health Act, 1875, with regard to level, width and construction, and plans are required to be deposited in the same way as for buildings.

Under Section 6 (1) of the Public Health Act of 1961 the Minister was given power to delegate to Local Authorities his power to dispense with or relax building regulations. By means of Regulation A13 the Minister has delegated to Local Authorities power to dispense or relax any requirement of the Regulations except those in Part A (General), Part D (Structural Stability) and Part E (Structural Fire Precautions). Dispensations or relaxations of the Regulations may not be made by a Local Authority in respect of its own buildings. They may be made only in any particular case if the operation of any requirement would be unreasonable in the special circumstances. Forms of application for dispensation or relaxation of Building Regulations are given in the Regulations.

Under Sections 6 (2) and 7 of the 1961 Act there now exists a right of appeal to the Minister against a Local Authority's refusal to relax. Notice of Appeal must be in writing within one month from the date of the Local Authority notifying their refusal.

The general law does not authorise the Local Authority or any of its officials to receive any fee for the examination of plans, the inspection of work or the testing of drains, but this may be permitted under local Acts of Parliament (e.g. the London Building Acts *).

Administration of Building Regulations.—Local Authorities, other than rural districts, are required under the Local Government

* The London Building Acts (Amendment) Act, 1939, Sections 91–93 and Schedules.

Act 1933 to appoint a Surveyor. The duties he performs for his authority normally include administration of the control of building operations covered by the regulations, as well as the construction and maintenance of council properties, highways, bridges, sewers and sewage-disposal works. He also has important duties in relation to refuse collection and disposal and town and country planning. Larger authorities appoint planning officers and architects for some of these duties, and the Surveyor (or Engineer and Surveyor as he is normally called) will be assisted by a Building Surveyor or Building Inspector. The latter is normally concerned with the administration of the Building Regulations.

Rural district authorities, though with more limited powers, also usually have a Building Surveyor with similar duties on a smaller scale. Town planning, highways and bridges would normally be under the control of the county authority.

These officials are employed to perform certain administrative and technical duties which are defined by building legislation. Whilst their primary concern is to ensure that all building work in their area complies with the regulations, they must interpret such regulations in a reasonable manner and must not exceed the statutory powers of the local authority.

The Factories Act 1961.—This Act consolidates the Factories Acts 1937 and 1959 and certain other enactments relating to the safety, health and welfare of employed persons. Certain building operations and works of engineering construction are subject to the provisions of the Act. It gives powers to fire authorities and local authorities to satisfy themselves with regard to the provision of means of escape in case of fire, sanitary conveniences, drinking water, washing facilities, and the size, ventilation and lighting of rooms used in factories and buildings of the warehouse class.

Factory inspectors appointed by the Secretary for Employment and Productivity have powers to enter factory premises and warehouses to ensure that the requirements of the Act are being complied with. They should be consulted on aspects of the Act which relate to the safety and protection of occupants and operatives where machinery, hoists, lifts, cranes and lifting tackle are installed in buildings.

Clean Air Act, 1956.—This Act makes it illegal to emit dark smoke from chimneys. Local Authorities, with the approval of the Minister, may create " Smoke Control Areas " in which the emission of any smoke from chimneys is an offence, and the Local Authority creating such an area may make grants towards the cost of converting fires in private dwellings and in certain other buildings in the area.

The Thermal Insulation (Industrial) Buildings Act, 1957.—This Act is administered by the Minister of Power, and the Regulations came into operation on 1st January 1959. They apply to any industrial building or to any extension commenced after that date. The Regulations exempt certain buildings such as boiler houses, buildings or extensions of buildings which are heated solely by any manufacturing or cleansing process carried out in them, and unheated buildings. A Local Authority must reject for the purposes of this Act any plans of a proposed industrial building which do not conform to the required standard of thermal insulation.

The Local Authority must give notice of approval or rejection of the plans within one month of their being submitted, subject only to an extension to five weeks where meetings of the Local Authority are not more frequent than once a month.

If an industrial building has been erected in contravention of the Act, the Local Authority has power to require the Owner to make the necessary alterations to comply with the Act. If the Local Authority approves the erection of a building or fails within the statutory period to reject an application and the building is erected in contravention of the Act or the building has been completed for more than twelve months the Local Authority cannot take any enforcement action.

There is a right of appeal to the Minister of Power in any dispute which might arise.

The Caravan Sites and Control of Development Act, 1960.—This Act institutes a licensing system for the establishment and operation of caravan sites. In general, no land may be used as a caravan site unless the occupier is the holder of a licence. An exception is made where a caravan is used incidental to the enjoyment as such of a dwelling house situated on the same land.

6

APPROVALS AND CONTROLS (*continued*)

LOCAL ACTS, SUPERIOR AUTHORITIES, MATERIALS CONTROL

Local Acts of Parliament.—Greater London and some provincial authorities have local Acts of Parliament which will supplement the ordinary law with regard to buildings and streets: they add to the normal provisions of the law rather than alter it. A copy of any provisions in a local Act relating to any matter about which building regulations may be made under the ordinary law must be appended to the printed copies of any building bye-laws in force.

London Building Acts (Amendment) Act, 1939.—This Act now relates to all streets and buildings situated in Greater London, and is divided into twelve parts and three schedules dealing with the naming and numbering of streets, buildings, &c.; the construction of buildings; special and temporary buildings and structures; means of escape in case of fire; rights and liabilities of building and adjoining owners; dangerous and neglected structures; sky signs; superintending architect, district surveyors and their fees; bye-laws; and legal proceedings. The introduction to the Act contains definitions of the various terms used. A good knowledge of the provisions of this Act is essential to the practitioner in London.

Before the passing of the London Government Act, 1963, the County of London was administered by the London County Council, the City Corporation and twenty-eight Metropolitan Borough Councils. The new Act, however, has created a new administration area, known as Greater London, which comprises 12 inner London Boroughs, 20 outer London Boroughs, the City and the Inner and Middle Temples. It is administered by a council known as the Greater London Council. This Council has now assumed the functions of the London County Council under the London Building Acts (Amendment) Act 1939 and the inner London Boroughs have the functions of Metropolitan

Boroughs. Part II of the Act extends to the outer London Boroughs as if they, too, were Metropolitan Boroughs.

By the London Government Act, 1963, the following provisions of the London Building Acts 1930 to 1939 cease to have effect:—

(a) Parts II and III and Sections 51 to 53 of the Act of 1930.
(b) Section 4 (i) (a) of the Act of 1935.
(c) Sections 128 to 131 and 156 of the Act of 1939, and Section 148 of that Act so far as it relates to other provisions of the London Building Acts 1930 to 1935 repealed by Section 43 (6) of the London Government Act 1963.

In matters relating to building and planning control, the Greater London Council is the responsible Authority. In order to administer and supervise the control of building, the Council makes the appointment of a " Superintending Architect of Metropolitan Buildings " aided by a number of " District Surveyors ", who are whole-time officers of the Council and are debarred from practising in a private capacity. The District Surveyors are required to supervise any building works which are in their own area, to ensure that they comply with the provisions of the London Building Act in respect of works " to, in, or upon a building or structure, width and directions of streets, the general line of building in streets, the provision of open spaces about buildings, the height of buildings and all work in persuance of Part V (Means of escape in case of Fire) ". A builder before commencing any work on a building is bound (under Section 83 of the Act) to give the District Surveyor two clear days' notice in a prescribed form: similar notice must also be given in the event of any work which is suspended for three months, or if, during the progress of the work, the builder is changed. In cases of emergency, work may be commenced immediately, but the " notice " must be served on the District Surveyor not more than twenty-four hours after work has begun. The builder is also required to notify the District Surveyor of the cost of the work within fourteen days of its completion.

Provision is made under Section 86 of the Act for the builder to appeal to the Council against any decision of the District Surveyor, and a further appeal may be made to a Tribunal of Appeal against the Council's determination, except in cases relating to the stability or the protection in case of fire of the building or structure.

Specific fees are payable to the Council by the builder or building owner in respect of the services rendered by the District Surveyor, and these are defined in the First and Second Schedules to the Act. In the main, such fees (other than for dangerous structures) are calculated on the cubic contents or cost of the building or alteration. In cases of default, provision is made for the recovery of any fees or expenses which are due to the Council.

It should be particularly noted that the local authorities in Greater London and not the Greater London Council are responsible for fulfilling the duties imposed by the Public Health Act, 1936 (e.g. drainage, ventilation of buildings, refuse disposal, &c.), the Water Acts, the Clean Air Act and the Noise Abatement Act. In addition, the Common Council of the City of London, not the Greater London Council, has powers in regard to all dangerous structures situated within the boundaries of the City.

Superior Authorities.—Under this heading come various authorities, from Government Departments to private individuals, who may have the power to criticise, amend or even prohibit a scheme. Some of these are mentioned below.

War Damage Commission.—The War Damage Act, 1964, came into operation on 1st October 1964. By it the existence of the War Damage Commission was terminated and the Commission's Duties transferred to the War Damage Office of the Department of Inland Revenue. The Act qualified the existing scheme of war damage compensation under the War Damage Act, 1943, by setting a four-year limit from 1st October 1964 for claiming payments of cost of works and for making applications for determination of value payments. This four-year period from 1st October 1964 to 30th September 1968 was called " the terminal period ".

A payment of cost of works could be made only where war damage had been made good. Any war damage repairs for which the owner intended to claim had therefore to be done and the claim made by 30th September 1968, if his right to receive a payment of cost of works was to be preserved. A " converted value payment " under Section 13 of the War Damage Act, 1943, might be paid in respect of war damage which had not been made good within the terminal period, provided that an application for a value payment determination had been made, in writing, by 30th September 1968.

The four-year limit applied also to applications for payments in respect of church buildings and other properties held for charitable purposes and to claims for payments in respect of site clearance under the War Damage (Clearance Payments) Act, 1960. The works again had to be completed and applications or claims for payments made by 30th September 1968. The War Damage Office will complete work on outstanding claims, but no claims made after the terminal period can be entertained.

Ministry of Housing and Local Government.—Though the architect's client may be a Local Authority having power in England and Wales to prepare and carry out housing schemes, these are subject to the approval of this Ministry, both as to design and cost. In Scotland the relative authority is the Department of Home and Health. House or flat plans and lay-out plans will have to be submitted for approval, and the work cannot go ahead until the Ministry has agreed the cost for the purpose of sanctioning a loan. As Local Authorities depend very much on the raising of loans for their capital expenditure, and as all such loans are under the control of the Ministry, they are bound to follow its dictates.

Department of Education and Science.—Though education, including the erection of schools, is in the hands of County and County Borough Councils, the D.E.S. has the same supervising authority in that sphere as the Ministry of Housing and Local Government has in Housing.

Department of Health and Social Security.—The D.H.S.S. is the Central Authority administering the Health Service and controlling hospital building in England and Wales. The country is divided into a number of Regions, each of which is controlled by a Hospital Board appointed by the Minister of State for Health. These Boards are responsible for the actual planning and erection of any medical buildings required and payment is made out of funds provided by the Department. Except for minor works, plans and estimates for medical buildings must be submitted to the Minister for approval before any building work commences, and programmes for such works must be forwarded annually with the Boards' estimated expenditure for the ensuing year.

Local hospital administration is undertaken by Hospital Management Committees who must apply to their Regional Boards for any building work which they require.

In Scotland the Central Authority is the Scottish Home and Health Department and in Northern Ireland the Northern Ireland Hospitals Authority.

Ministry of Public Building and Works.—On the 22nd October 1962 it was announced that responsibility for construction work at home and abroad, including maintenance work of the War Office and Air Ministry, would be transferred to the Ministry of Public Building and Works. On the 7th December 1962 a further announcement stated that the construction and maintenance work of the Admiralty would be similarly transferred. The Architects', Engineers' and Surveyors' sections of the Service Departments are now sections of the Ministry of Public Building and Works.

Church Authorities.—In the case of the Church of England, approval will probably be required from the appropriate Diocesan Finance Board as well as the Church Commissioners of England, who have their own architectural advisers. Other Churches and religious denominations will each have their own governing bodies who will deal with their building work.

Leasehold Property.—In the case of leases it is usually provided that the lessee shall not alter or add to the buildings without the written approval of the lessor. This means that plans and specification must be submitted to him, and he will, through his architect or surveyor, give his approval. He may make conditions as to supervision of the work in progress by his representative to see that it is in accordance with the approved drawings and specification, and he will require the fees of his technical adviser to be paid by the lessee.

Adjoining Owners.—The erection of a building often affects owners of adjoining property. In the Administrative County of London procedure is laid down for giving of notices of the work and negotiating agreement.* Elsewhere negotiation is a private matter. One cannot place foundations on adjoining land without permission nor overhang the boundary line at a higher level with a gutter or other obstruction. There may be rights of light attached to the adjoining building, a right to run drains across the building owner's site, a chimney-stack which would not be effective if a taller building were erected adjoining it, and so on. These are all matters which can usually be settled by friendly negotiation, the building owner realising that if his proposal causes damage to his neighbour he must put it right, paying any cost involved.†

Control of Materials.—The supply of many materials was controlled during the war period and immediate post-war years by some form of licensing or quota. As materials became more plentiful these controls were gradually withdrawn. Price, too, of many materials in common use, such as bricks and timber, was controlled by Statutory Instruments, but, again, such Government control has been removed. There are still recognised fixed prices for certain materials, such as cement, stoneware pipes, standard metal windows and structural steel, usually fixed by the trade association concerned, sometimes after consultation with Government Departments.

This tendency towards monopolies, in other spheres besides the building industry, caused some public concern, resulting in the appointment of a Commission to hold enquiries into the subject. In some cases price control has already been affected by the

* London Building Acts (Amendment) Act, 1939: Sections 44–59.
† See page 236.

C

Restrictive Trade Practices Act, 1956, which followed reports of this Commission.* The Act requires all such restrictive practices to be registered. In January 1957 the Commission reported on the supply of standard metal windows and doors and found that the common price system of the Metal Window Association,† as operated, was not against the public interest, though they made some minor recommendations. Since then the Restrictive Practices Court has investigated a number of price agreements in the building trade. A price-fixing scheme of the British Constructional Steelwork Association was withdrawn after reference to this Court.‡ In the case of the Cement Makers' Federation Agreement § fixed prices were found not contrary to the public interest, except restrictions as to rebates to large users which were therefore declared void. The restrictions of the Linoleum Manufacturers' Association ‖ were found to be contrary to the public interest.

The Building Control Act, 1966.—This Act is intended as a permanent measure, the object of which is to enable the Government to control the start of work on certain major building projects. This is so that the total level of demand on the building industry may be regulated to suit the industry's resources and also so that priority may be given to urgent and socially important projects over less essential building.

The Act came into force on 9th August 1966, but the Minister of Public Buildings and Works subsequently made an order which suspended building licensing from 20th November 1968. It should be noted, however, that the Act is still on the Statute Book, and the Government retains the power provided in the Act to make an order reimposing licensing if it became necessary and at short notice.

For this reason the general requirements of the Act are outlined here. Although the control covers all work carried out in the construction or alteration of a building, maintenance and repairs which do not involve alterations are excluded from control and also the following types of project:—

---

* See *Report of the Monopolies and Restrictive Practices Commission on the Supply of Buildings in the Greater London Area:* H.M.S.O.
† *R.I.C.S. Journal,* March 1957, page 488.
‡ (1959) 1 W.L.R. 306.
§ (1961) 1 W.L.R. 581.
‖ (1961) 1 W.L.R. 986.

1. Projects costing less than the Cost Exemption Limit (including the cost of preparing the site and ancillary works, but excluding the cost of land and professional fees). This was £100,000 at the time building licensing was suspended.

2. Private dwellings.

3. Industrial buildings as defined by Section 21 of the Local Employment Act, 1960.

4. Buildings used for scientific research in the course of a trade or business.

5. Buildings providing services or facilities reasonably required for the use of a contiguous or adjacent building exempt under categories 2, 3 and 4 above.

6. Where a project consists partly of work exempt under categories 2 to 5 and partly of non-exempt work, the whole project will be exempt, provided that the gross area to be used otherwise than for exempted purposes does not exceed 20% of the gross floor space of the building or 20,000 square feet, whichever is the less.

7. Work in localities specified as development districts for the purpose of the Local Employment Act 1960 or as development areas under the Industrial Development Act 1966.

8. Work carried out at the expense of certain public bodies, including local authorities, development corporations for new towns, the Commission for the New Towns, harbour authorities in respect of harbour development works, nationalised industries and undertakings, statutory water undertakers, universities, schools and other establishments of education in receipt of grants provided by Parliament, hospital authorities in respect of hospital or research work and any other bodies whose income consists mainly of moneys provided by Parliament.

9. Projects carried out on behalf of the Crown.

10. Buildings containing more than 3,000 square feet (10,000 square feet outside the Metropolitan Region) of office premises for which the Board of Trade have issued an Office Development Permit.

11. Work which is the subject of an outstanding cost of works War Damage Claim.

12. Work for which the Minister of Power has issued a pipe-line construction authorisation.
13. Work begun or contracted for before 28th July 1965.

It is necessary to add to the cost of constructing a new building the cost of constructing any other building contiguous or adjacent to it, if any work has been done in the construction of the other building within two years and the two buildings are used for the same undertaking or constructed for the same client.

For alterations it is necessary to add to their cost that of any other alteration in the same building carried out within two years and also the cost of constructing the building itself if it was carried out within two years. Earlier work is not taken into account if it is exempt under the Act other than on cost grounds alone.

When issued, a licence will generally contain the conditions that the work is started not before and not more than six months after the approved starting date and that the cost does not exceed the approved cost by more than 5% or £20,000, whichever is the less.

Offices Shops and Railway Premises Act, 1963.—This Act makes provision for the safety, health and welfare of people employed in these premises which have now to be registered by the employer with the authority responsible for enforcing the Act's provisions. These are the councils of county boroughs, London boroughs, county districts and the City Corporation of London. For offices of local authorities, government departments, certain factory and railway premises the existing Factory Inspectorate will be the enforcement authority.

Responsibility for complying with the provisions of the Act is laid generally on the occupier of premises to which it applies, although the actual employer of persons working in the premises has certain specific responsibilities. In certain buildings some of the occupier's responsibilities are transferred to the owner of the building, who is also responsible for complying with provisions relating to " common parts ", e.g. entrances, passages, stairways and lifts.

The Minister has power to exempt by order a class of premises from certain requirements where in his opinion it would be unreasonable to require compliance because of special circumstances. If the enforcing authority are satisfied that compliance is not reasonably practicable they may exempt individual premises from certain requirements. Application for an individual exemption must be made to the enforcing authority on Form OSR.5. If it is refused there is a right of appeal against the refusal within twenty-one days to a Magistrates' Court.

The provisions securing health and welfare lay down minimum space standards to prevent overcrowding paying regard to space occupied by furniture, fittings, machinery, &c., as well as to the number of persons. They lay down reasonable environmental standards in terms of temperature, lighting and ventilation which must be provided.

Sanitary conveniences, washing facilities and drinking water must also be provided in accordance with the requirements of this Act.

The safety provisions are based upon those set out in the Factories Act, 1961, with reference to sound construction of all floors, stairs and passageways and freedom from obstructions. Hand-rails must be provided to all stairways and fencing and fixed guards provided for dangerous machinery.

The Act lays down detailed fire precautions in relation to means of escape, alarm bells, &c., and for certain classes of premises a Fire Certificate must be obtained before it is lawful to employ anyone in them. The local Fire Authority is responsible for enforcing the Fire Provisions and application for a Fire Certificate should be made on Form OSR.3 together with copies of plans showing the proposed means of escape. The authority may refuse to issue a certificate unless certain alterations are made within a specified time (which may be extended if necessary). There is a right of appeal to a Magistrates' Court against the decision within twenty-one days. Any order which the court may make will be binding on the authority, but the applicant may further appeal against the order to a court of Quarter Sessions.

7

BUILDING CONTRACTS

Generally.—The detailed study of the law of contract and of building contracts in particular is a separate subject for the student and cannot be given anything like full treatment within the scope of a book of this type.   In this chapter the principal forms in use are noted and some attention is drawn to those clauses which most affect the practice of the architect and deserve his special study.   Some text-books and reference books will be found quoted in Appendix 2.

Contract Documents.—A building contract is usually composed of a set of drawings, a bill of quantities in the case of larger works (or a specification for the smaller) and articles of agreement with detailed conditions of contract. All these documents read together form the contract.   With the Government form of contract a specification is part of the contract in addition to the bill of quantities, but not with the R.I.B.A. form referred to below.

The drawings will consist of plans, sections and elevations, with such details (the more the better) as can be made available. The ideal to be aimed at is to supply all drawings that will be required for the job, so that on the contract being signed they can be handed over with the feeling that " it is all there ", and that there is nothing further to do but supervise the erection, deal with the incidental administration and solve any minor problems that may arise as the work progresses.

The bill of quantities is, in effect, a detailed and priced *pro forma* invoice for the building, provided in advance and setting out all its parts individually priced, so that omissions or additions, if decided on, can be made at fixed rates.

In smaller works where there may be no bill of quantities its place is taken by a specification, which sets out the description of materials and workmanship and describes the work to be done, but gives no quantities.   The builders tendering must estimate the quantities for themselves and prepare their tender by reference to the drawings and specification.

The articles of agreement and conditions of contract will probably be in one of the standard forms referred to below.

Lump-sum Contracts.—The architect will have to consider what form of building contract is suitable. Mostly, full information being available, a lump-sum contract will be used, i.e. one in which the contractor undertakes to carry out the work specified for a fixed sum. The usual form adopted in private practice is that issued under the sanction of the R.I.B.A. and the National Federation of Building Trades Employers, the R.I.C.S. and the various Local Authorities' Associations.* This form is prepared by a Joint Contracts Tribunal, on which the above-mentioned bodies are represented. It is therefore generally acceptable. This and other forms prepared in this way are known shortly as R.I.B.A. forms.

The Tribunal has decided to issue a new print of the contract form each year on July 1st, incorporating any amendments made during the previous year. Amendment sheets will be published annually on January 1st and July 1st (the latter also included in the new print).

There are two alternative versions of this form available for use—with and without bills of quantites—and the architect will have to decide which is to be used. The builders' federations had a rule that their members should not tender for contracts to a value of over £8,000 unless a bill of quantities was supplied. This rule was found to be contrary to the public interest by the Restrictive Practices Court † and has been dropped. However, the figure may be taken as an approximate guide to the limit above which it would not be reasonable in normal circumstances to ask more than one contractor to do all the work in preparing an estimate without a bill of quantities. If, therefore, the contemplated work exceeds this amount in value, the architect should take the steps referred to in the next chapter for the appointment of a quantity surveyor. Whereas for a small contract, such as a pair of cottages, builders can be expected to take their own measurements, anything beyond the suggested limit would place an excessive burden on their staff. Moreover, the margin of error due to differences in interpretation of the specification and drawings increases with the size of the contract.

---

* *Agreement and Schedule of Conditions of Building Contract* (alternative forms for use with and without quantities) 1963 (revised 1969): R I.B.A.

† (1963) 2 A.E.R. 361.

A variety of the lump-sum contract is the contract with an approximate bill of quantities, or even only a schedule of prices, in both cases subject to measurement of the whole work as it is done. The approximate bill is prepared by the quantity surveyor to the best of his ability from the information available—the more accurate and complete the information the more accurate and complete will the bill be, and the nearer its total to a definite tender. The schedule of prices is merely a list of the items which are expected to arise, with a unit rate for each, on which a measured bill can be based. Having no quantities, there is no total, so comparison of tenders is difficult, and depends on a study of the relative importance of the items in the particular job. But, whether with approximate bill or only schedule of prices, the contract will still be one for a lump sum, but the sum has not been determined on signature of the contract. It will be determined in due course in accordance with provisions made by the contract. These types of contract are necessary only where the drawings and specification cannot be fully worked out and a start is urgent. The architect should, however, bear in mind that an early start does not necessarily imply early completion. It will be found well worth while to spend a little longer completing drawings and details for a fully thought-out scheme, instead of making a hurried start to be followed by delays due to insufficient or inaccurate data.

The form of contract to be used with an approximate bill of quantities or a schedule of prices will be the same as for a definite tender, with suitable amendment to cover the necessity for measurement and valuation on completion.

Prime Cost Contracts.—It sometimes happens that requirements are so uncertain that it is not reasonable to ask a contractor to give a fixed price, either in advance or after measurement and valuation as the work is done. The alternative then is for the contractor to be reimbursed his " prime cost "—i.e. actual expenditure on the works—and be paid a fee to cover his overhead charges and profit. This fee can normally be a fixed sum or sometimes it is in the form of a percentage on the expenditure.

The disadvantage of a prime-cost contract is that the contractor, having no fixed rates for his work, has not the same incentive to buy in the cheapest market or to watch economy on the site. He will get the same fee irrespective of such considerations; in fact, if the fee is a percentage, the more he pays the more he gets. Many contractors, of course, will not be consciously influenced by this, and where the need for this type of contract arises, the architect will be best able to protect his client by selecting contractors well known to him and whom he can trust.

A suitable form for prime-cost contract is published by the R.I.B.A.*

Public Authorities' Contracts.—Public Authorities, such as County, Borough or District Councils or the nationalised Boards or Corporations, may occasionally have their own standard form of contract, which may be based on the R.I.B.A. form or be entirely different. A version of the R.I.B.A. form is published for use by Local Authorities and is now accepted by most Authorities.† There are various requirements which such Authorities have to incorporate in all contracts under their standing orders which are not in the ordinary R.I.B.A. form. Clause 17A and 25 (3) of the special R.I.B.A. form (1963) for Local Authorities will indicate some of the items.

Government Contracts.—Government contracts are usually let on the basis of the official conditions of contract.‡ These conditions are more lengthy than the R.I.B.A. form, and are drafted for use in any of the types of lump-sum contract or in prime-cost contracts. They cover a number of special requirements of the Government Service, including emergency powers, secrecy, warnings against corruption, &c. There are no formal articles of agreement, the tender being submitted on a special form which with the acceptance constitutes the Contract.

Government Departments also make considerable use for maintenance work of term contracts. These are contracts, let competitively by which a builder undertakes to carry out all repair and maintenance work on Government buildings within a

---

* *Fixed Fee Form of Prime Cost Contract:* R.I.B.A.
† *Agreement and Schedule of Conditions of Building Contract (Local Authorities Edition)* 1963 (revised 1969): R.I.B.A.
‡ *General Conditions of Government Contracts for Building and Civil Engineering Works (Form CCC/Wks/1):* H.M.S.O.

stated area for a particular period or term, usually two or three years. Competing contractors state a percentage on or off a published schedule of prices. The Ministry of Defence have a published schedule,* which is also used by some other Government Departments.

R.I.B.A. Form (1963) (revised July 1969).—The following are some of the main points which should receive the attention of students:

Clause

1. Requires the Contractor to complete the works " to the reasonable satisfaction of the Architect ". The words " in accordance with the directions " (of the Architect), which were in the previous edition, have been dropped. How the work is done is for the Contractor to decide, but the result must satisfy the Architect.

2. This clause is important as defining procedure for the instructions which the Architect, elsewhere in the contract, is authorised to give. They must be in writing. Verbal instructions must be confirmed by the Contractor to the Architect and if not dissented from in writing in seven days they become binding instructions.

   Under subclause 2 the Contractor may request the Architect to specify in writing the clause which is his authority for the instruction; he must therefore be careful that he does not issue instructions *ultra vires*.

3. The contract documents are defined and there is a requirement that the Architect shall supply a specification, schedules or other like document.† It should be noted from subsection 7 that the contract documents are confidential, particularly, of course, the Contractor's prices in the priced bill of quantities.

4. This is the clause which governs payment of their charges to Statutory Authorities (so far only as their statutory work is concerned). If an Electricity Board quotes for the wiring of a building they are normal nominated subcontractors for this (clause 27), but their charge for bringing in their mains is paid under this clause.

---

* *War Department Schedule of Prices for Works Services*: H.M.S.O.
† See page 96.

5. The Architect must provide full information by giving levels and fully dimensioned drawings to enable the Contractor to set out the works.

6. The Architect is given authority to order the opening up of work which he may think was not done in accordance with the contract. Unless it is found that the Contractor was at fault, the cost may be added to the contract sum. The Architect, of course, owes a duty to his client not to order such opening up recklessly.

8. The general foreman is established as the Contractor's agent for receiving instructions from the Architect.

9. There is power reserved for the Architect to enter upon the works or workshops (where otherwise he would be a trespasser).

10. This clause makes clear that the Clerk of Works is only an inspector. Any instructions he gives are of no effect unless confirmed in writing by the Architect within two working days.

11. Subsection 1 authorises instructions for variations which are defined by subsection 2. They must not be so extensive as to change substantially the nature of the contract. If they are, the Contractor cannot be held to his rates.

  The rest of the clause is mainly of concern to the quantity surveyor, but is of importance to the Architect where there are no quantities.

  Under subsection 6, any loss or expense that the Contractor suffers as a result of a variation or adjustment against a provisional sum, which the normal methods of valuation would not meet, must be assessed and allowed to the Contractor.

12. Subclause 1 relates the quality and quantity of the work to the bill of quantities and subsection 2 provides for errors of the quantity surveyor (not in the Contractor's prices—see clause 13) to be corrected.

14. This clause governs the inclusion of unfixed materials in interim valuations. They must be on or adjacent to the works, and on being included in a valuation become the property of the Employer.

  Although not specifically mentioned in this clause, the Architect may include unfixed materials before delivery to the site under the conditions set out in clause 30 (2A).

15. Under subclause 1 the Architect must issue a certificate of practical completion of the works, from the date of which the defects liability period will run (the period within which defects appearing due to faulty materials and workmanship must be remedied). Clause 30 (4) (b) requires release of part of the retention money at the same time.

Under subclause 2 the Architect must within fourteen days of the expiry of the defects liability period deliver to the Contractor a schedule of outstanding defects to be remedied (he may point out defects earlier, but is not bound to).

Subclause 4 requires the Architect to issue a certificate that all defects have been made good.

16. This clause provides for the completion of the contract in stages and governs the handing over of each stage, the making good of defects and release of the outstanding retention money in respect of each stage.

17. The consent of the Employer is necessary for the assignment of the whole contract, as the Contractor would be assigning his obligation and the Employer must have a say. The consent of the Architect is sufficient for subletting part of the contract, since the Contractor is still responsible and approval can, therefore, reasonably be delegated.

18. This clause requires the Contractor to indemnify the Employer against claims for

(*a*) injury to person (unless the fault of the Employer);
(*b*) loss or damage to any property due to the negligence of the Contractor or those for whom he is responsible.

19. Subclause 1 requires the Contractor to insure his liabilities under clause 18.

Subclause 2 requires insurance in the joint names of the Employer and Contractor against claims for loss or damage to property, which is not due to negligence for which the Contractor would be responsible under 18 (2). As it is not practical in many cases for the risk to be assessed in advance, it is required that such insurance shall be covered by a provisional sum.

20. This clause covers insurance of the works themselves against loss or damage by fire and certain other risks. It will be seen to be in three sections. [A] would be the normal section applicable to new works and [C] to alterations to an existing building. In the latter case, the building being already insured by the Employer, he can arrange with his Insurance Company for alteration in the cover. Subsection [B] applies to a case in which the Employer requires to insure a new building himself.

21. Provides for date for possession of the site and date for completion, the actual dates in each case being filled in to the Appendix.

22. Provides for liquidated damages for delay beyond the date of completion, again referring to the Appendix. The amount should bear a relation to the loss which the Employer would incur and should generally be fixed in consultation with him.

23. This clause sets out the reasons for which the Architect may extend the time. It should be noted that reasons for extension must fall within the list given. Extension cannot be given because the Contractor says he has lost, say, a month: he must satisfy the Architect that *completion date* is delayed. It is no argument for him to say that he was aiming to finish three months early (the Employer might not want it—perhaps not have the finance arranged to suit).

Subclause (*j*), a hang-over from war-time conditions, would normally be deleted.

24. This clause is one the Architect should note carefully, particularly subclause 1 (*a*). The " due time " is a matter to be determined with each contract. The Contractor cannot demand all drawings at the beginning of the contract (though to supply all of them should be the aim of every architect), and then complain because they are not forthcoming. He must be reasonable having regard to the date for completion, and he must make his claim within a reasonable time of its becoming apparent that the works are affected.

25. The Employer is given power to determine the contract if the Contractor

    (a) suspends work on the contract;

    (b) does not proceed with reasonable diligence;

    (c) refuses or deliberately neglects to remove defective work;

    (d) fails to get the required approval to assignment or subletting;

    (e) is bankrupt or goes into liquidation or commits certain acts implying an approach to such condition.

The reasons (a) to (d) require fourteen days' notice: in the case of (e) determination is automatic.

Procedure is then laid down to be followed in any such case.

26. The Contractor has power to determine the contract forthwith if

    (a) the Employer fails to honour the Architect's certificate for payment.

    (b) the Employer obstructs the issue of a certificate;

    (c) the works are suspended for more than periods specified in the Appendix for the reasons set out;

    (d) bankruptcy or liquidation or implication of it as in the case of the Contractor.

As in the case of determination by the Employer, procedure is laid down.

27. This very long clause governs the employment of specialist sub-contractors nominated by the Architect, often responsible for a substantial proportion of the whole contract, and needs very careful study. It is important in inviting tenders from firms for such work to notify them that they will be nominated sub-contractors under this form of contract and that they must comply with all the requirements of this clause.

Subclause (a) (viii), lines 5 to 8, may seem rather obscurely worded, and something further is said of this in the chapter on Certificates.* It is made clear that retention is held on trust (so not available to a receiver for the Contractor in bankruptcy).

* See page 145.

Subclause (e) is the authority for early release of sub-contractors' retention if considered advisable.

Subclause (g) permits the Contractor in certain circumstances to tender for work covered by a p.c. sum. It should be made quite clear whether the tender is to be on the same basis as a proposed nominated subcontractor or whether he should include the profit he has included in his tender on such p.c. sum, which would accordingly be deducted.

28. This clause sets out the terms on which orders are to be placed with merchants supplying goods to be fixed by the Contractor who, being selected by the Architect, are termed " nominated suppliers ".

It is important to remember in obtaining quotations to stipulate that the estimates must be subject to 5% cash discount. There is no provision for payment on the Architect's certificate. Such merchants are in the same position as most other merchants, i.e. they must be paid in the month following delivery.

29. Provision is made to allow artists, &c., employed and paid direct by the Employer to come on to the works.

30. This is an important clause defining procedure in making interim payments and issue of the final certificate. In the Appendix are to be filled in the intervals for certificates, the percentage of value to be retained as a reserve and a limit at which the sum retained shall remain at the same figure.

Subclause 2A gives the Architect discretion to allow the value of materials intended for inclusion in the works and ready in all respects, but stored off the site, to be included in interim certificates, on condition that the provisos listed are complied with. The Tribunal felt that the restriction to pay only for such " materials and goods delivered to, placed on or adjacent to the works " was inadequate under modern conditions of construction. Such application, made in the first instance to the quantity surveyor, would be referred to the Architect with a report that the provisos of the clause have been complied with, and it would be for him to decide if he can give his consent.

Subclause 4 (a) makes it clear that retention sums are

held on trust (so not available to a receiver for the Employer in bankruptcy). 4 (*b*) and (*c*) provide for release of retention in two stages on the basis of the latest available valuation, leaving any balances (either way) to be covered by a final certificate (subclause 6). Subclause 7 defines the finality of such a certificate.

31A–D. These clauses set out the conditions under which fluctuations in the contractor's costs are to be admitted for adjustment of the contract price. Either 31A or 31B should be deleted. Clause 31A provides for adjustment of fluctuation in rates of wages, prices of materials and in any "type and rate of contribution, levy and tax" payable by the contractor as employer under any Act of Parliament. Under clause 31B fluctuations in rates of wages and in prices of materials are excluded, so that only the above-mentioned statutory contributions are adjustable. Detail of these clauses is largely a matter for the quantity surveyor, but in contracts without quantities the Architect would be responsible for checking the detail and should, therefore, be acquainted with the requirements.

32 & 33. These clauses, one hopes, will not have to be applied. Perhaps one can say " sufficient unto the day ".

34. The Contractor must be reimbursed for any loss or expense involved in preserving antiquities, if not otherwise covered.

35. The parties are left to appoint their own arbitrator and, in the event of failure to agree within fourteen days of notice, reference is to a person to be appointed by the President of the R.I.B.A. Except as provided by subclause 2, the arbitration will not be opened until after alleged practical completion of the works.

CCC/Wks./1.*—There are not, as in the R.I.B.A. Form, separate forms for use with and without quantities. Clause 5A provides for a schedule of rates to be deposited by the Contractor where no bill of quantities is supplied. There are no Articles of Agreement: the form of tender and acceptance constitute the

* See footnote on page 59.

contract. The clauses in the Conditions of particular interest to architects are:—

Clause

1. The definitions should be understood.

3. Everything on the site becomes the property of the Authority. Under the R.I.B.A. contract unfixed materials only become vested in the Employer when included in a valuation paid.

4. Unlike the R.I.B.A. form, this contract makes the Specification a contract document.

5. The bill of quantities. The effect of the subclauses on correction of errors is similar to that of the R.I.B.A. form. It will be noted that the same Conditions of Contract are applied with Provisional or Approximate Quantities or with a Schedule of Prices.

7. S.O.'s Instructions and the conditions under which the relative work is chargeable.

8. Failure of Contractor to comply with Instructions.

9. Valuation of variations.

10. Valuation by complete measurement.

11. This clause (Price Variation) has been withdrawn from the printed document, but is added as a supplementary clause for contracts with price adjustment.

12. Setting out of the works.

13. Quality of materials and workmanship.

14. Statutory fees, &c. There is no requirement for provisional sums: tenderers are expected to ascertain their liability.

20. The Contractor must not allow in his prices for being able to use such material as sand from the excavation. What he uses will be valued and he will be charged.

21. Approval of foundation bottoms.

22. The Contractor is to give notice before covering up. This would probably normally mean keeping the Clerk of Works informed of such matters. Although there is usually a Clerk of Works on such works, there is no mention of him as such in the Conditions. The reference to the " S.O.'s representative " in clause 13 is, no doubt, to him.

23. S.O.'s control over suspension of work for frost.

24. Rendering of daywork accounts.
25. There is no requirement for fire insurance, &c., in the case of Crown property. The Government are their own insurers (see clauses 1 (2) (*h*) and 26 (2) (*b*) (ii)).
26. Damage to Works, Plant, &c.
28. Delay.
29. Damages for Delay.
31. Subcontractors. There is no provision for " nominated " subcontractors in the sense of the R.I.B.A. contract. In practice, more specialist work is probably measured out and fully specified and detailed for the general contractor to price than in private work. There is, however, provision for p.c. sums in clause 38.
32. Defects.
33. Agent (general foreman).
36. Power of the S.O. to dismiss the Contractor's servants.
37. Attendance of the Contractor for measuring.
38. Prime cost items. The cash discounts under the Conditions are the same ($2\frac{1}{2}\%$) for both suppliers and subcontractors. They are not guaranteed, being described as " obtainable ".
39. Provisional lump sums and provisional quantities.
40. Advances on account. The percentages to be retained and maximum amounts are fixed and not left to be determined in each case, as in the R.I.B.A. form.
41. Payments on completion.
42. Certificates.
43. Recovery of Sums due from the Contractor.
44. There is a unilateral power to determine the contract and full instructions as to the procedure to be followed. The Contractor does not get compensation for loss of profit, but subclause D (5) makes provision for an *ex gratia* allowance in case of hardship (which is usually interpreted as losing money, not failing to make it).
45. Determination in case of default or failure of the Contractor.
46. A clause applicable to all cases of determination.
47. Injury to person and property. The Contractor's liability is defined. There is no reference to insurance: that is his affair.

48. The Contractor is not responsible for damage to highways, &c.

61. Arbitration.

It should be noted that there is no Appendix as in the R.I.B.A. contract. The material information is given in an " Abstract of Particulars " which accompanies the tender documents.

Comparison of R.I.B.A. and Government Forms.—The R.I.B.A. form, being one negotiated between the building owner (represented by architects and quantity surveyors as well as officers of Local Authorities) and the contractor, is one mutually agreed by or on behalf of the parties to a building contract. The Government form, unilaterally prepared, is a good deal longer, as, besides providing for the special circumstances of Crown property, it is for use in both building and civil engineering works. Moreover, it seems to be elaborated in an attempt to cover as many unforeseen conditions as possible: the more that decisions which involve individual judgment, and perhaps prejudice, can be reduced, the less likely are inconsistencies between the rulings of different officers, possibly resulting in injustice. The tendency, accordingly, is for the Government contract to be more onerous on the contractor than the R.I.B.A. form.

Neither form of contract defines " p.c. items " or " provisional sums ". The implied meaning is that p.c. sums are sums to be expended either on materials to be supplied by merchants or on work to be done on the site by sub-contractors, to be included in the tender and set against the relative account, with adjustment of any profit, &c., added by the contractor. Provisional sums are lump sums to be included provisionally in the tender, usually for uncertain needs such as the contingency sum, against which may be set measured work, daywork and/or an outside account, with a profit for the contractor.*

Form of Sub-contract.—A form of sub-contract has been prepared for use between contractor and nominated sub-contractor under the R.I.B.A. contract.† This is agreed between the

---

* This meaning is confirmed by a definition in the *Standard Method of Measurement*, 5th Edition, clause A7, which will apply to bills of quantities, unless otherwise provided.
† *Standard Form of Sub-contract (1963):* N.F.B.T.E.

N.F.B.T.E. and the Federation of Associations of Specialists and Sub-contractors, with the approval of the Committee of Associations of Specialist Engineering Contractors. If prospective sub-contractors are warned on invitation to tender that they will be required to enter into this form of contract, conditions should be absolutely clear.

Fixed Fee Form of Prime Cost Contract, R.I.B.A. Form.*— This is a form on much the same lines as the standard R.I.B.A. contract, but provides for the contractor's remuneration by payment to him of his prime cost plus a fixed fee instead of a stated lump sum. The method of calculating the prime cost is fully defined in a Schedule to the form. An estimate of the prime cost is to be made before signature of the contract, and this and the amount of the agreed fixed fee are to be inserted in other Schedules. There is no provision for variations, except for cost of disturbance under clause 20 (corresponding with 24 of the standard form) or expense under the " antiquities " clause.

It is one of the conditions (clause 3 (1)) that there shall be no alteration in the nature or scope of the works. The architect should therefore be sure that he does not alter the character of the work nor materially increase the prime cost beyond the estimate that has been made beforehand.

Form of Agreement for Minor Building Works.†— This is a four-page document of thirteen clauses, being a very abbreviated form of the standard edition, intended for work which is not technically unusual or complex. It is especially suitable for contracts to carry out maintenance on existing buildings or for simple conversions, provided that no work of a specialist nature is involved. It is not possible to put a limit to the financial value of contracts in this form. For example, it could be used for a maintenance contract on a school building amounting to £12,000, whereas for a new house costing £6,000 the Standard Form should be used.

A specification, with or without drawings, is prepared for the builder to submit a lump-sum tender for the work, which will usually be completed in a short period. It is not appropriate to

---

* *Fixed Fee Form of Prime Cost Contract:* R.I.B.A.
† *Agreement for Minor Building Works:* R.I.B.A.

use the form for work where bills of quantities have been prepared, or where a schedule of rates is required for valuing variations, or where fluctuations in prices are admitted. In such cases the Standard Form should be used.

The form is not applicable for work in Scotland.

Other Forms of Contract.—Forms of contract other than the above are unusual, but if the architect meets a form which is strange to him, he must study it, particularly to see what differences have been made from what is in his experience normal practice.

Firm Price Contracts.—With the greater stability in cost of labour and materials which it is hoped has come, there is a tendency for contracts to be placed on a firm price basis without any fluctuations adjustment clause. In order that the contractor may reasonably tie himself, it is more than ever essential for the project to be thoroughly thought out and not extend too far into the future. The Joint Consultative Committee of Architects, Quantity Surveyors and Builders published their recommendations (*R.I.B.A. Journal*, September 1958, p. 386). Briefly they recommended:—

1. thorough preliminary planning;
2. acceptance of a tender within two months;
3. complete documentation;
4. notification to the architect by the contractor at the earliest stage of his future requirements.

When, after experiment, this procedure was decided on for Government work, the Minister of Works stated in the House of Commons (30th April 1957) that it would be limited to cases where the estimated contract period was not more than two years. This period, confirmed by the N.F.B.T.E.* and the Banwell Report (8.4) is generally regarded as a limit beyond which it would not be reasonable under present conditions to ask contractors to quote a firm price.

All-in Contract.—A development of recent years is the all-in contract, sometimes referred to as a " package deal "

* *Firm Price Tendering, A Statement:* N.F.B.T.E.

in which the building contractor undertakes the whole of the services required for the erection of the building from the first designs, so dispensing with the independent architect, consultant and quantity surveyor. Their technical work is, of course, required, but is provided by the contractor's own staff, permanent or specially commissioned. It is suggested that the unity of control speeds up administration, but, on the other hand, such a contract is not normally on a competitive basis, and may, therefore, be at a higher price than if it were let in the normal way. Price, however, is not always the primary consideration of the building owner.

A modification of this procedure allows the building owner's own appointed architect to be employed, giving him the advantage of consultation with the contractor from the very start.*

The services of the quantity surveyor in this type of contract will be under the direction of the contractor, though a building owner's quantity surveyor may have either a watching brief or a more definite share in control.

Consortium.—The term "consortium" has only recently appeared in connection with the Industry, and is used of the association of a number of contractors to carry out large contracts. They may give a joint tender under normal procedure, or they may adopt the all-in contract principles referred to above. Sometimes a development group is formed for large projects with parent, holding and development companies incorporated. The intricacies of company law are not here our concern, but the outlook of the architect may vary according to the organisation of the consortium.

A similar association may be formed by the professional advisers: architect, consultants and quantity surveyor.† Such a consortium may include the contractor as well, the contract price being negotiated with him in advance. This has the advantage that the procedure to be adopted in carrying out the work can be discussed with the contractor and the requirements of his organisation can be known at an early stage and work planned accordingly.

Very Small Contracts.—When dealing with very small works the architect may feel that he can dispense with the use of formal conditions of contract. There will, of course, still be a contract, constituted by the written tender and acceptance. The specification should cover any of the subjects in the standard conditions which are applicable, otherwise, as in the sale of goods, the purchaser will be entitled to have what the seller has agreed to sell—neither more nor less—at the price agreed, which will be payable on completion. There would be no question of interim payments, variations, price fluctuations, damages for delays, &c. As such a method would only apply to the very smallest contract, these would not be important. Anything over, say, £500 in value should preferably have a formal contract.

8

THE QUANTITY SURVEYOR—HIS USE AND NEEDS

Work of the Quantity Surveyor.—The work which the quantity surveyor does cannot be better set out than in the booklet entitled *The Services of the Chartered Quantity Surveyor* published by the R.I.C.S., which reads as follows:—

1. Advise on what a project would cost.
2. Advise on what size and standard of structure can be erected for any given expenditure.
3. Advise on the economics of a project and the preparation of a budget.
4. Co-operate with the designers to ensure that a building can be erected within an approved expenditure.
5. Advise on tendering procedures and contractual arrangements. Prepare documents for obtaining tenders and arranging a contract.
6. Exercise control during the construction so that the cost is not exceeded without authority.
7. Act with the Architect or Engineer to ensure that the financial provisions of the contract are properly interpreted and applied so that the Client's financial interest is safeguarded and that the Builder is paid a proper price for the work.

Use of the Quantity Surveyor for Advice.—The architect will realise that in order to get full value from the quantity surveyor's assistance, the question of his employment should be raised with the client at an early stage. Even if no appointment is made, the architect will usually be in touch with a surveyor, who will help him in any difficulty on matters within his province. Such advisory services are particularly valuable in the early stages of a scheme, when approximate costs are being considered, or later where, perhaps, there being no quantities, the architect has to deal himself with builders' accounts. The quantity surveyor will usually give advice on a first approximate estimate without charge, but a subsequent cost planning service, involving as it does a substantial amount of work, is the subject of a fee to be agreed. Where there are no quantities, it may be possible to get the client's approval to the appointment of a quantity surveyor to deal with the adjustment of accounts, and to have him named as surveyor accordingly in the building contract.

Appointment for Preparation of Bill of Quantities.—
When it comes to the preparation of quantities, the approval
of the client to the appointment should be ensured, and something is said of the legal aspect in Chapter 16. The terms of
employment should be made clear to the client, and any conditions or qualifications on the subject received from the quantity
surveyor should be communicated to him in full. If the architect
will see that the client has information in writing as to the
appointment of the quantity surveyor, it is likely to save trouble
later. Much of the difficulty on this subject in the past has been
due to the architect not broaching the matter to his client
beforehand, but making the appointment on his own initiative.
If the architect is satisfied that the employment of a quantity
surveyor is of value, he must explain the need to his client, and
the above-mentioned booklet published by the R.I.C.S. will be
found very useful for this purpose.

The above applies mainly to a private client. Public Authorities may have their own system of appointment, possibly from a
panel of surveyors regularly employed by them.

Architect Preparing Bill of Quantities.—Though quantity surveying has become more and more a specialised profession,
there are occasions when an architect may decide to prepare
quantities himself. In a provincial practice, where there may
not be sufficient work for the architect to confine himself to
architecture proper, he may supplement his main work by dealing
with surveying in some of its branches—from estate agency and
property management to the work of the building and quantity
surveyor. He has, however, to face the difficulty of qualifying
himself properly in the branch concerned or risking trouble from
his lack of knowledge and experience. There are also, of course,
the large firms who run different departments under qualified
heads, including, perhaps, one for quantity surveying. The main
objection to the architect for a scheme also acting as quantity
surveyor is that he is bound to find it more difficult than the
separate quantity surveyor to adopt an independent view-point.
The architect is already in a difficult administrative position in
having to act impartially as between client and contractor on
many points. Apart from the natural distaste of many designers
for the routine work of measurement and accounts, it relieves

the architect of part of his problem if the quantity surveying work is in independent hands. Where the architect does act as quantity surveyor, he should be sure that his client is aware of the fact, as otherwise he may have difficulty when he renders his account.

Time for Preparation of Quantities.—The quantity surveyor's work is the last stage before receipt of tenders, except the estimating by the builder. Consequently, there is a tendency for the cumulative result of delays during the earlier stages of a scheme to have its effect on the time suggested for preparation of quantities. With drawings completed and everything apparently cut and dried, it is sometimes difficult for the client to understand further delay, and the surveyor is accordingly pressed. The surveyor can and will work at high pressure when necessary, but he and his staff cannot do so for *everybody* and *all the time*. He is, after all, preparing a document which will define the contract work precisely, and accuracy in the bill depends on a systematic checking of each stage and a very careful reading through of the final draft. Excessive pressure can only result in work being done hurriedly or in part omitted, with dangerous results. An extra week or two can, in most cases, make little material difference to the client, but may make all the difference to the quality and accuracy of the bill.

It is a great help in shortening the time required for preparation of a bill if the quantity surveyor has full and accurate warning of when the documents will be ready for him. All preparation of quantities being, with few exceptions, for some reason in a rush, the surveyor may not always have the staff available to take on an unexpected job, and he cannot shelve it— at least, not for long. He cannot keep a number of takers-off doing nothing, waiting for new work, so a job sent him without warning is bound to disorganise his plans, and consequently take longer. He may even not be able to do it at all. If the surveyor has been approached at an early stage, he should be kept informed of the programme and probable date when he can start, as well as of deferments resulting from controls, or otherwise, as they arise. When drawings approach the final stages he should be given a definite date, which, once given, will be adhered to. He will then be able to plan his work so that the job can be done in the minimum of time. If he is definitely anticipating drawings on a fixed date, this may make him refuse other work ; so it is most important to adhere to promised dates. Moreover, if the surveyor, expecting drawings on a certain date, says he can do the work in six weeks, the same period may not be sufficient if drawings turn up a fortnight late, or if they come slowly in batches. The period is fixed having regard to the work expected to be in hand at the time, and assuming that all particulars will be available together, unless otherwise arranged. The architect may be confident that the surveyor, for his part, will do the work as quickly as possible, as it is in his own interest to do so.

Procedure in the Quantity Surveyor's Work.—In order that the architect may appreciate the requirements of the quantity surveyor in the way of drawings and particulars, it is necessary to give some idea of how he sets about his work.

There are two systems in common use by quantity surveyors in preparing bills of quantities. One is to take the measurements trade by trade in the usual order of trades. He would start by measuring all excavation, then all concrete, then all brickwork, &c. This method is very difficult to adopt except in small buildings because of the complicated nature of building construction, though some surveyors claim that they do so even for large buildings.

The second and certainly more general method in London and the South of England is to divide the building into sections structurally, and measure one section at a time. A list of sections in a typical building might be :—

1. Foundations up to damp-proof course.
2. Brickwork (superstructure).
3. External facings.
4. Floors.
5. Roofs.
6. Fires and vents.
7. Internal finishings.
8. Windows and their openings.
9. Doors and their openings.
10. Openings (without window or door).
11. Fittings.
12. Plumbing.
13. Heating and hot-water service.
14. Electrical work.
15. Drains.
16. Paths, fences, &c.

This list is naturally elastic, and a particular building might introduce additional sections, e.g. lifts, cooking plant, &c. It will be seen that the list is in a logical order, following, more or less, the construction of the building. The surveyor in going through these sections sees the erection of the building carried through in his mind's eye and must see *every* detail, or his building is not complete. If the architect does not show him any particular detail (and even the fullest drawings will not show everything), he must decide for himself what that detail is, for he cannot measure without something definite in mind.

It will be realised that if he is to adopt the first system abovementioned, the surveyor must have all drawings and particulars before he starts. Otherwise he is bound to take much longer going back over his dimensions when new drawings are made available, and, apart from the time lost, the risk of error is much increased.

With the second system it is obvious that if certain drawings are delayed the surveyor will not be held up. But it must be the right drawings which are kept back. The surveyor may be able to do without joinery fittings or drains and not upset his organisation, but if he is sent foundation drawings and told by the architect, " You will have to wait for depths ", they are worse than useless. Even if he says, " It is all there, except reinforcement, which I am awaiting from a consultant ", the surveyor is bound to lose time. He would normally measure reinforcement whilst the foundations are fresh in his mind. If he has to go over the whole again, there is much wasted effort. He would much rather wait and start at a definite level (say damp-proof course— assuming the superstructure drawings are ready). If widths of concrete are also dependent on the consultant, the surveyor cannot start foundations, as such widths also govern the excavation.

Where complete drawings are not available the surveyor should be consulted as to priorities, so that the progress is suited in that. What he can wait for may depend on how many assistants he can put on to the job. In the list above, if two takers-off were engaged, A would take No. 1–6, B Nos. 7–10. Whichever was first available would possibly take 12–15, whilst the other would take 11 and 16. If, however, three were employed, the third would start at once on 12–15, so that drawings for only 11 and 16 would not be pressing.

Advantage of Complete Drawings.—The ideal is, of course, for drawings to be handed complete to the surveyor. Generally, he would much rather wait till they are all ready than tackle the job piecemeal. The time saved by having drawings sent in instalments is mythical, unless they are supplied according to a prearranged plan fully understood and agreed by the quantity surveyor. In any case, a list of the drawings which will be available should be made and handed to the quantity surveyor with the first drawings, so that he knows exactly what is to follow and can arrange his work accordingly. A drawing received " out of the blue " can be most disorganising. The surveyor will have settled points from the information he has, and the architect's development of the detail may be quite different from what he expected. If important details of construction are entirely omitted the same trouble arises, only at a later stage. If the architect is doubtful, the quantity surveyor will be more so. The architect must draw his sections to show the difficult points, not to dodge them. There may be little difference in the actual value between the quantity surveyor's solution and the architect's, but the surveyor will be dissatisfied with quantities which are wrong, and, if amendment is not made, explanation will have to be given to the contractor later and his agreement obtained that adjustment is not necessary.

Again, it is little use giving a surveyor 1 : 100 drawings and telling him that 1 : 20 details are to follow. The 1 : 100 drawings will be fully figured, but there is presumably some reason for preparing larger-scale drawings (e.g. to show and work out details of construction which cannot be clearly shown on the smaller drawings). Moreover, the architect's experience will tell him that in drawing out the 1 : 20 details he will nearly always find some improvement in design or construction that he wants to incorporate. If the quantity surveyor has to review all his dimensions on receipt of the 1 : 20 drawings and make adjustments, again much time will be wasted. Incidentally, unusual scales should be avoided. A 1 : 15 scale should not be used just because the resultant drawing fits more conveniently on the sheet in question.

As to the supply of " preliminary " or " advance copies " of the drawings for the quantity surveyor to get on with, they are (except where it is agreed that only a schedule for complete re-measurement is to be provided) most unsatisfactory. Being probably incomplete, apart from giving the surveyor a lot of extra trouble, they will increase the amount of eventual adjustment of variations, so wasting the client's money on unnecessary extra fees. Even if they are prints from pencil drawings given with the assurance that " they only have to be traced ", it is most likely that amendments will be made before they are.

Except in the very smallest jobs, at least two copies should be supplied to the surveyor of all general drawings and main details. One copy will probably be sufficient of any specialised or large-scale drawings (e.g. those of drains, fittings, &c.) or full-size details of special items. On the larger jobs three copies of the general drawings will be wanted. Again the quantity surveyor should be consulted, as the number of copies will depend on the number of assistants he will have measuring. The comparatively low cost of extra prints is more than balanced by the time saved in measurement. That the prints should be clear ones may seem obvious, but illegible prints from rough pencil drawings, which the surveyor has to go over to make the lines and figures clear, are not unknown. Blue prints should be avoided ; it is a good deal more difficult to measure from a blue print than from a dye-line or black-and-white print.

Perhaps one might add that there is a limit to the need for completeness in detail drawings. The detail of, say, a flush door, which must be fully given in examination to prove the candidate's knowledge of its construction, is not necessary for contract purposes, where the detail is largely covered by the specification or, perhaps, a British Standard incorporated in it.

Figured Dimensions.—Figured dimensions on drawings may be divided into three categories :—

(a) Over-all dimensions of the buildings.
(b) Subdivision of the last for setting out, showing spacing of structural frame, windows and doors, &c.
(c) Internal dimensions of rooms.

The quantity surveyor will require (a) and (c). He uses (a) to calculate the girths of the walls, and a whole series of items dependent on that girth—trench digging, concrete foundations, brickwork, damp-proof course, facings, copings, &c. He must have (c) to set down the measurements of ceiling and floor finishes and to get the girths of rooms for wall plaster, skirtings, &c. The architect should see, therefore, that he gives over-all dimensions of all sides of the building and that the exact dimensions of every room in either direction can be seen at a glance. Where there is a range of rooms of similar dimensions, obviously the figuring need not be repeated for each, but otherwise the two dimensions of each room should be clearly given on the plan. The dimensions of piers, recesses, cupboards, &c., should be clearly marked. The figuring of heights on sections must not be forgotten, with no doubt as to whether they are floor-to-floor or floor-to-ceiling heights. Category (b) of the figured dimensions is not of interest to the quantity surveyor but, of course, is absolutely essential on the drawing from which the builder is to set out.

The builder, too, requires the over-all dimensions (except where setting out is from a steel frame), as he will be setting out the corners of the building before he has to think about the positions of window or door openings, &c. In the same way, the inside sizes of rooms will help him to set out the internal walls and partitions.

All figured dimensions on plans will normally be of the shell of the building—i.e. between wall faces before plastering. In the case of heights, it should be made quite clear whether dimensions are to finished level or surface of the structure : the allowance to be made for thickness of finishings should be definitely given, so that the foreman has figures to follow. The architect must, however, remember where there is any requirement of minimum height for rooms, that such minimum will be between finished surfaces, and he must make allowance accordingly. It may be found convenient to mark floor-levels on each floor in relation to some datum, particularly where they vary on a floor. It should be made clear by a note on the drawing whether these are finished or slab levels (usually the former).

Whilst on the subject of figured dimensions, the width of the cavity of hollow walls should be clearly indicated. The change from imperial measure means that the convenient description " 11" hollow wall " (often actually $10\frac{1}{2}''$) will have gone. It is understood that the standard thickness of a brick will be 102·5 mm, so with a 50 mm cavity the description would be " 255 mm hollow wall ". There would then be no doubt as to the width of cavity.

Specification Notes.—Drawings must be supplemented by further information of a descriptive nature. This may be either a full specification such as would be used if there were no quantities, or in the form of notes expressing the architect's requirements and leaving the gaps to be filled in by the surveyor, who perhaps knows the architect's usual standard requirements. Where the Government form of contract (CCC/Wks/1) is to be used, the specification is a contract document, and is therefore usually supplied to the surveyor in full. In the case of the R.I.B.A. contract, the specification is not part of the contract, and so need not be in such a full form, and its preparation can be delayed, as it is not required until the building work starts. The fuller the information given to the quantity surveyor, the more will the bill represent the architect's requirements and the less trouble there will be in answering questions raised by the surveyor. The surveyor, as already explained, having to pass the whole building before his mind's eye, must decide every detail, if not according to drawings and specification supplied, by enquiry from the architect or by using his own common sense—but somehow or other an answer must be found.

Whatever form the architect's specification takes, it should preferably be in type, and the same number of copies should be supplied as of the general drawings. If two or three assistants are measuring, they all want to refer to the specification probably at the same time, and much time is wasted if they have to share a single copy. Further, even the best handwriting has not the clarity of type, and when handwriting is not of the best the serious loss of time is obvious.

Specification notes are sometimes found written all over the drawings. If then they are at all full, they hinder easy reading of the drawings, particularly if the same note is repeated in several places. For instance, a note " 255 mm hollow wall " is sufficient, if the bricks are known to be 102·5 mm thick. Detail as to bond, ties, &c., is not for the drawing but for the specification.

Corrections to Drawings.—The very detailed analysis made by the surveyor is in one way of great assistance to the architect, in that it will bring to his notice any errors or inconsistencies in the drawings or specification requiring correction. Even if not definite errors, points raised by the surveyor may sometimes involve alteration. After the bills of quantities have been completed it will be found a good plan to ask the surveyor to lend a copy of the drawings marked with any amendments which have been discussed and agreed, so that the necessary corrections can be made to the architect's drawings before they are issued to the contractor. In this connection a word of warning is necessary. The contract drawings *must* correspond with the bill of quantities, so if, as sometimes happens, alterations are discovered to be necessary at a late stage, and the surveyor is told to leave the alterations to be adjusted as a variation, it is most important that the drawings to be signed with the contract should not show the alteration. It has been known for the original drawing to have been altered in such circumstances, so that all further prints show the alteration. When it comes to signing the contract, prints of the original drawing cannot be made, or the architect, not realising the discrepancy which arises, supplies the revised prints, so causing inconsistency between drawings and bill of quantities, both part of the contract.

If during the preparation of the bill of quantities the architect proposes to alter drawings, he should give immediate warning to the quantity surveyor. Even one line altered or erased may involve quite substantial alterations to the surveyor's dimensions. Such changes as reducing the length of a building by 0·250 m or the pitch of a roof by 5° involve complications not apparent at first sight and cannot be, as an architect once suggested, " put on a postcard ". Alterations made during the progress of the measuring are not only waste of time in themselves, but mean that, when it comes to adjusting variations, it is necessary to hunt in two or three places to find what is in the contract, and so the adjustment is complicated. If revised prints are sent to the quantity surveyor to correct drawings which he has, it is most useful if the architect circles the revisions in coloured pencil. Otherwise, a lot of unnecessary time is spent looking for the corrections and there is no guarantee that minor alterations will not escape notice.

"**Cut and Shuffle**".—In many quantity surveyors' offices an administrative revolution has been lately and is still in progress, so perhaps a word of explanation may be given of this

D

phrase, which may come to the ears of architects. The traditional method of preparing a bill of quantities included an intermediate process between putting down the measurements and writing the draft bill, in which the measurements were sorted and classified into the proper order on an abstract. Somebody had the bright idea that if each item of the bill were measured on a separate slip of paper the same result would be achieved by sorting the bits of paper, a pile of which in the right order could be given to the printer, from which to type the finished bill direct. In short, by this method a certain amount of time can be saved and a good deal of the junior staff, whom it has been difficult to get, can be eliminated. On the other hand, more time is necessary for the takers-off, the more skilled and expensive members of the staff, who must do the bulk of the work.

Importance of Full and Proper Particulars.—It may seem that these suggestions, in the writing of which a surveyor has evidently played a large part, are prejudiced! But this is not the case : the suggestions are not made merely to save the surveyor time and trouble (much as that would be appreciated), but because they are thought to be in the best interests of improved contract procedure. It is only common sense to say that the fuller and clearer are the particulars supplied by the architect, the closer and more accurate will be the tenders, and the less will be the subsequent adjustment of variations, with its delay and unnecessary expense imposed on the client. It is an evident fact, for which proof will hardly be expected, that the more the architect does in the pre-contract stage, the less there will be to do later.

In 1944 was published a report of the Central Council for Works and Buildings entitled *The Placing and Management of Building Contracts*,* often known as "The Simon Report". After reviewing the system of placing contracts before the war, the report says :—

" 24. This system has been gradually built up as a result of long experience. We regard it as being in general the right system, subject to certain conditions and modifications which we discuss in this and the following chapters. Any inefficiency can be traced to one or other of the following causes :

    (*a*) Insufficient pre-contract preparation of the particulars of the work to be carried out.

           * H.M.S.O. (now out of print).

(b) Extensive variation orders after the contract is placed.

(c) Indiscriminate competition tending to place work in the hands of those builders who adopt the lowest standards.

(d) Indefinite relationship between the general contractor and the various sub-contractors nominated by the architect."

" 55. We are satisfied that bills of quantities prepared from the particulars supplied by the architect afford the best basis for estimating cost. . . . Bills of quantities are highly technical documents which must necessarily be prepared by a quantity surveyor who has had a long training in all matters of building construction and building surveying, and their purpose is to put into words every obligation or service which will be required in carrying out the building project."

A Working Party on Building Operations was appointed by the Government in 1948, and the following extracts are from their Report :— *

" 69. . . . we think that the highest degree of efficiency cannot be achieved in any building operation of considerable size unless it is planned in detail before work is commenced. It is only in this way that the substantial economies to be derived from the proper phasing and pro-gramming of the work can be realised. Moreover, the delays and disorganisation due to inadequate pre-planning not only add to the immediate cost, but tend to undermine the general morale and so have an influence extending much beyond the particular job."

" 84. . . . we have stressed that all the information necessary must be in the hands of contractors before tenders on a truly competitive basis can be ensured, and that the efficiency of running a contract must be impaired unless complete information is available before work is started. The primary duty of the architect to ensure that the details and drawings are available may be hampered by the incompleteness of instructions given him by his client. From the evidence before us it would appear that this lack of decision and failure to supply fully informative drawings and particulars are increasing. The numerous variations and alterations so often introduced in the course of construction add to the cost of building. We hope therefore that both clients and architects—as business men realising the effect upon the cost of work as well as the efficiency of the industry—will strive mutually to remedy it."

In their Summary of Recommendations they say :—

" 7. In view of the control which the architect exercises over building operations, it is important that his training should give him adequate knowledge of the practical aspects of building. . . .'"

A later Working Party, investigating the difficulties of con-tractors in financing work because of delays in payment, attributes

* *Working Party Report—Building:* H.M.S.O. (now out of print).

their difficulty in part to inadequate planning in the first instance. One of its conclusions * is

> " . . . all possible steps should be taken to let contracts on the basis of a clear-cut scheme with full drawings and, where appropriate, accurate bills of quantities, so as to avoid the complications which otherwise arise."

This importance of full and proper particulars is emphasised by the Report of the Productivity Team which visited the United States in 1949.† Though there is a difference in system, in that in the U.S.A. the quantity surveyor's work is mostly done by the builder, the value of full particulars is the same in both cases. Whether the particulars are to be interpreted by the builders tendering or by an independent quantity surveyor, the fact remains that they must be interpreted with certainty. The following quotations from the above-mentioned report may be of interest :—

> " 3. 16. . . . It is usual for the design and specification of the specialist items to be dealt with by the architect before the tendering stage is reached, and not by any specialist contractor who may be selected later. There is consequently no danger that the orderly progress of the job will be dislocated by the late arrival of the specialists' designs. This example of pre-planning before the contractor comes on the scene is an important time-saving factor."

> " 3. 17. . . . In the *Handbook of Architectural Practice* it is laid down that :
>
> > ' The architect owes to the owner, and to all who may be connected with the work, the duty of making the working drawings and specifications as complete, clear and thorough as it is possible to make them. . . .'

> " 3. 19. The working drawings for any substantial building are considerably more numerous and more detailed than is customary in Britain."

> " 3. 20. Whenever possible, and certainly in all cases in which a lump-sum bid is required, all the working drawings, specifications and schedules are completed in every trade and specialist service *before tenders are invited.* . . . The contractor knows further that, once the work is begun, it will not be held up, possibly for weeks or months, by delay in receipt of the necessary drawings and instructions. When his tender has been accepted, the contractor can and does make arrangements for the purchase of all materials and fittings, and can place all his sub-contracts to enable the sub-contractors to do the same, before work starts on the site. . . . In short, the contractor is given by the architect every item of information requisite for the complete and proper organisation of the job at the earliest stage."

---

* *Retention Moneys on Building and Civil Engineering Contracts* (1954), § 32 (iv): H.M.S.O.

† *Productivity Team Report—Building:* British Productivity Council (now out of print).

" 3. 21. It was emphasised to the Team in the strongest terms by both architects and contractors that *the early supply of complete and detailed information is a fundamental factor in securing speed of construction.* The time required by the architect to assemble and prepare the necessary documents is more than made up by the rapid progress the contractor is able to make when the work begins."

" 3. 22. The American building owner is as anxious as his counterpart in Britain to see his building begun and finished, so that it may become revenue-producing. The American architect has been able to convince him, however, by practical experience, that thoroughness and completeness in the preparatory stages result in savings both in time and cost. It would be unthinkable in America for a contractor to be instructed to send half-a-dozen labourers to a site to start excavating, at a time when the final designs were no more than half sketched out in the architect's office, merely to satisfy the owner's desire to see work in progress."

" 3. 24. The business-like attitude of the American architect to his profession is reflected in his office administration, which is usually more elaborate than in Britain and is organised to enable the procedure set out in the preceding paragraphs to be followed. . . ."

" 3. 33. *Variations of the work during the progress of the job are discouraged by all parties ' as a source of delay, annoyance and loss '* (*Architect's Handbook*) and are not made to anything like the same extent as in Britain. This is due, no doubt, both to the extra care and time given to settling the client's requirements at the pre-contract stage and to the fact that the cost may be disproportionately high. . . ."

The whole report is well worth study, but the above extracts will indicate that the emphasis laid in this chapter on the importance of proper particulars for tendering is neither axe-to-grind enthusiasm nor the whim of a lunatic.

Finally, the view of an important Study Group: —*

" . . . by far the greatest single factor causing difficulties is the extent to which variations are introduced. Many of these could, and would, be avoided if all concerned with contracts were more acutely aware of the serious harm caused by the introduction of variations either to agreed plans or to work in progress, and were to make determined efforts to avoid them."

And lastly, the Report of Sir Harold Banwell's Committee † reiterates and confirms much of the above, laying additional emphasis on the need for cooperation by all branches of the Industry.

* *Building Contracts of Local Authorities:* Royal Institute of Public Administration, 1958 (§ 5). See also *Plan Before You Build:* Joint Consultative Committee of Architects, Quantity Surveyors and Builders.
† *The Placing and Management of Contracts for Building and Civil Engineering Work:* H.M.S.O.

9

CONSULTANTS AND SPECIALIST CONTRACTORS

Need for Specialist Services.—The erection and equipping of a modern building is a highly intricate operation which demands a considerable degree of scientific knowledge from the designer. By his training and experience the architect acquires a good deal of this knowledge, but obviously there is a limit to the number of subjects of which he can make a specialised study. Even if he had the genius to absorb all this knowledge he would not, in fact, have the time to practise it, and it is therefore becoming more and more common for him to consult experts in connection with certain of the more specialised items of the building. The fact that such experts can and do exist is in itself ample proof of their value to the architect. The principal fields in which they work are :—

1. Structural engineering (structural steelwork and reinforced concrete).
2. Mechanical and electrical engineering (heating, hot water, ventilation, gas, refrigeration, lifts and all electrical services).
3. Sub-soils and sub-structures (piled and raft foundations and soil mechanics).
4. Acoustics (including the use of acoustic materials).
5. Special finishings and materials (flooring, roofing, &c.).
6. Landscape design.

When the architect requires such expert assistance he can either approach a professional consultant or else nominate a specialist firm to carry out the particular work. There are important distinctions, however, in the employment of each of these specialists, and it is very necessary to appreciate these before deciding which of the two alternative methods to choose.

The Professional Consultant.—The consultant is a professional man like the architect himself, and is qualified to undertake the design, specification and supervision of the execution of the particular service on which his advice is sought. He undertakes these duties for a specific fee, which is usually governed by a scale of charges laid down by the particular professional Institution concerned. The responsibility for payment of this fee depends largely on the circumstances of the work, and here again a clear understanding should be reached before any commitments are entered into.

If the specialist is consulted with regard to any matter which might reasonably and customarily be considered to come within the province of the qualified architect—for example, calculations for determining the thickness of brick walls or the specification for a simple electrical installation in a small building—then the architect would normally be liable for the payment of the fee, as the consultant would, in those circumstances, be relieving the architect of certain of his accepted duties. If, however, the work involved was of a highly complex nature and outside the normal practice of the architect—for instance, the design of the reinforced-concrete framework or the mechanical engineering services in a large building, which demand complicated calculations and specialised knowledge—then the architect would be entitled to recommend to his client that a consultant should be appointed. In this case the fee of the consultant would be paid by the client and some reduction may be made by the architect in his own fee on the cost of the work on which the consultant was employed. The R.I.B.A. Scale of Fees no longer includes a clause providing for reductions in the architect's fees when consultants are employed, as on some highly complex designs the work entailed in co-ordination and checking and the architect's consequent responsibilities are not reduced and may even be increased. As this depends on the job, the new Scale of Fees permits architects, at their discretion and by prior written agreement, to reduce their fees by up to one-third of the percentage fee on the cost of the particular service, provided that the architect's total fee is not reduced by more than one-sixth. The architect, as the co-ordinator of the whole building project, will then instruct the consultant, and will have frequent discussions with him in order to ensure that the particular requirements of the building are fulfilled. The nomination of the consultant will usually be made on the recommendation of the architect, but he may equally well be an expert who the client himself will wish to nominate.

As already stated, the consultant is a professional man, and not a contractor. His services are offered in an advisory and super-visory capacity, and apart from the expert advice which he is able to give, he is also able to arrange for the invitation of com-petitive tenders from specialist firms based on his own design and specification. The client can therefore expect to get the best or most suitable service for his particular requirements at a competitive price. It cannot be emphasised too strongly that if competitive quotations are to be obtained from more than, say, three specialist firms, drawings or a specification or both should be prepared by the architect or a consultant, so that all the firms can tender on the same basis and their prices can be fairly and accurately compared. Except on the smaller and simpler schemes, it is unfair and unsatisfactory to invite competitive quotations unless this procedure is followed. If designs and specifications are prepared individually by the firms competing, it may well be that a firm might through lack of sufficient information submit a low price and obtain the contract, and then either produce an inferior scheme or else involve the building owner in additional cost to bring it up to the required standard.

The special finishings referred to under (5) above are in a different category. They do not usually involve the advice of a professional consultant, and are dealt with below under the heading of specialist firms.

Design by Specialist Contracting Firms.—If a consultant is not employed to prepare the design and specification, invitations should be limited to not more than two or three firms of an equal and known standing, who should be asked to prepare individual schemes based on given requirements and to submit their tenders with a detailed specification. The architect (if suitably qualified) or a consultant must then check the specifications in order to arrive at a fair and reasonable comparison of the tenders. Even this, however, is not wholly satisfactory, as it is difficult to make an accurate comparison of specifications which will inevitably not be identical, and consequently there are bound to be some differences in quality for which it is difficult to make an adequate allowance. It is also rather unfair to the contractors who are not successful, as they will have given a lot of time and may have incurred appreciable expense in preparing a design for which they will receive no payment.

Specialist Firms as Sub-contractors.—Something should be said of the term " nominated sub-contractors " used in the R.I.B.A. Form of Contract * and appearing in other forms of contract, either under this name or otherwise. The nominated sub-contractor is selected by the architect to carry out specialist work *on the site.* The general contractor may object to the employment of any firm who will not enter into a sub-contract with him on terms consistent with the general contact, as the general contractor is responsible for the sub-contractor's work. Payment is made through the general contractor, but the sub-contractor is protected under the R.I.B.A. form in case of failure by the general contractor to pay any moneys included for him in an architect's certificate,† as authority is given to the architect to certify such payment to him direct by the employer and to deduct it from moneys due to the general contractor. As mentioned above, these firms will either tender on a given specification or will also undertake the preparation of the design, if required to do so, when the design fee will be included in their tender as an overhead charge. If the specialist firm are to design as well as estimate, it may be possible to appoint them in advance as prospective nominated sub-contractors, and if a reputable firm is approached there will be little risk of their price not being a fair and reasonable one (which is not necessarily the same as the lowest competitive tender). However, there cannot be a sub-contractor until there is a contract, and the client's authority would be required if he is to be committed to the employment of a particular firm. It should be made clear that the client is not bound to proceed with the work, and, if the scheme is extensive, an arrangement could be made for some design fee to be paid in case of abandonment.

It will be the duty of the architect to instruct the specialist firm, approve their scheme and be responsible to the client for its satisfactory execution. For this reason he will not be expected to make any reduction in his fee as is the case when a consultant is appointed. The specialist's work will be included in the bill of quantities as a prime cost sum. The contractor will be required to provide any " general attendance " which the sub-contractors need, and provision will be made in the bill of quantities for him to add for this in his tender. The term " general attendance "

---

* See R.I.B.A. Form of Contract, clause 27.

† It should be noted that this protection is not afforded to a " nominated supplier ", see page 94.

must not be confused with builder's work in cutting away and making good, or specific work such as ducts, &c. These will all be measured in the bill of quantities for the contractor to price. " Attendance " is that indefinable work which is necessary to organise the sub-contract and provide the sub-contractor with such sundry facilities as he requires. If the sub-contractor wants to borrow a hammer, the contractor cannot say, " It is not in my contract to lend you one ". *The Standard Method af Measurement* (B 20(b)) extends the term to include use of standing scaffolding, messrooms, sanitary accommodation, welfare facilities, office and storage space, light and water and clearing away. Any supplementary special requirements must be specifically described.

The amounts due to nominated sub-contractors at each interim payment should be clearly specified on the architect's certificate valuation, but the general contractor will be responsible for making the actual payment to his sub-contractor and the building owner will in no way be liable unless the contract provisions in the case of default come into effect. The general contractor, in turn, will be allowed $2\frac{1}{2}\%$ cash discount by the nominated sub-contractor, if payment is made to him within a specified period (fourteen days in the case of the R.I.B.A. form) of receiving the architect's certificate (not the cash).

The selection of specialist contractors, whether for the purpose of making a single nomination or of preparing a list of tenderers, will usually be made by the architect with the concurrence of his client. The architect's choice will normally depend on his own experience or knowledge of the firms, but if a consultant is employed the architect will naturally ask his advice.

Invitation of Quotations.—Whenever quotations are asked for, the architect should endeavour to provide the specialists with as much information as possible, and should include drawings as well as a specification and, where practicable, a bill of quantities, so that every competitor is able to tender on the same basis. A standard form of Estimate for Nominated Sub-contractors can now be obtained from the R.I.B.A. which if properly completed by both the Architect and the tenderers should ensure that tenders are based on complete and identical information.* The Archi-

---

* *Standard Form of Estimate for Nominated Sub-contractors:* R.I.B.A. These forms are supplied in sets, including a *Form for Nomination of Sub-contractors* for use as instruction on acceptance.

tect should also try to select firms of equal standing, so that the fairest possible comparison can be made of the prices submitted. The list of tenderers should also be prepared with due regard to the size and complexity of the job and of the quality of work.

Whether a bill of quantities can be supplied will depend on the nature of the work. In the case of the specialist finishings referred to under (5) on page 88, a separate little bill of quantities can usually be prepared by the quantity surveyor and sent out in advance of the main bill, so that tenders on this can form the basis of a prime cost sum in the main bill. Where a consultant is employed the preparation of quantities is sometimes undertaken by him, particularly in the case of such services as electrical work, which need in the measurer expert technical knowledge of the design. On the other hand, structural steelwork and reinforced concrete are quite normally measured by the quantity surveyor, where proper drawings are available.

Adequate time should be allowed for the preparation of tenders, and the competing firms should be given full particulars as to the name of the general contractor (if known), the location of the site, the form of contract to be used, the name of the building owner, the latest date for the submission of tenders and the address to which they are to be delivered. It should be made clear to tenderers what cash discount they must include.

It is important to notify the tenderers that the nominated firm will be sub-contractors to the general contractors and will be bound by the same general conditions of contract. If the R.I.B.A. Form of Contract is being adopted, it will usually be sufficient to mention this, but the tenderer will also require to know how the blanks in the Appendix have been completed. Many Local Authorities have Standing Orders and other General Conditions of Contract of their own, and when they are the employers, a copy of these conditions should be sent out to, or be available for inspection by, the firms tendering. However, these are now largely covered by the special clauses (17A and 25 (3)) of the Local Authorities' Edition of R.I.B.A. contract.

Many specialist firms have their own Conditions of Contract, which are generally printed on the back of the tender, and these should be checked to see that they are not at variance with the conditions of the general contract. If they are, the proposed sub-contractor should be requested to amend them as necessary before the general contractor is instructed to enter into a sub-contract with them.

It should particularly be verified that the proper cash discount is included. Auditors tend to object to the cash discount being adjusted at the settlement of accounts, and to refuse to read into clauses 27 and 28 of the R.I.B.A. contract any warranty that estimates obtained by the architect will be subject to the proper discount, though it is obviously his duty to see that they are. The contractor has the right to object to the employment of any firm which does not allow the proper discount (see R.I.B.A. contract, clauses 27 (*a*) (vii) and 28 (*b*) (iv)), and his agreements to the appointment can be taken as a waiver of any objection.

It sometimes happens that a firm is both a nominated sub-contractor and a supplier (e.g. a steelwork firm may erect part of their steelwork, whereas part may be in plain beams for erection by the contractor). In such cases the estimate should be in two sections, each with its proper discount. The same point sometimes arises in variation orders. A metal-window firm may have quoted for supply and fixing of windows, and it may be decided that some part is to be fixed by the contractor. The estimate should be requoted with correct discounts, unless the fixing by the contractor is done as a mutual arrangement between contractor and sub-contractor.

It is advisable to ask for five copies of estimates, one copy for the architect, one for the quantity surveyor, one for the clerk of works and two to be sent eventually to the contractor with instructions for acceptance. Quantity surveyor, clerk of works and contractor should, of course, also have a copy of any drawings or specification.

Nominated Suppliers.—The name of " nominated suppliers " is given by the R.I.B.A. contract * to those firms which are nominated by the architect to supply special materials or goods but *do not carry out any work on the site* of the building contract. They are not sub-contractors to the general contractor, and are neither bound by the same conditions of contract nor protected so far as payment is concerned, as are nominated sub-contractors. The architect selects the goods they supply and nominates the firm, but, apart from this, nominated suppliers are in just the same position as any other merchant supplying the contractor.

* Clause 28.

The nominated supplier's estimate would not be subject to the fluctuations clause of the main contract under the R.I.B.A. form, as the materials concerned would not be in the " list " referred to in clause 31 (*c*) (i).   However, quotations at the present time are usually given with a time limit for acceptance, or else to be subject to fluctuation in price.   The supplier would then be expected to provide evidence of the correctness of any price variation.   As in the case of the nominated sub-contractor, any special conditions, printed or otherwise, appearing in the estimate of a nominated supplier should be scrutinised to avoid misunderstanding later.

All payments by the general contractor for materials or goods of nominated suppliers must, under the R.I.B.A. contract, be made in full and paid within thirty days of the end of the month during which delivery is made, less only the cash discount, if the payment is so made.   The cash discount to which the general contractor is entitled in this case is 5% under the R.I.B.A. contract ($2\frac{1}{2}$% under CCC/Wks/1), and when inviting competitive quotations, all the tenderers should be advised of the terms of payment and be instructed to include the proper cash discount in their price.

The R.I.B.A. has prepared in conjunction with the R.I.C.S. and N.F.B.T.E. a standard Form of Tender for nominated suppliers,* which can be commended as embodying all the information which is required to secure better tendering and to ensure that the conditions of tender do not conflict with the conditions of the main contract.

Information for the Quantity Surveyor:—It is essential that all the component parts of a specialist's estimate should be sent to the quantity surveyor.   A copy without the printed conditions of the specialist or without the drawings may only cause misunderstanding.   It is not sufficient to telephone and say X's estimate is £550.   The specialist's work must be dovetailed in with that of the general contractor and unless the quantity surveyor is quite certain of the exact extent and nature of the specialist's work and his requirements of the builder, something may be omitted or duplicated.

* *Form of Tender for use by Nominated Suppliers:* R.I.B.A.

10

SPECIFICATION WRITING

Character of the Specification.—There are three separate cases where a specification is required :—

1. Where it will form part of the contract without quantities.
2. Where quantities are part of the contract and the specification is not.
3. Where both quantities and specification are part of the contract.

In (1) the specification alone will be read with the drawings to set out the quality and quantity of materials and the quality of workmanship required in the building. It must therefore be so full and clear that doubt cannot arise later as to what is and what is not included in the contract. It must have the same water-tightness as a lease or other legal agreement. Otherwise, the contractor will find loopholes which may form the basis of claims for extras. In the case of (2) and (3) the specification is merely a supplement to the bill of quantities (in which everything affecting price should have been included). Its purpose then is to instruct the foreman as to location of the items in the bill of quantities and other points he must know but which do not affect price, e.g. the spacing of timbers in floors, &c.

The Specification without Quantities.—The architect preparing a specification for use without quantities must remember that he is drawing up some of the terms of a building contract, a supplement to the articles of agreement and general conditions which will bind both parties as to the extent, character and quality of the work. It is not a document to be scribbled quickly, but it must be drafted with an orderly method as a basis, and every care to be both clear and comprehensive without repetition. On the other hand, any gap which there may be is a potential basis for claim by the contractor.

The first need is a mastery of language. Arguments may arise as to the meaning of a single word, and the architect must therefore be careful to use words in their right sense. Not only words but phraseology must be clear. Sentences should not be long and involved, and the language must be suited to the least educated of its readers—probably the builder's foreman—and not drafted as if to be read by a University Professor of Architecture.

The architect will probably write his specification for a new building trade by trade, and in doing so he will find the same difficulty as does the quantity surveyor when he measures on that principle. In a draft only one side of the paper should be written on, and plenty of space should be left between each trade, or section of a trade—in fact, except in the smallest work, a new page should be started for each. The architect can then go back when necessary to make additions, either at the end of the sections or on the back of the sheets, with clear reference to the proper positions these additions are to take when being typed.

The specification divides itself into two parts. The first (corresponding with the preambles to the trades in a bill of quantities) deals with the description of the materials to be used (i.e. the bricks, cement, sand, timber, &c.) and the character and quality of the workmanship (e.g. the proportions of the ingredients in concrete, the method of mixing and depositing, precautions against frost, &c.). The second part is the description of the actual work to be done (e.g. that certain places are to have mass concrete, others reinforced concrete—giving particulars of rein-forcement). If not scheduled, sizes and location of such things as lintels, structural timbers, copings, &c., must be given and the extent of finishes defined. In short, everything must be set out which, read with the drawings, is necessary to define exactly how the building is to be erected.

Each trade would begin with general clauses describing mater-ials and workmanship in the trade, and these would be followed by the clauses describing the works to be done. Alternatively, it is sometimes found convenient to group all the general clauses together under one heading (though the sequence of trades would be maintained) and follow them by all the " works " clauses. Which method is adopted is a matter of choice.

The whole specification will be preceded by a series of Pre-liminary Clauses, corresponding to the Preliminary Bill in a bill of quantities. These clauses set out all items of general application not covered by the Conditions of Contract. The architect must be very careful to see that he does not introduce into the specification anything at variance with the Conditions of Contract, as nothing in the specification will override the Conditions (see R.I.B.A. form, without quantities, clause 12 (1)). A list of the main items required in the " Preliminaries " section of a specification is given in Appendix 1.*

The Specification where Quantities are Part of the Contract.—Where quantities are to be part of the contract, the specification may be prepared in two stages. The first step is to make a series of notes for the quantity surveyor setting out as fully as possible the materials and workmanship required, but in the disjointed form of notes under trade or other headings. The quantity surveyor will supplement the notes as necessary in consultation with the architect, and incorporate everything affecting price in his bill of quantities. The final stage in preparation of this specification need not be considered until the quantities have been prepared unless, as suggested below, it is incorporated in the bill of quantities.

Where quantities are part of the contract there is not the need of a full document which, quite independently of the bill, describes everything fully. This would involve a lot of repetition of matter already in the bill, which wastes both labour and the additional cost of reproduction of copies.

There are three forms in which the specification may be prepared :—

(a) It may be incorporated in the bill of quantities ; i.e. the surveyor may include in his bill all matters of location, &c., referred to above, either in the description of individual items or in separate sections suitably grouped in his document.

(b) It may be prepared as a supplement to the bill of quantities, i.e. as a separate document, which can conveniently be abbreviated by references to the item numbers in the bill.

(c) It may be written as a full and complete document, exactly as it would be if quantities were not part of the contract.

The alternative (a) is in many ways convenient. It brings everything together into one document, avoiding discrepancies

* Page 278.

and the trouble of referring to two, so that no separate specification is required at all. Being part of the bill of quantities, it is, however, *ipso facto*, part of the contract. It has the disadvantage that it must be prepared at the time that the bill is written for reproduction with it, causing delay, whereas (b) and (c) can be written or completed afterwards, in the interval between the issue of the bills and the signing of the contract. It is possible to avoid delay with (a) by having the specification notes typed only into those bills which will be used during progress of the contract, an appropriate number of copies being kept unbound until tenders are in and a decision is made to proceed.

The difference between alternatives (b) and (c) is principally a matter of length. Type (b) supplements and is to be read with the bill, whereas type (c) is independent and full.

The R.I.B.A. Scale of Fees makes it part of the architect's duty to prepare a specification, but appears to give him discretion as to its extent. Clause 2.30 describes the architect's normal service in respect of the final design of new works as:—

> " Preparing, in collaboration with the quantity surveyor and consultants if appropriate, a scheme design consisting of drawings and outline specification sufficient to indicate spatial arrangements, materials and appearance. . . ."

And under clause 2.40 the architect's normal service in respect of design details and production drawings is:—

> " Completing a detailed design, and specification where necessary, incorporating any design work done by consultants and nominated sub-contractors. Obtaining estimates and other information from nominated sub-contractors and suppliers. Preparing information necessary for Bills of Quantities, if any. . . ."

Though there is no doubt that the architect's fee includes for the specification when there are no quantities, there is no mention of payment for the specification referred to in the R.I.B.A. Form, with Quantities, Clause 3(3), which reads :—

> " . . . the Architect without charge to the Contractor shall furnish him . . . with two copies of the specification, descriptive schedules or other like document necessary for use in carrying out the works."

This appears to be whatever the architect deems " necessary ", bearing in mind the information already embodied in drawings, schedules and bills of quantities. The Scale of the R.I.C.S. likewise makes no mention of a specification in such circumstances.

In the case of Public Authorities it will be found that either they supply the full specification to the quantity surveyors, which serves both purposes, or they require the quantity surveyor to prepare one and recognise this as an additional service for which they make payment.

The tendency now is for the architect to prepare more drawings and schedules than was the practice in the past and so explain the construction of the building graphically rather than by description. As the specification of materials and workmanship is included in the preambles to the various trades in the bill of quantities, the contractor or his foreman should be able to manage without the lengthy and detailed description of the works which was previously contained in the specification. Something, however, is essential to indicate the grouping and location of the items in the bill of quantities, and there may be minor points of procedure which, since they do not affect price, do not appear in the bill of quantities. This is all that is necessary for the " specification " required by clause 3 of the R.I.B.A. form of contract. It may either be shown in the architect's schedules or described in a separate specification, which is often prepared by the quantity surveyor as a separate document or may be included in the bills by annotation. A lot of duplication of the subject matter is saved by that means, and a document results, which when complete gives information to clerk of works or foreman for carrying out the work.

It is useful to have standard headings for consideration when preparing a specification. A large organisation may have its own system, but a suitable form is published.* This has spaces provided under a great variety of headings which serve as a reminder of what may be necessary. Naturally, with a form applicable to any type of building there will always be headings which do not apply to the particular case. It is easier to discard a heading than to rack one's brains trying to think what has been forgotten.

Both Specification and Quantities as Part of the Contract.—In the Government form of contract (CCC/Wks/1) and in the contracts of some other public authorities the specification is a contract document as well as the bill of quantities. It

---

* *Specification Notes:* Crosby Lockwood.

is usually supplied to the surveyor in full (though draft) form, and afterwards reproduced with any amendments agreed between him and the architect. As both documents are part of the contract, it is absolutely essential that their wording should agree. The quantity surveyor may, in the interests of economy in typing costs, shorten his descriptions by cross-reference to the numbers of the specification clauses, so avoiding the repetition of identical wording. However, it is more satisfactory for the contractor, as it will save him time in estimating by avoiding constant cross-reference, if the bill can be in full and the specification abbreviated.

Form of the Specification.—The specification should be divided into trades following the standard order,* though this is sometimes modified to suit individual requirements. Each subject should form a separate paragraph with a marginal heading given, and all headings should be numbered either serially from beginning to end or following the standardised system of numbering.

Some change in arrangement, at any rate where there is a bill of quantities, has resulted from the 1963 revision of *The Standard Method of Measurement of Building Works*. The bill of quantities which was formerly divided into trades is now classified, to a certain extent, according to sections of the work. For instance, there is a " Roofing " section which includes lead and copper flats, formerly billed under " Plumber ". Carpenter's ironwork, such as straps and bolts, now come into the " Carpentry " section. It seems a necessary consequence that the specification should follow suit.

In the same way, if an elemental bill is being used, the specification would probably follow the same grouping.

The specification will usually be typed on one side of the paper, and it will then be found convenient to put marginal headings on the right, with only a binding margin on the left. If typed on both sides, the marginal headings would be on the outer edges of the pages. An index (or rather table of contents) is a very useful adjunct to a full specification, particularly where there is no bill of quantities. It should precede the first page, be prepared in tabulated form and be typed with two columns to a page, so that as much as possible is visible at one page opening. It is much

* B.S. 685.

simpler to find something if there are only two pages to look at than if there are four (see example in Appendix 1 *).

Different views are held as to the value of underlining. Though this makes a particular sentence stand out, it has no specific legal effect. If the sentence is there the contractor is expected to have read it. The danger of underlining is that it gives a prominence which the contractor might expect elsewhere. He might say, " You underlined that, so I should have expected this to be underlined ". It is much better to regard the specification, when part of the contract, as being one of the contract documents whose terms the contractor must be assumed to have studied in detail and understood before entering into the contract.

One of the commonest faults in specifications is their incompleteness, either through the entire omission of something or its incomplete description. The writer may prepare the materials and workmanship clauses of the " Concretor " and forget one mix of concrete, or he may specify somewhere " waterproofed concrete " without any indication of how the waterproofing is to be done.

It is often a saving of time to use an old specification as a draft for a new one, but such use needs great care. Each clause re-used must be checked to make sure that it is applicable : it may quite likely be forgotten a year or two afterwards that in the old case water was from a well and not from the mains ; a special clause drafted particularly for the former job may be left in and make nonsense. Further, it may be forgotten that the special circumstances of the former case required a clause to be cut out which should now be reinstated. One must keep the mind constantly alert when drafting from old clauses, to avoid, for instance, the repetition of a stock description such as "The bricks to be sound hard *well burnt* . . ." when they are all to be sand-lime bricks !

Vagueness and Impracticability:—The specification must be definite. The writer must remember that the contractor has to estimate scientifically the cost of the work required, not guess it. He must not be given the opportunity of saying to himself, " What the —— does the fellow mean ? " It follows that to express himself properly the architect must himself know what he wants, otherwise he can hardly expect the contractor to esti-

* Page 280.

mate for it. Of course, everything may not be obvious, and the architect is entitled to rely on the tenderer using his technical knowledge and judgment (e.g. in pricing "spot" items*) but he should not ask for a firm price for work which cannot reasonably be estimated. If it is not reasonable to ask for a firm price, a provisional sum should be included to cover the work being done as day-work.

Metrication.—From January 1969 a beginning should have been made in preparing drawings to metric dimensions, and it is anticipated that gradually all drawings and contract documents will use metric terms and that the bulk of the change should have been made by the end of December 1972.†

It will be realised that the change for most manufacturers is a difficult and expensive one, and one which cannot be made quickly. It is therefore inevitable that for an interim period both imperial and metric measures will appear together. The metric equivalent of a $4'' \times 2''$ timber is 102×51 mm. Whether this will become 100×50 remains to be seen, especially as the Scandinavian trade is geared to imperial measurements, since so much of their timber is exported to Britain. Pipes at the time of writing can still only be described as $2''$, $3''$, &c. There is no object in converting these to metric sizes until metric sizes are available on the market. The Joint Contracts Tribunal have recommended in a Practice Note‡ that, where either imperial or metric measure is specified in a contract document and is not available, the use of the alternative should be allowed and adjustment made as a variation. The architect must, of course, ensure that the alternative proposed suits the design. If, for instance, for $\frac{1}{2}''$ steel bar reinforcement (equivalent to 13 mm) the alternative were 10 or 15 mm the design might affect choice.

Order of Sizes.—When giving sizes in a specification it is important to keep a consistent order. Width is usually

---

* See page 110.
† *Programme for the Change to the Metric System in the Construction Industry* (PD 6030): B.S.I.
    The Use of the Metric System in the Construction Industry, 2nd Edition (PD 6031): B.S.I.
    Building Drawing Practice (Metric Units) (B.S. 1192): B.S.I.
    Metric Guide: R.I.C.S.
    Metric Conversion Tables: R.I.C.S.
‡ No. 14.

given before height, so that 150 × 300 mm road kerb is understood to be set on edge, a 300 × 100 mm laid flat. A 150 × 300 mm stone band would be worked on the 300 mm face, a 300 × 150 on the 150 mm face. Doors should be described with width first. It will be found that metal-window manufacturers maintain the reverse order, but the order given above has been a recognised custom for many years, and is confirmed by the *Standard Method of Measurement of Building Works*. In the case of metal windows it may be advisable to add *wide* and *high* to each dimension, to avoid the possibility of misunderstanding by the dissenters.

When sizes of timber scantlings are given, some prefer to give the thickness first (e.g. 20 × 80 mm architraves); others give the larger size first (e.g. 80 × 20 mm architraves, &c.). As the order has no special significance in these cases, it is immaterial which system is followed, but the specification writer should be consistent, and not follow both practices. When we are accustomed to metrication we shall, no doubt, be as used to talking of 100 × 50 timber rafters as we have been of 4 × 2.*

Nominal Sizes of Timber.—The scantlings of timber as supplied by the merchant will not actually measure the full dimensions by which they are described. Timbers of the ordinary sizes used are converted from larger scantlings, and there is inevitably loss from the saw-cut and planing. In the case of softwood timbers the usual allowance is 3·2 mm or $\frac{1}{8}''$ for each wrought face, the standard one followed in the preparation of bills of quantities.†

It will be found much more convenient to use nominal sizes in specifying. Though, of course, full-size details must be drawn to finished sizes, or the parts would not fit together, these finished sizes should be worked out from the nominal, bearing in mind the sizes and thickness in which timber is available. An eye on the sizes in which timber is supplied will help in economy. The width is not so important as thickness, because what is cut off in width can have another use, whereas reduction in thickness is wasted and must be paid for in full.

One thing which must be avoided is to mix nominal and

* See B.S. 4471: 1969. Metric Dimensions for Softwood (M).
† *The Standard Method of Measurement of Building Works*, 1968, N 1 (*b*), P 1 (*b*). R.I.C.S.

finished sizes of timber when figuring them on drawings. It is best to keep to the nominal in figuring, even on full size drawings : that is the size the builder wants to know, and it will be obvious in scaling the full size that allowance has been made in the drawing out.

Another application of the principle of nominal sizes is to steel tubing. If tubing to B.S. 1387 is to be used, say, as railing standard, it should not be marked " 1″ outside diameter ",* because the standard classification for such steel tubing is by the bore. It is not likely that the architect would object to $1\frac{1}{16}$″ outside diameter, which is the measurement for $\frac{3}{4}$″ bore tubing. Steel tubing for structural purposes is classified by outside diameter, but it will be seen from B.S.1775 that there is no tube of exactly 1″ outside diameter.

Verification of Facts.—The writer should never be satisfied to specify some material with a proprietary name without having from the merchants full particulars about it—not merely pictures of buildings where it has been used, but a sample and solid facts as to its qualities, the standard sizes in which it is supplied and the practical methods of fixing. He will then be able to specify the fixing properly and make provision for the proper grounds or other builder's work involved.

Not only proprietary materials need verification. In such a matter as stoneware drain-pipes it is surprising how often it is not realised that there are five different qualities, as follows (in order of cost, cheapest first) :—

Seconds ;
Best quality ;
British Standard ;
Tested ;
British Standard Tested,

and that the builder must know exactly which one of these is required. Moreover, there is no such thing as " first-quality " pipes: the recognised trade name is " best quality " (actually, as will be seen above, the fourth quality).

Full use should be made of merchants' catalogues or British

---

* Metric sizes of tubing not being yet available, the imperial sizes have been left to illustrate the principle.

Standards for reference when specifying, and care taken to adopt the standard sizes of ordinary materials and goods. It is careless to specify an intermediate size of, say, shelf brackets or tee hinges, which it can be verified from a catalogue is not available. It is not likely that the exact dimension is essential: if it is, the item should be described as purpose-made, to emphasise the need. Otherwise, the contractor is fairly certain to price for a stock size.

Care must be taken to see that registered trade names are not used in a general sense, as they apply only to a particular manufacturer's material. Such names as "Sirapite plaster", "Copperlite glazing", "Bitumastic paint", &c., are seen used without the intention of limiting the material to a particular maker's product (Keene's cement is, however, a general name of a material manufactured by various firms). A general term should be substituted such as "copper came glazing", "gypsum plaster" or "bituminous paint", if a choice is left open to the contractor.

It sometimes happens that some material is mentioned by a client or builder by its trade name with which the architect may not be acquainted. The more usual of such trade names, with names and addresses of makers, will be found in such books of reference as :—

> Specification;
> Laxton's Builders' Price Book ;
> The Architects' and Contractors' Year Book.

Those in London have easy access to The Building Centre, where information can often be obtained on such special materials, and there are similar Centres in several large towns.* When reading glowing descriptions in the manufacturers' literature, one must make due allowance for the natural bias of sellers.

Under present conditions the question of availability of materials often needs serious consideration. It is no use to pick an article from a catalogue (particularly an old one) and specify it, if there is a possibility of its not being obtainable. A catalogue or list may show paving-tiles made in red, buff, black, brown, &c., and even quote prices for them, but on enquiry from the makers the reply may be, "Sorry, we are only making red at present". Again, a material may be available, but delivery be so much delayed that it is useless to specify it.

* See page 269.

If the writer feels at all hazy about what he is specifying, he *must* look it up or make enquiry. What is haze to him will be fog to the builder.

P.C. Prices for Materials.—It is often convenient to give p.c. prices for certain materials (e.g. facing bricks, roofing tiles, coloured glazed tiles, &c.). A p.c. price is a prime cost for the material which the builder is to assume for purpose of tendering. It should be avoided as a substitute for taking the trouble to select a material. However, even though the material may have been selected, a quotation obtained for the selection can be used in this way to save a number of contractors each making enquiry : they will all be given the same basis on which to tender. There are three important points to bear in mind in connection with p.c. sums :—

(*a*) If a p.c. price is given for a material, suitable prices must be given for all forms of the material which will be used. It is no use saying that facing bricks are to be p.c. 350/- per 1000, if bull-nosed and splayed bricks are also required. P.C. prices must be given for these or any other specials, including their angle and stop bricks (if any). In the same way, a p.c. price for roofing-tiles must be accompanied by prices for eaves-tiles, tile-and-a-half, hip-tiles, ridge-tiles, &c.

(*b*) Prices should preferably be " delivered site ", and this should be made clear. If a quotation is " ex works ", either a suitable addition must be made to cover transport, or the contractor must be told where he is to collect from. It is not good enough to say " add for carriage ", which might be from the next town or the other end of the country.

(*c*) If the contract makes provision for the p.c. prices to allow a certain cash discount, the estimate must be checked to see that it includes the proper discount. The word " net " does not necessarily mean that no cash discount is allowed, nor can the absence of any mention of discount be taken to mean that what is usual will be allowed. If the discount is not clearly stated, definite confirmation should be obtained, and a revised estimate asked for, if necessary.

Prime Cost Sums for Specialist Sub-contractors' Work.—
The remarks in the preceding paragraph about cash discount
apply equally to p.c. sums for the work of nominated sub-contractors. The difference in the discount between clauses 27 and
28 of the R.I.B.A. form of contract should be noted.

When estimates are invited for work of specialists who will be
nominated sub-contractors under the R.I.B.A. contract, they
should be told that this will be the case, and that they will be
required to enter into a sub-contract on terms consistent with
that contract.*

Where a quantity surveyor is employed and the information
is available to measure specialist work (e.g. asphalt work, terrazzo
or other special flooring and skirtings, &c.) it will assist competitive tendering if the quantity surveyor prepares a little bill to
send out to the specialist firms.

The builders' work in connection with such specialist sub-
contractors as Heating Engineers needs careful specifying, where
there is no bill of quantities. Apart from a general item for
attendance, cutting away and making good (which without the
position of radiators, boilers, &c., and runs of pipes shown on the
drawings cannot be priced), there are such items as boiler bases,
pipe-ducts or casings, plumber's work, painting, &c., which must
be described in detail. The easy way out—a provisional sum for
adjustment against daywork—should be avoided.

Provisional Sums.—The term " provisional sum " is now
defined by *The Standard Method of Measurement* (A7 (i)) as " a sum
provided for work or for costs which cannot be entirely foreseen,
defined or detailed at the time the tendering documents are
issued ". This would cover sums included for general contingencies, for some builder's work of uncertain nature which it is
known will arise or for specialist work which cannot be given
with sufficient particulars to enable the tenderer to price his
profit and attendance.

Schedules.—Much of the information to be given by a
specification can be provided in the form of schedules (see Appendix I).† The tabulated form greatly facilitates reference, as

---

* E.g. *Standard Form of Sub-contract :* N.F.B.T.E.
† Pages 281 and 305 (and see B.S.685, Appendix A).

one can run one's eye over a list of rooms or sections of a building and quickly grasp—say—their finishings. This saves much thumbing of pages which would be necessary to search through the trades, looking for block floors in Joiner, granolithic in Concretor or Plasterer, tile and terrazzo in Plasterer, &c. The attempt made to simplify uncertainty as to trade by establishing a trade of "Pavior" was not a great success, as the same material used for pavings is often used for other purposes—e.g. window-sills, cappings, &c.— which are illogical in a " Pavior " trade. Such a trade no longer appears in the *Standard Method of Measurement*.

Standard Specifications and Codes of Practice.—The wordiness of a specification can be considerably reduced by reference to the British Standard Specifications or Codes of Practice.* Standard Specifications refer to materials and manufactured articles and are given serial numbers and the date of publication (e.g. the standard for Portland cement is B.S. 12). In specifying it will be found convenient to insert a clause such as :—

" The initials ' B.S.' refer to British Standards published by the British Standards Institution, of the serial number quoted and issue current at date of tender."

This will save repetition of the year of issue every time. Codes of Practice are similarly referred to (e.g. the Code for Normal Reinforced Concrete is C.P. 114).

But the architect must not look on reference to B.S. or C.P. numbers as an easy way out of writing the specification. It is essential to read what is being incorporated in the specification by these references, or the architect may find that something becomes specified which he does not want. Further, the specifications and codes often contain alternatives. It is no use saying, " The cast-iron rain-water pipes are to comply with B.S. 460 ". This specification covers three different weights, therefore there should be added : " (medium weight) ". Again, the same material may be covered by two specifications (e.g. asphalt for roofing). There is a big difference in cost between asphalt to B.S. 988 and that to B.S. 1162. Asphalt for damp-proof courses has yet a different specification (B.S. 1097).

* *Sectional List of British Standards (Building) :* B.S.I.
  Sectional List of British Standard Codes of Practice for Buildings : B.S.I.

An up-to-date list of all British Standards and Codes of Practice will be found in the *Year Book of the B.S.I.**

Works of Alteration.—One of the most difficult jobs of the builder's estimator is to give firm prices for works of alteration or " spot " items. Spot items are those which the estimator cannot properly value from the drawings, but for which he must examine the existing building to see what is visible (and guess what lies behind the surface). He can only visualise the proposed alteration and judge how many hours it will take for bricklayer and mate, or whatever trades are involved, and what materials they will require ; in other words, he must make an advance estimate of a day-work job. Where such spot items are very extensive and a substantial part of the whole contract, serious consideration should be given to the advantages of a prime-cost type of contract, which with a reputable contractor and proper supervision will probably give a better result than firm competitive tenders.

Where it is necessary to obtain firm prices for spot items, often, of course, arising as a minor part of a contract, it is important to be absolutely clear as to the requirements, and not leave them to the tenderer's imagination. The writer should visualise each step in the proposed alteration, putting himself in the position of the foreman doing the job, and describing what is to be done as seen through the foreman's eyes. He should draw attention to those matters which he has noted in his survey of a building and which the estimator might not easily see (e.g. wall surfaces which are battened out, floors which are double-joisted, &c.). In general, it is not necessary to state thicknesses of walls, as in the " spot items " of a bill of quantities, but it is, of course, a help to do so. The estimator tendering on a specification only will expect to use his measuring-rod, whereas with a bill of quantities it should be almost unnecessary.

The National Building Specification.—The R.I.B.A. has recently undertaken to set up an organisation to prepare and publish a National Building Specification. This was at the

---

* Free to subscribers to the B.S.I. Convenient references to those most used in building are given in *Specification Writing for Architects and Surveyors* by A. J. and C. J. Willis (Crosby Lockwood).

request of the Government's Economic Development Committee for Building which represents all sections of the Building Industry. It is intended to produce a " library " of clauses covering quality of materials and workmanship so that specifications for particular projects can be assembled rather than be written anew or adapted from previous jobs. The R.I.B.A. has set a target date in September 1971 for publishing the National Building Specification.

Responsibility for Economy.—The architect when specifying must always do so having regard to his client's instructions as to expense. One client may want a strictly utilitarian building at the absolute minimum cost, whilst another may be prepared to be more lavish, spending money on more expensive finishings and ornament.

There are two reasons which lead an architect to expense beyond the absolute minimum :—

1. He is a designer, and as such he strives for originality: originality is usually expensive—a painted portrait costs more than a photograph. A new material is perhaps introduced, which builders are unused to handling and which almost always costs more than the traditional, or decorative features are added ($x + y$ can never equal x, as long as y is a significant figure). *But* scale and proportion cost nothing, surface-colour and texture little, and much can be done with them. The good architect adapts himself to his client's pocket, but still maintains his reputation for good design.

2. The architect feels his responsibility for the structure. He may be blamed for defects arising later, as having been caused by faulty constructional design. This concern is but natural, and to a certain extent unavoidable. His client expects a more substantial building than a speculative builder would give him. But the fear may result in over-caution, and the extra reinforcement, or whatever the result may be, costs money.

Some Causes of High Cost.—A number of other points may be mentioned as being responsible for high cost :—

1. The employment of specialists for work which the contractor is quite capable of doing.
2. Departure from standardisation. The standardised or mass-produced article is always cheaper than one specially made for the job. Even adopting a standard within the job itself helps cost, e.g. keeping the same section of frames, architraves or skirtings, so far as possible.
3. Insufficient forethought and detailing (or lack of supervision of draughtsmen) involving variations (and even alterations after work is built).
4. Something shown on the drawings which looks simple on paper, but which a little thought on *how* it is to be done would show to be expensive.
5. Too theoretical specifying (e.g. a variety of mixes of concrete when, perhaps, two would do ; several gauges of metal where one would be sufficient and reduce the amount of waste).

Summary.—The essentials for writing a good specification can be summarised in a few words :—

KNOW practical building construction.
Write LUCIDLY.
VISUALISE the work.
VERIFY your references.
Be DEFINITE.
Be CONSISTENT.
ARRANGE carefully.
OMIT NOTHING.
DO NOT REPEAT yourself.
Putting yourself in the ESTIMATOR'S PLACE, you should have NO DOUBTS.

And, finally, remember you are your client's AGENT, not the PRINCIPAL, in the matter of EXPENDITURE.

11

TENDERING PROCEDURE AND LETTING THE CONTRACT

Procedure in Preparing a Tender.—The preparation of a builder's estimate may be divided into two parts: the ascertaining of facts and the application of his judgment. The facts are the nature and quantity of the materials and workmanship required, which must be set out in a form suitable for pricing. These are provided by the bill of quantities. Where no bill of quantities is supplied, the tenderer must, with the guidance of the specification, prepare his own quantities from the drawings.

The deciding factor in the preparation of a tender when quantities are supplied is the tenderer's judgment on prices. He should not follow rule-of-thumb or price books (though some inexperienced firms do), because every contractor's office has to take into account different circumstances. The tenderer will probably have from his own records the actual cost on different jobs of the main components of a building, and these costs will help him as a basis. He may have particularly good workmen in some trade, or may have special opportunities of buying some materials advantageously. He must consider the particular location of the job in question, its distance from his office and from a railway station, its accessibility for heavy road traffic, and adjust his costs accordingly. An isolated site involving transport and travelling time for his workmen will make a big difference to the real cost of an hour's work. There will be many items for which he must obtain quotations for materials and build up suitable rates. He will even adjust his tender according to his need for new work. If he is short of work, he may be satisfied with the prospect of a very small profit. If he is very busy, he may not want the work, unless he can have it at an exceptionally advantageous price.

It is important to remember that in submitting competitive tenders a mistake by the tenderer may involve very serious financial loss. It is, therefore, most important that he should have all possible information available and every facility to acquire as full knowledge as possible of the circumstances of the proposed work.

Documents for Tendering.—Where a bill of quantities is supplied, it is customary to issue with it a copy of the general 1:100 or 1:50 scale drawings. The supply of these gives the tenderer a better idea of the nature of the job and his probable commitments than a hurried look at them in the architect's office. Where no quantities are supplied, each contractor must, of course, be given a complete set of the drawings from which to prepare his estimate.

In the case of works of alteration, a set issued to each tenderer is almost indispensable. If, however, for some special reason each is not issued with a set, one should be available on the premises to be altered; the difficulties of an estimator going round a building pricing spot items without a drawing must be appreciated. Where there are substantial alterations to be priced, a set of drawings to be inspected at the architect's office is *no* use. Moreover, if the tenderer has a set he has a reminder of the conditions when he is pricing in the office.

Perhaps it may be emphasised here that in works of alteration, where rooms are divided or two or more are thrown into one, rooms should be given serial numbers on the drawings according to the *existing* plan. The specification and bill of quantities will be similarly referenced. The numbers then have a clear meaning to the estimator walking round the building before any alterations have been made. If identification of the new rooms is required in a similar way, a series of letters could be used (or *vice versa*).

Where there are no quantities, a full specification will be supplied to each firm for tendering, but with quantities there is no need for a specification at this stage, as everything affecting price should be in the bill.

Selection of Builders.—The selection of builders to tender for each job should be made with full regard to its size and nature. The architect should aim to have builders of the same standing tendering to make tenders properly comparable. A small house will need a different list from that for a Town Hall, and builders who may be suitable for a Town Hall may not be suitable for a reinforced-concrete factory. Whereas many builders could tackle a dozen houses in a Housing Scheme, the number in the locality who could undertake a contract for 200 houses is probably very limited. The nature of the work and financial capacity must always be taken into consideration. Reference should be made to *A Code of Procedure for Selective Tendering*.*

In many lists of tenderers there are some who are ineffective. A firm will, perhaps, agree to tender because they think (often quite wrongly) that they might offend the architect or prejudice future work if they did not do so. They might feel that the work is not " in their line " or, though quite suitable, they may be so pressed with other work that they cannot undertake the job. The result is the practice of " taking a price " from another tenderer (i.e. somebody who has prepared a genuine tender gives a price somewhat higher than his own, which, therefore, is certain to be rejected. The tender-form is filled in accordingly, and, if the priced bill of quantities is to be delivered sealed with the tender, it will be found, if opened, to be blank).

Certain public authorities are required by their standing orders to advertise their contracts publicly. This results in a mixed list, and many of the better firms, as long as they have plenty to do, will refrain from tendering in such circumstances. They have to compete with inexperienced firms, who may cut the price merely to get a start in the contracting business. As they are unknown, tendering in this manner is the only way in which to make a start. The lowest price in such circumstances is not necessarily the best—or even the most economical in the end. If the authority could be persuaded to advertise that it will select a list from the applicants, there would probably be an effective saving of ratepayers' money instead of a saving apparent but often illusory.

Where open invitations are issued, it is quite usual for the building owner to require the successful contractor to provide a guarantee bond, and this may be obligatory to comply with the standing orders of some public authorities. The guarantor undertakes to meet any deficiency due to the failure of the contractor to carry out his contract, up to an agreed limit specified. The details of the bond are a matter for the building owner's solicitor and are outside the province of the architect.

Time for Tendering.—With the object of ensuring that builders have every opportunity of preparing a proper tender

* N.J.C.C. (revised 1969).

which they can stand by, the time allowed for tendering should be as long as possible.   An excessively short period results in rushed work, inability to get estimates in time and consequently increased possibility of errors.   It is sometimes said that builders asked to tender put the bill aside " on a shelf " when they get it, from which it may be thought that they need not be given so long. In fact, the usual procedure in a builder's office, when a bill is received, is for the estimator to go through it and mark those parts for which quotations are required—either for the supply of materials or for work to be sub-let.   A typist copies out the marked portions with any adaptation necessary, and these extracts are used for competitive enquiries.   The bill must then be put " on the shelf ", because it cannot be priced until all the replies are in, as to do so piecemeal is a waste of time.   It may therefore be that nothing more can be done for a fortnight. Then the replies received are sorted, examined and the most suitable used, with the necessary additions for profit and fixing (where applicable).

Whilst it is always advisable to ask contractors in good time if they would like to tender, where time is for some reason short they should be given warning of when documents will be sent out and the date for delivery of tenders.   The *Code of Procedure* (Appendix A)* makes provision for such a preliminary invitation. Any firms who cannot tackle the job in the time will then be able to say so and avoid last-minute applications for extension of time.   Four weeks should be regarded as a minimum time for tender.

It is obvious that when builders are tendering on a specification only they will need longer to tender than when a bill of quantities is supplied for a similar building, as they will have to prepare their own quantities.

Sending Out Documents.—If there is no bill of quantities, the architect will send out to each firm tendering a copy of the specification and tender form and a complete set of drawings, with a covering letter which should state :—

> (*a*) Invitation to tender (if the firm has not been previously invited).

* Page 282.

(b) List of enclosures.

(c) Date and place for delivery of tenders.

(d) Whether the site is open for inspection or what arrangements should be made to see it.

(e) Request for acknowledgment.

If Appendix* B of the *Code of Procedure* is used for (a) above, items (b) to (e) will be found included in it.

Tenders will usually be delivered to the architect, unless the employer particularly desires them to be delivered direct to him. In the case of Public Authorities both the sending out of documents and the receipt of tenders are usually dealt with by the Clerk to the Authority. Recommended tender form from the *Code of Procedure* is given in Appendix 1.* The documents should be accompanied by a suitable envelope for delivery of tender, ready addressed and marked " Tender for ——— " on the face. These envelopes will on receipt then be recognised as containing tenders and be kept unopened until the time stated for delivery has passed and a check has been made that all have been delivered.

Where there is a bill of quantities much the same procedure is followed, though the documents are usually (except in the case of Public Authorities mentioned above) sent out by the quantity surveyor on receipt of the bills from the duplicating firm, so saving a little time. A selection of small-scale drawings with, perhaps, typical details will usually be sent to each contractor to indicate broadly the scope and quality of the work, and the covering letter will state where further drawings may be seen (usually the offices of the architect or surveyor). Proper accommodation should be provided to enable the tenderers to make a full examination of the drawings.

If the priced bill is to be delivered with the tenders, as is sometimes required by Public Authorities, the documents must include an envelope of suitable size and strength to hold the bill, addressed in the same way as the envelope to contain the tender. The tenderers should be notified in the covering letter that they must put their name on the outside of the envelope containing the bill and enclose this with the tender envelope, each separately sealed, in a single parcel. They should also be told that if their tender is not considered for acceptance the envelope containing the bill will be returned unopened.

* Page 282.

Opening of Tenders.—It is important before opening the tenders to see that all have been delivered, and care is necessary if any tender is delivered late. After the time fixed for delivery there may be enquiries from one builder to another on the telephone as to figures, and one must accordingly be sure that no late tenderer has taken advantage of this. If the lowest tender is delivered late, tenderers could be advised that this was the case and that an extension of forty-eight hours is given for reconsideration if required. If the late tender is not likely to be considered for acceptance, there would be no need for this.

If tenders are delivered to the architect, he will open them and prepare a list, arranged in order of price, for submission to his client. Any special conditions attached to the tender should be noted and entered against the tenderer's name in the list. If tenders, as is sometimes the case, state the time required, this, too, will be entered against each. The same procedure will be followed by the Clerk to a Public Authority for submission of the result to his Council or Committee.

It was once the custom for tenders to be opened at the appointed time in the presence of any of the contractors who cared to attend, but this procedure is now very rarely adopted owing to the need to study the complex detail of a tender before acceptance.

Reporting of Tenders.—In considering tenders other factors than the tendered price may be of importance. The time required to carry out the work, if stated on the form of tender, may be compared, as time may be very important financially to the client. Although there may be reasonable excuses for failing to keep to the time arranged, and loopholes for avoiding the liquidated damages provided for by the contract, the time stated by a reputable contractor may be taken as a reasonable estimate, having regard to the circumstances as he knows them.

If the contract is subject to adjustment of the price of materials the schedule of basic rates of materials must also be considered and the question asked: Has the tenderer assumed reasonable basic prices for materials? If he has based them too low he will be getting excessive " increased cost " on a rising market or allowing too little in " reduced cost " on a falling market. Where tenders are close the schedules of basic rates should be compared, as the lower tenderer may have less favourable rates. Only a preliminary examination will be made at this stage to ascertain which tender or tenders should be considered for acceptance, a fuller report, after supporting estimates are produced, being made later by the quantity surveyor.

The architect, having considered these matters in consultation with the quantity surveyor, or the Clerk to a Public Authority in consultation with both the technical advisers, will report the tenders to the client or committee concerned and set out clearly for their consideration the arguments in favour of acceptance of one tender or another, if there is any doubt. It should be mentioned that, when tenders are invited from a limited number of builders, the lowest, or potentially lowest, should be accepted. All go to a good deal of trouble and expense in preparing a tender, and the object of such tendering is to decide which amongst a number, all acceptable to the building owner, will do the work at the lowest price. Whether expressly disclaimed in the invitation or not, there is no legal obligation to accept the lowest or any tender, but there is in a limited invitation a moral one to accept the lowest, if any. When tenders are advertised and any Tom, Dick or Harry who can find the required deposit and surety may submit a tender, the circumstances are different. One can justly say "I didn't ask you and I don't want you," though even then, when the expenditure of public money is involved, there may sometimes be repercussions.

Examination of Priced Bill.—If the employer decides to proceed with the work, the tenderer whose offer is under consideration will be asked to supply a copy of his priced bill (if it has not already been delivered with the tender), a blank copy being sent him for the purpose. Sometimes to save time he is asked to send his original bill, but a copy is sufficient. This should be examined by the quantity surveyor for mathematical errors, and he will also look through generally for any possible serious errors in pricing. If there is no serious error, acceptance of the tender can be recommended. The attention of the tenderer should be drawn to any bad mistake and confirmation obtained that he will stand by his tender.* He may consider the mistake so seriously against him that he will withdraw, when the next tenderer must be dealt with in the same way. It is not

* See page 179.

usually good policy to press a contractor who has made such an error to stand by his tender. The inevitable effort to recover his position is fairly certain to give trouble.

Though the tenderer agrees to stand by his tender, corrections of any material errors should be made, solely for the purpose of providing a fair schedule of prices for the adjustment of variations. The principle to be followed is that the total of the bill must be unchanged and agree with the contract sum : the adjustment due to correction of errors will be treated as a rebate or plusage on the whole of the prices (except p.c. and provisional sums) and appear immediately before the final total on the summary. The actual corrections will be made by the quantity surveyor.

Reductions.—It is unfortunately not uncommon for tenders to be higher than expected, sometimes due to too optimistic an attitude of architect and quantity surveyor at the approximate estimate stage, or, more probably, because a full cost-planning exercise has not been carried out. If the employer is not prepared to meet the higher cost, ways and means have to be found to come down to his figure, and at the same time meet his requirements as to accommodation, &c. The architect will have to re-examine his drawings and specification with this in view. Here the help of the quantity surveyor will be useful, as he may be able to suggest, from the analysis which his bill provides, where the architect's requirements are expensive and might be cut down. A list of possible reductions will be prepared and valued in consultation with the quantity surveyor. He will prepare a bill of omissions and any counter-balancing additions, from which the tender sum can be adjusted. It must be realised that, for what sounds quite a simple reduction, adjustment on a bill of quantities may be quite lengthy. To take 150 mm off the length of a building (which may only mean a few broken lines and figured dimensions on the architect's drawings) affects a large number of items through many trades in the bill of quantities, from the area of stripping surface soil to the paint on ceilings and walls.

There is one cause of excessive tenders and consequent reductions which should be avoided, viz. the inclusion of something which the architect wants, in the hope that the client can be persuaded to want it, when he discovers it is included in the tender. The architect may feel that it is easier to cut such an item out when tenders come in than to add it afterwards, but unless there is a reasonable hope of keeping within the client's price, it should be cut out in the first instance. Reductions in a tender only make additional, unnecessary and unremunerative work for architect and quantity surveyor in altering drawings and specification and preparing reduction bills, and, moreover, involve the client in additional fees and expenses. The importance of cost planning at the earliest stage of the project cannot be emphasised too strongly, if the unfortunate consequences of an unsatisfactory tender are to be avoided.*

Publication of Tenders.—A tender may be withdrawn at any time before acceptance, but once accepted is binding. The list of tenders is not therefore normally published until one has been accepted. It would reveal the difference between the lowest and the next tender, and therefore might affect any negotiations due to errors or reductions. However, once a decision has been made, the result of tenders should be circulated to contractors. This gives them a guide as to their position, so to speak, in the market, and is the least one can do for the unsuccessful contractors in return for the work they have done in tendering. When circulating the result of tenders to the unsuccessful contractors it may be thought preferable to list the amounts of the tenders and not the names of the tenderers, except that the successful contractor could naturally be named.

Contract Documents.—If the aim suggested in Chapter 8 as to supply of particulars has been attained, there will be little to do in the way of preparing documents on acceptance of a tender, except to obtain prints of the drawings and prepare the contract. The quantity surveyor will supply the priced bill of quantities, and all the documents which will form part of the contract must be prepared for signature. The method of doing this and of preparing the contract itself is referred to in Chapter 17.† Where the specification is not part of the contract it may not have been completed, and, if one is necessary, this must now be done. The architect's next task will be to issue instructions to the contractor and to undertake the supervision dealt with in the next chapter.

* See page 22. † Page 180.

Negotiated Contracts.—This is perhaps the place to say something of negotiated contracts. They may be of two classes—original contracts or extension contracts.

There may be good reason in a particular case why a contract should not be let on competitive tender—perhaps the building owner has an association with some firm and is prepared to give them the contract on a recommendation that the price is reasonable. If that is the case, a bill of quantities can be prepared in the normal way and sent to the builder to price. When priced, the bill will be returned to the quantity surveyor for examination and report. He will examine the rates and make notes of points on which he wants further information and then arrange an appointment with the builder to go through them. He will probably ask for production of estimates for the principal materials and for any work proposed to be sublet and for the build-up of any rates which he feels should be queried. The surveyor will get any adjustments agreed with the builder and then report that a tender of £x is in his opinion reasonable. This does not necessarily mean that it is as low as would be obtained in competitive tender, when profit may be cut below the normal, but that a fair price is being asked.

Another occasion for a negotiated contract is the addition of further substantial work on a site where a contract is already established. There are practical difficulties in employing two contractors concurrently on the same site, so it may be decided to negotiate a second contract with the same firm on the basis of the first. It may even be preferable to negotiate a price with the same contractor for a similar building on another site rather than invite new tenders, if the contractor has given satisfaction and his price is considered reasonable. In either of such cases the bill will be prepared as before and priced, so far as practicable on the basis of the rates in the existing contract, adjusted, if necessary, for fluctuation in labour and material costs which have arisen in the interval. The second building may be of quite a different type from the first, so that many items will appear in the bill of quantities which did not appear in the first bill. Rates for these items will be negotiated as before. Consideration will also have to be given to such economies as should arise by employing a contractor already established on the site and this, with any other change of circumstances, will probably be reflected in the pricing of the Preliminary Bill. Even with a contract which is to be subject to price adjustment, it may be advisable to bring the measured rates up to date and fix new basic rates for labour and materials, bearing in mind that the contractor has no profit on additions by way of increased cost brought into account.

A contract may also be negotiated after first obtaining competitive tenders on a " notional " or approximate bill of quantities, so that the contractor can be appointed before working drawings are completed. The advantages of that procedure are discussed in Chapter 4.*

* Page 28.

12

THE WORKS IN PROGRESS

Instructions to Contractor.—The contractor must be supplied with two sets of the contract drawings (on larger contracts he may ask for more copies, but only two will be supplied to him free of charge) as well as of all detail drawings which may be necessary. These latter, in the ideal job, will be all ready, having been prepared to give the quantity surveyor full information. If they are not ready, their completion should be the first task. Copies of the specification which, as explained in Chapter 10, may or may not be a contract document must also be supplied to the contractor.

A copy of all drawings and the specification will also be required by the clerk of works referred to below, if one is being appointed.

An early opportunity should be taken to check over the nominated sub-contractors' estimates to ensure that they meet requirements and are consistent with the terms of the main contract. They may have been rather hastily perused in the rush to complete documents for tender ; a long period may have elapsed between the date of the estimates and the starting of the contract, involving a change in conditions ; the architect or client may have changed his mind. Specific instructions for acceptance must now be sent to the contractor (which it will not be possible to countermand later without loss to the client) with a copy of each estimate to be accepted and any relevant specialist drawings and specification (see Appendix 1).*

The contractor, under clause 27 (*a*) of the R.I.B.A. contract may make reasonable objection to the employment of a particular nominated sub-contractor. The list of such sub-contractors proposed should in any case be sent to him at an early stage, if estimates for acceptance are not being sent at once, to give him an opportunity of making any such objection. It may by that an objection will be based on previous financial relations or experience of dilatory work resulting in delay in completion. If such objection is made, the architect may be able to obtain

* Page 286.

assurances from the proposed sub-contractor which will satisfy the contractor, or otherwise smooth out the difficulties. Apart from objection to the firm of subcontractors, as such, there may be objection to some specific condition in the particular estimate. This must come within subclauses (i) to (ix) of clause 27 (a). If, when inviting tenders, the architect has stated that the successful tenderer will be required to enter into a subcontract on terms consistent with the main contract in the R.I.B.A. form, such further difficulty should not arise.

A copy of the letters of instruction for acceptance of sub-contractors' estimates should be sent to the quantity surveyor as well as of any relative documents which are different from those used for preparation of quantities. It is important that the quantity surveyor should have this information at an early stage, as he has to base his valuations for interim certificates on it. Failure to advise him of changes has before now resulted in over-certification and trouble in a case of bankruptcy of the contractor. Priority of need must not be overlooked : work required in the early stages must have first attention and full time must be allowed for possible delay in delivery of materials.

The estimates of nominated suppliers must be treated in a similar way.

Once all these instructions have been disposed of, the main duty remaining to the architect will be supervision of the work in progress.

Scope and Purpose of Supervision.—Supervision is by no means the least of the architect's duties, for on this will very largely depend the quality of the finished building. It is important, however, that the duty of supervision should be carried out in a positive manner, and not only as an insurance against faulty workmanship or the use of materials which are not in accordance with the specification. By his interest and personal explanation the architect can help the builder to interpret his design and produce the effect that he particularly desires. The proper execution of the details of the building is of paramount importance from an æsthetic as well as a practical point of view; if care is devoted to the details of construction, the main structure will look after itself. Defects are invariably caused by minor faults in the first instance. This again emphasises the importance of thinking out the details and preparing a full set of drawings before the building work starts. Nothing is so likely to contribute to defective work as alterations and improvisations found necessary after the work has commenced on the site because of lack of forethought or the absence of sufficiently detailed drawings.

The architect will need to carry out inspections to suit the exigencies of the work and any instructions, criticisms or observations which he may give verbally should always be confirmed in writing and copies distributed to the clerk of works and quantity surveyor. Any instruction which constitutes a variation to the contract should be confirmed by the issue of a formal " Architect's Instruction " as soon as possible.*

Site Meetings.—The architect should arrange regular site meetings attended by the general contractor and his principal subcontractors, any professional consultants employed by the architect or employer, the quantity surveyor, Clerk of Works and any other persons who might be specifically required for the business to be discussed. The architect should issue an agenda a few days before the site meeting and should arrange for the distribution of minutes not later than a week after the meeting has taken place. The first site meeting is particularly important, and the architect should use this opportunity to give a clear indication of the way in which the contract is to be administered. A specimen agenda for the first site meeting is given in Appendix 1.†

Apart from the site meetings, the architect will require to make intermediate visits which may be undertaken informally, but with no less meticulous recording of any instructions given.

The Clerk of Works.—The architect must give adequate supervision to ensure that the building is erected in accordance with the provisions of the contract, but normally the terms of his appointment do not require him to give constant superintendence. If this is necessary, a clerk of works must be appointed by the client. He is generally appointed on the advice and recommendation of the architect, but is paid by the client, and, although

---

* See page 150.   † Page 287.

he takes his instructions from the architect, he is the servant of the client and must act solely in his employer's interests. The architect has to act impartially between his client and the builder, but the clerk of works is only responsible to the building owner. The architect must therefore maintain a delicate balance in his dealings with the clerk of works and the builder, and although he must preserve the authority of the clerk of works, he must not allow him to dictate unfairly to the builder.

The clerk of works' duties and limitations should be clearly understood, and it is the responsibility of the architect to see that he is properly instructed. A good clerk of works can be of the greatest assistance to the architect, who should make a point of getting to know him well and gaining his confidence at the earliest stage. He is usually a man of considerable practical experience who has graduated from a particular trade—the training of a carpenter and joiner is probably the most useful background—and the architect should not hesitate to seek his advice on practical matters when the occasion demands.

The primary duty of the clerk of works is to ensure that the work is carried out in strict accordance with the drawings and specification, and he is not expected, or indeed authorised, to give any instructions which are not covered by the terms of the contract. His authority is limited to ensuring that the standard required under the terms of the contract is maintained, and he has the power to condemn any work or materials which fall short of this standard. He must be on the site throughout the hours that the builder's men are there, and, further, must endeavour to be everywhere at once! It is a most difficult job to do well, and requires both tact and knowledge. The architect should recognise this, and do all that he can to help him.

The clerk of works can also be of considerable assistance to the quantity surveyor, by keeping, for instance, a record of any work which is likely to be covered up before his visits to the site, so that the measuring can be correct. This applies particularly to foundations and any items which are shown as " provisional " in the bills of quantities, and which are therefore subject to re-measurement on completion.

Besides these duties, there is a variety of records which the clerk of works should keep. He will have day-work sheets submitted to him, when works are to be valued on a day-work basis, and he will be required to certify that the time and materials are correct. He is not concerned as to whether the item is an extra or not, nor whether day-work is the proper method of valuation. He is only concerned with the facts. When he knows that the item will be charged on day-work sheets, he can keep notes of the time spent and material used as the work goes on. If he has no record, or to amplify his own information, he will examine the contractor's records on the men's time-sheets or otherwise.

Again, where the contract price is adjustable for fluctuations in cost of labour and materials, he, as the man on the spot, will certify the contractor's statement of hours of labour worked, on the basis of which adjustments will be made. He will do this by checking with the contractor's pay-sheets, and, knowing the men individually, he can certify the correctness in a way which architect or surveyor, who has not the same close contact, cannot. In the case of materials, too, he may himself keep a record of deliveries, or will see the record made by the contractor's agent, and therefore be able to give information on fact on points that may arise.

The clerk of works will also be on the look-out for variations. The contractor will no doubt watch for extras, but will not always be so keen on drawing attention to savings. Whilst a broad view and a certain amount of give-and-take on minor variations are to be commended, the clerk of works should draw the attention of architect or quantity surveyor to any variations which he may think might be overlooked.

In fact, the clerk of works should make any records in connection with the building works which he thinks may be of value later. For instance, the positions of any unexpected water- or gas-mains, &c., should be fixed, or any changes made from the drawings, such as a variation in drain lines. These help the architect to amend his drawings and so leave a correct record of the work done.

Indeed, the clerk of works should have a note-book constantly in his hands, and his diary will be a most valuable record of the work. Any verbal instructions which the architect may give on the site should be recorded by the clerk of works and be included on his weekly report if they are not confirmed within two days in writing by the architect.* Needless to say, the architect should keep the clerk of works fully informed of any instructions which he may issue to the contractor.

* See R.I.B.A. contract, clause 10.

The clerk of works should keep a set of drawings, bills of quantities and files of all letters, written instructions, &c., issued by the architect or himself, available for reference during the architect's visits, and he should be provided by the contractor with a table, chairs, cabinet, drawing-board and tee-square in his office, so that he may have full facilities for keeping his records or making drawings. It is highly important that the clerk of works should have his own office and a separate telephone, so that he may, if necessary, speak privately to the architect, quantity surveyor or building owner.

In view of the large number of records which he has to keep, the architect should not make any unreasonable demands on the clerk of works in the way of reports, but a simple progress report, made out on a suitable form which tabulates the essential information, should be prepared and submitted weekly. These reports, besides giving a brief description of the general progress of the work during the current week, should include a summary of the work completed to date in each trade. Other information should include the number of men employed daily (by trades), the weather, names and dates of visitors, unfixed materials on the site, drawings received during the week, further drawings needed and any matters requiring urgent attention. The reports should be dated and numbered consecutively. An example of such a Report Form is shown in Appendix 1.*

The Agent or General Foreman.—The man in charge on the site on behalf of the contractor will be the agent or foreman (according to the size of the job and sometimes the self-esteem of the holder of the post). Whichever he is called, he is the representative of the contractor on the job, to whom the architect can give instructions (R.I.B.A. contract, clause 8). He will frequently be a practical man brought up as a tradesman (probably a bricklayer or carpenter). His opinions on practical problems, as well as those of the clerk of works, should be given full consideration by the architect. Much of value can be learnt from both by those who do not mind admitting that they are not infallible. In the larger and more complex contracts the agent's role is that of a Project Manager, and he will need to be trained in the more sophisticated techniques of management, such as

* Page 288.

programming by critical-path network and computer. If the foreman or agent is inefficient, the architect can order his dismissal, as he can of any workman (R.I.B.A. contract, clause 6 (5)). But such action must, of course, have reasonable grounds, and should be taken only for serious cause.

The Builder's Surveyor.—The builder's surveyor will mostly have dealings with the quantity surveyor appointed by the building contract, but when there is no such quantity surveyor the architect will have to deal with him over the preparation and checking of the final account. In the smaller firms, at any rate, he will probably be the estimator who has prepared the tender and will have been watching the progress of the contract in his employer's interest. He will represent his firm under clause 11 (4) of the R.I.B.A. contract when the quantity surveyor measures variations and will do any negotiating of prices in the final account. In larger firms the duties of surveyor and estimator may be in different hands.

Architect's Site Visits.—The frequency of the architect's visits will depend on the nature, situation and complexity of the work, and no hard-and-fast rules in this connection can be laid down. The importance of adequate supervision has already been stressed, and if the work is within reasonable travelling distance of the architect's office it should be quite easy to arrange this. There may be occasions, however, when the architect has to travel a considerable distance—possibly even overseas—to visit the work, and in such cases it will be necessary to make less frequent visits but to spend several days at a time on the site. In these circumstances the clerk of works' weekly reports take on an added importance, and will probably have to be supplemented by frequent or even daily correspondence.

The architect's visits will not necessarily take place at regular intervals, but will be made to suit the exigencies of the work. They will probably be less frequent during the earlier stages of the work than the later—unless the peculiar nature of the site or the subsoil present particular problems. The setting out of the works, however, is especially important, and should be carefully checked by the architect or his clerk of works. It is the architect's responsibility to furnish the contractor with levels and accurately dimensioned drawings to enable him to set out the enclosing walls of the building at ground level.* After the initial setting out has been checked, the contractor is responsible for the accuracy of the work, and will be held liable for the correction at his own expense of any errors arising from his setting out.

It is advisable to arrange with the main contractor for periodic site meetings to be held with the nominated sub-contractors—the first of which should be shortly after work begins on the site—at which programmes of work can be arranged and the specialists' work co-ordinated. This will be invaluable in helping to smooth out the difficulties of each sub-contractor and in integrating their work. At these meetings it will, of course, only be necessary to invite the sub-contractors who are directly interested at each stage of the work, but at the first meeting it will be useful to arrange for as many as possible to be present, so that everyone can be properly briefed and " put in the picture " from the beginning.

Site Office.—On large contracts the architect may have an assistant permanently on the site and a drawing office where details can be prepared on the spot. The architect will be responsible for the acts of his assistant within the scope of his authority, so it should be made clear to all concerned what duties the site architect will have. He is always, of course, at liberty to say that he must reserve a decision for his principal.

Progress Schedules.—A Progress Schedule is usually drawn up by the contractor at an early stage of the work—probably following the first site meeting with the principal sub-contractors —and kept up-to-date week by week. It should be made on a large sheet of paper, so that all the information can be clearly tabulated, and should be posted up in a prominent position in the site office. It must not be too complicated, but must give a precise indication of the progress planned by trades each week, together with the actual progress maintained. An example is given in Appendix 1,† on which the chart is " squared off", with the trades or operations arranged in a column on the left-hand side and the weeks inserted along the top. A line is drawn in black (or any other colour selected) against each trade or operation, commencing at the week during which the particular work

* See R.I.B.A. contract, clause 5.   † See page 305.

is due to start and continuing through the number of weeks that it is expected to proceed. This may not, of course, be a continuous line, as it may be necessary to suspend the particular work whilst some other operation is proceeding and then return for a second spell. In a domestic building the bricklayers will probably take the walls up to first-floor level and then have to transfer to another section of the work whilst the carpenters are fixing the first-floor joists. As soon as the carpenters have finished they will return and carry the brickwork up the plate level whilst the carpenters are preparing for the roof-fixings.

The actual progress achieved should be recorded in a line of a different colour under the " scheduled " line.

The value of a Progress Schedule is that it will enable the contractor to plan ahead, give early and precise notice to sub-contractors, avoid the risk of overlooking the ordering of materials or fittings in good time and enable him to take adequate steps to reinforce or reduce his labour force as the occasion demands. Finally it is a constant pointer to contractor, foreman, clerk of works, architect and client as to whether the work is proceeding at a satisfactory rate or not. On large contracts it is becoming customary for the contractor to include in his Progress Schedule the dates by which he requires: (a) full details of the various sections of the work from the architect and structural engineer, and (b) instructions with regard to the placing of orders for all work covered by p.c. and provisional sums. As the contract proceeds it may be necessary to expand the progress schedule to show in more detail the co-ordinated installation and commissioning of complex engineering services.

The requirement of a Progress Schedule, or critical-path network in a more complex contract, should be made in the bill of quantities (or specification where there is no bill), as it is not included in the subjects on which the architect is authorised to give instructions under the R.I.B.A. form of contract. Though co-operation in preparing such a schedule may be valuable, responsibility for progress is the contractor's. Any comment by the architect on the contractor's schedule can only be advisory.

Progress Photographs.—Apart from the valuable record of the progress of the work that will be provided by photographs being taken at regular intervals, it will be found that they can be of considerable assistance to the architect in his supervision of the work, particularly if it happens to be at some distance from his office.

To be of value, however, a definite series of photographs must be planned, and each one must be carefully annotated and dated. A better progress record will be kept if a number of photographs are taken at regular intervals from fixed viewpoints, which should be selected to give a slight overlap, so that they can be related to one another. Other photographs can be taken of any work which is to be covered up, such as roof construction hidden by a ceiling, fixing devices, pipe-ducts, &c., or of any special details of construction or finish.

Photographic records of this sort may provide very useful information if alterations or extensions are carried out in the future, and they may also be of considerable value as evidence in a legal action. Further, they may form a useful supplement to those drawings showing the main lines of essential services, which the architect provides for his client on completion of the work, if requested to do so.

The architect may take progress photographs himself, or he may commission a professional photographer. They need be no more elaborate than snapshots, and should be taken for their intrinsic and not their æsthetic value.

The cost of photographs would normally be regarded by the architect as part of his overhead expenses, but if a specific series of photographs were taken on the client's instructions, he would be entitled to charge them as an out-of-pocket expense or they might be included in the contract, particularly if, as might be the case on a large scheme, a professional photographer is employed.

Foundation-stone Laying.*—The ceremony attending the laying of a foundation-stone has been evolved by tradition without being governed by any specific ritual. The procedure may be adapted to suit particular circumstances, but the following notes will serve as a general guide.

The position of the stone should be determined as soon as possible after the contract has been let. Traditionally it should be in the north-east corner of the building, but this may not always be suitable : if not, some prominent position should be

* These notes have been compiled from notes for guidance issued by the R.I.B.A.

chosen where it will be seen by people passing or entering the building. When the position has been decided, the size and type of stone should be settled, as it may be necessary to inspect it at the quarry, or to make special arrangements for its transport and handling. At the ceremony the stone can either be handled by a lewis with chain and pulley block suspended from a gantry of steel scaffolding, or in certain circumstances electrical mechanism may be preferred. In any case one should make quite certain that the mechanism is strong enough for the purpose and yet causes as little obstruction as possible to the onlookers at the ceremony. It will be advisable to arrange a thorough test of the equipment before the ceremony takes place, and to ensure that the stone fits accurately on its bed to avoid having it re-set afterwards.

The person who will perform the ceremony will be approached well in advance by the employer, and it is also important to decide at an early stage the number of distinguished guests to be invited, as it will usually be necessary to erect a platform to accommodate them and, possibly, an awning as well in case of inclement weather. The lay-out of the platform and arrangements for accommodating other spectators should be carefully considered. Steps must be taken to clear and tidy up this portion of the site and its approaches, as at this stage a site is usually muddy and obstructed by heaps of spoil, stacks of bricks and other building materials.

The selection of those to be invited, including a clergyman for the religious aspect of the ceremony, will be made by the employer with such consultation as he finds necessary. He will usually discuss with the architect the printing of invitation cards and the inscription to appear on the stone. This latter should be carefully checked before the carving is put in hand, as any mistakes are extremely difficult to correct.

For the ceremony the stone should be in position on the handling equipment, and the foreman mason should have all the implements ready together with some fine mortar, free from grit. The implements required will be a clean trowel, mallet, level and plumb rule. It is customary for the contractor, the architect or the employer to present a special trowel and mallet to the person performing the ceremony, and these implements should actually be used. The trowel may be of silver in a presentation case, and the foreman mason should be responsible for washing it immediately after it has been used and for replacing it in the case.

It is quite common for a box containing current coins, plans, papers and other documents to be placed under the stone, and for this purpose a suitable recess must be formed in the bedstone or brickwork under the stone, and possibly even in the underside of the foundation-stone itself. The box should be made of stout copper, lead, silver or other non-ferrous metal and may be either rectangular or cylindrical in shape. Many boxes of beautiful design have been used for this purpose in the past. Some responsible person (often the architect) should have charge of this box before the ceremony and should ensure that all the contents are inserted and the box properly sealed.

On the day of the ceremony the guests will assemble on the platform shortly before the person who is to lay the stone. He will be escorted by the employer and will be introduced to all the guests on the platform. The ceremony may open with the singing of a hymn, accompanied by a band for preference. The employer will then make a short speech describing the purpose of the building to be erected and will ask the invited person to lay the stone. The trowel and mallet will be presented to him by the respective donors. The foreman mason will then spread the mortar evenly on the bed and the box containing the documents will be inserted under the stone. The person performing the ceremony will usually complete the laying of the mortar with the presentation trowel and then the stone will be slowly lowered into position. The contractor or the foreman mason will plumb the sides and the person invited will tap the top two or three times and declare the stone to be well and truly laid.

A dedicatory prayer may then be offered where appropriate. The employer will thank the person who has laid the stone, and he will reply with a short speech. The doxology may then be sung and the proceedings be concluded with the Benediction and the National Anthem.

Different rituals will be observed in ecclesiastical or masonic functions, and the architect should in such cases consult the respective authorities for guidance as to the special arrangements and order of service.

The Opening of a Building.—No definite procedure is laid down for this ceremony, and the elaborateness of the ritual will depend on the importance of the occasion and the rank of the principal guest invited to make the formal opening.

As in the case of the foundation-stone laying ceremony, the employer will also ask other guests to attend the function and invitation cards will be sent out to them. A gold or silver key or other suitable token will often be provided for presentation to the principal guest.

The ceremony will sometimes take place outside the main entrance, but it is equally common for it to be in one of the important rooms of the building or in the entrance hall, if suitable. A dais may be erected and decorated to accommodate the leading personages, and, possibly, music provided to entertain the company before the arrival of the principal guest as well as after the ceremony. The employer will meet the principal guest at the entrance to the building and will introduce him to others taking part in the ceremony. If he is accompanied by his wife, she will usually be presented with a bouquet of flowers. The principals will then take their places on the dais and the employer will make a short speech inviting the principal guest to open the building and presenting him with the key or other token, accompanied sometimes by an illuminated address. The principal guest will reply, and declare the building open, using the presentation key to open the main door if the gathering is outside, or otherwise such inner door as may be appropriate. Alternatively, he may simply unveil a commemorative plaque.

The employer will then conduct the principal guest over the building. The other invited guests may accompany the principal guest on this inspection or may be asked to go round after the principal guest has completed his tour. The procedure to be adopted will depend on the importance of the principal guest, the number of other guests present and the size of the building. Royalty are usually conducted over the building alone. Refreshments should be provided for the guests after the ceremony.

The Time Factor.—Most forms of building contract will provide for a period of time after the practical completion of the works (usually known as the defects liability period) during which the contractor will be liable for making good any defects which may occur due to the workmanship or materials not having been in accordance with the contract. This clause is necessary because it may take several months after a building has been erected before such defects become apparent. Moreover, the time factor has a direct bearing on the cost to the client. Extended time may involve additional cost of the building contract itself, but more important may be consequential extra costs. In a private house delay in completion may mean that the building owner, having sold his house, must move to a hotel and store his furniture. In the case of a trading establishment loss may be much more serious: loss of business for several weeks may be disastrous, particularly in a period when extra Christmas trade is expected.

Maintenance Inspections.—The contractor is bound to make good such defects at his own cost, though the R.I.B.A. contract * gives the architect the opportunity of taking into consideration factors outside the contract which have contributed to the fault. In such cases he will have to decide as fairly as possible the respective liabilities of the contactor and the employer.

In any case, whether the contractor is held to be wholly responsible or not, he must carry out the work if so instructed in writing by the architect (if necessary, under the provisions of the contract relating to extra works). The architect must allow a reasonable time for the work to be undertaken, however, as the contractor will have to bring men (and possibly plant as well) back to the site, and they may not be immediately available owing to other commitments.

It is worth bearing in mind that the guarantee of a merchant supplying goods is normally limited to replacing the goods and does not include the removal and refixing nor consequential damage. This does not, however, relieve the general contractor of his responsibility.

The contractor is not normally held liable for damage due to frost after the completion of the work, unless the architect decides that this damage was due to injury which had taken place before the completion.

Under the R.I.B.A. form of contract, clause 30 (4) (b), the employer is protected against failure of the contractor to make good any defects by the withholding of one half of the retention sum until the work has been carried out satisfactorily and if, after due notice has been given in writing (preferably by registered letter), the contractor still fails to carry out his full obligations under the terms of the contract, the architect may employ some

* Clause 15(2).

other person to undertake the work and may deduct the cost so incurred from the Final Account.

The architect will carry out an inspection, preferably accompanied by the contractor, shortly before or upon the expiry of the defects liability period, and will send to the contractor within fourteen days of such expiry a list of the works to be undertaken, differentiating between works which are wholly the responsibility of the contractor and those which may either be a shared liability or be extra works.

The inspection will have to be thorough, as once the defects liability period has expired, and the certificate of satisfactory completion of making good has been issued, the contractor's liability is at an end, except in case of fraud, dishonesty or fraudulent concealment or the discovery of any defects and insufficiencies which could not have been disclosed by a reasonable examination.* Even then it may require recourse to law before the contractor can be induced to undertake the work. After the defects have been made good to his satisfaction, the architect must, under the R.I.B.A. contract (clause 15 (4)), issue a certificate to confirm this.

It will take an experienced eye to detect some of the defects which may occur, but the following are some of the items which should be looked for :—

1. Damp. This may be revealed by actual wet patches, discoloured or blistered paintwork, flaking distemper, &c. Examination must be made to find the cause.
2. Damp-proof courses, flashings, gutters, roofs, pointing— for faulty workmanship or omissions.
3. Cracks or looseness in plaster or floor finishings, which may be due to damp, faulty preparation, shrinkage (or expansion) or settlement.
4. Cracks in brickwork, which may be due to settlement, seasonal variation in the subsoil, expansion, unsuitable mortar.
5. Paintwork—blisters, cracks, flaking, rust marks, &c.
6. Plumbing installation—check joints, water-seals, ball-valves, flushing cisterns, &c. Check falls on floor channels.
7. Drainage—examine manholes and sewage-disposal plant, if any, and check falls in paved areas, terraces, &c.
8. Timber—shrinkage or warping in windows, doors, tables,

* R.I.B.A. contract, clause 30 (7).

draining-boards, cupboards, floors. See that window-sills are not split. Check for any evidence of rot or disease in timber.

9. Precast or reinforced-concrete work—cracks, chips, inadequate cover to reinforcement.

If the architect suspects that any materials used have not been in accordance with the contract—e.g. plaster, mortar, &c.—he may have samples cut out and sent away for analysis. Also, if he suspects that a damp-proof course or cavity gutter, for instance, has been omitted, he may order the work to be opened up for inspection. If his suspicions are found to be correct, the contractor will be liable to rectify the defect in accordance with the architect's instructions, but otherwise the cost of opening up and making good must be allowed as an extra.

13

CERTIFICATES

Responsibility for Certificates.—It usually falls on the architect under a building contract to certify from time to time the amount of instalments on account to be paid to the contractor and to certify the final total of his account. It is generally provided that his interim certificates shall include the value of the work properly executed and unfixed materials on the site, less a specified percentage to be retained which is known as the retention sum or reserve. His legal position in certifying is dealt with in Chapter 17.

In most public work the quantity surveyor is appointed by the authority concerned to make valuations and recommend to the architect the amount to be certified, but the architect is nevertheless responsible for the issue of the certificate, the surveyor's recommendation being possibly affected by deductions for unsatisfactory work, delays in payment to sub-contractors, &c. In private work of any size the architect may get his client's authority to employ the quantity surveyor for such valuations, but unless his authority is obtained such employment may involve the architect in meeting the surveyor's charges. A certain amount of unofficial help may be given by the surveyor, but on a substantial contract he cannot be expected to advise the architect without charge. A standard valuation form is published by the R.I.C.S. for completion by the quantity surveyor and is reproduced in Appendix 1.* Public Authorities may have their own form.

On smaller contracts the architect should be able quite easily to make his own assessment. Where there are no bills of quantities the builder can be asked for his original estimate as a guide to the subdivision of the contract sum, if a copy has not been supplied (the R.I.B.A. form without quantities, clause 3 (2) (b), only asks for a " schedule of rates ", and such schedule may have no quantities or pricing out, and therefore not serve this purpose). Provision can be made in the contract for the builder to submit a detailed statement with each application, when these can be checked.

* Pages 292 and 293.

Method of Valuation.—How the architect makes his valuation will depend on the size and complexity of the contract. In the case of repetitive housing he may be able to fix values per house at each of half-a-dozen stages—say :—

(*a*) damp-proof course ;
(*b*) first floor joists fixed ;
(*c*) roof plate ;
(*d*) roof completed ;
(*e*) plastering finished ;
(*f*) fittings fixed, plumbing finished—all ready for decorators.

As a valuation is only approximate, it would not be necessary to distinguish between types of three-bedroom houses, though different figures would be necessary for two-bedroom or four-bedroom types. The proportion done of such work as drainage would also have to be assessed.

In contracts for larger buildings the architect, if without the help of the quantity surveyor, will have to go through the bill of quantities and, taking one trade at a time, pick out in a general way (without bothering about minor items) the work which has been done and its value. A total will thus be built up. A suitable proportion of the Preliminary Bill should, of course, be included, and a percentage addition made pro rata with any sums for insurances, &c., shown in the summary.

Unfixed Materials.—Most forms of contract provide for interim payments to include the value of unfixed materials on the site. The builder should be asked to prepare a priced list of these as at the date of the valuation, which can be checked by the clerk of works (if any) or architect. If verification of cost of any items is required it can be asked for. It is important to note that, as these materials when paid for become the property of the employer, it is usually provided that they must be on the site (i.e. within the physical control of the clerk of works). Being the employer's property, they must not, of course, be removed without permission, and in the event of the contractor's bankruptcy they would not be an asset vesting in the trustee, but could be removed or used by the employer.

A matter that needs careful consideration is the inclusion of unfixed materials that are not on the site and so outside the physical control of the building owner and his agents.*

There may be circumstances where with a contractor of sound financial standing the Architect might well agree to include materials not on site in an interim payment, but if there is any doubt as to financial stability, a firm refusal is the only thing. Otherwise, a working party sent on the contractor's bankruptcy to collect materials may find barred doors. The employer's right confirmed by a Court six or twelve months later would be of little use, when he is anxious for another contractor to get on with the job at once—in fact he would then be landed with something he does not want.

Nominated Sub-contractors.—The architect when issuing his certificate must notify the contractor of the amounts included for nominated sub-contractors. A form is published by the R.I.C.S. for use by the quantity surveyor, which sets out this detail,† and space is provided in the R.I.B.A. certificate form for the information to be included. The R.I.B.A. also publish a form for individual notification to each sub-contractor.‡ It is only by notifying these amounts and asking for production of receipts that the architect can enforce the authority given by the R.I.B.A. contract (clause 27 (c)) to certify payment of the accounts of nominated sub-contractors direct by the employer.

If payments are made direct by the employer to nominated sub-contractors under the above-mentioned clause, the employer, not the general contractor, would retain the cash discount, as the latter has not complied with the terms of payment. Contractors are sometimes apt to forget that it is a *cash* discount, but say that it is their profit, and that, having done everything except spend twopence on the cheque, they should have it.

Price Adjustment.—Where provision is made for price adjustment on account of fluctuations in cost of labour and materials, this must be taken into account in the valuation, under clause 31D (4) (c) of the R.I.B.A. contract.

Before any increased cost is included under the price adjustment

---

* See R.I.B.A. contract, clause 30 (2A) and page 65 above.
† *Statement of Amounts included in respect of Nominated Sub-contractors:* R I.C.S. See page 294.
‡ *Notification to Nominated Sub-contractors:* R.I.B.A. See page 297.

clauses, the contractor should submit a statement of particulars of the increases and decreases in a form which can be checked with his vouchers. If the time ever comes again when markets are falling, the architect will have to see that such statements are rendered regularly to avoid over-payment.

The contractor must have actually paid any increased cost before it can be included in an interim certificate and no profit may be added (provisos (i) and (ii) of the above sub-clause).

Nominated Suppliers.—There is no such protection given to nominated suppliers by clause 28 of the R.I.B.A. form as is given to nominated sub-contractors by clause 27 (c). They are on exactly the same footing as other merchants, except that they have been selected by the architect. There is no obligation for him to notify the amounts due to each, and he has no power in their case to certify direct payment.

Retention Sum.—In preparing his valuation the architect will have to take into account the sum to be retained under the contract. If the quantity surveyor submits a statement, the amount retained will be shown. In the larger contracts the same percentage will not be retained throughout, but a maximum sum will be fixed, and this will have to be remembered when preparing valuations for certificates. The retention sums out-standing on his various contracts are a substantial part of a contractor's capital. Whilst they are part of the financing which he is expected to do, he should not be expected to do more than his contract requires. The architect should therefore see that, so far as he is concerned, there is no delay in releasing balances at " practical completion " and at the end of the defects liability period. To this end he should be prompt in making his final inspection and giving notice to the contractor of defects to be remedied.

The Appendix to the R.I.B.A. form of contract makes provision for stating the percentage to be retained of value of work done and the limit of such retention, and footnotes suggest figures which are those commonly adopted. It should be noted that the limit must be a specific sum, though it can be expressed as a percentage of the contract sum (which only needs a slight mathematical calculation to make it a specific sum). Such sum will not be affected by variations.

A complication arises with maximum retention on subcontractors where a subcontractor comes in at a late stage, e.g. to lay wood block flooring. The contract retention may by then have reached its maximum some time before. Since the same rule is to apply to subcontractors as to the general contractor, the flooring subcontractor will have 10% deducted until *his* retention has reached 5% of *his* subcontract. The general contractor scores slightly. On the other hand, there might be a subcontractor, e.g. for piling, finishing at an early stage and entitled to a maximum retention before the general contractor is, in which case the latter loses. It is understood that the authors of the contract form contemplated such swings and roundabouts.

In some forms of contract (e.g. CCC/Wks/1, 40) the percentage retained of the value of unfixed materials is different from that retained from the value of work done, and the statement must be prepared accordingly.

Price adjustment is usually made without deduction of retention, though there may be no specific provision in the contract to say so. Such adjustments have in recent years been largely increases, and being regarded as an out of pocket expense of the contractor, on which he gets no profit, it would not be reasonable to make the same deduction from them as is made from a value which includes a profit.

A careful check should be made to ensure that the figure shown as already certified is correct, as a slip here may make a serious error in the valuation.

Release of Part of Retention.—It is usually provided that half, or some part of, the retention shall be released when the work is complete, the balance being retained till the end of the defects liability period. The R.I.B.A. contract clause 30 (4) (*b*) provides for this release on " practical completion " of the works, the architect being required to issue a certificate of practical completion under clause 15 (1). It is not, therefore, necessary for the contractor to have completed his contract. There may be odd things left to do, but the work should be substantially complete, or any outstanding work only delayed (as is sometimes the case) at the request of the employer.

It sometimes happens that a request is received from some nominated sub-contractors, whose work may have been completed at an early stage—e.g. asphalt damp-proof courses or structural floors—for release of their retention (in part or whole) some time before this is due in the case of the general contractor. Special powers are given to the architect to do this by clause 27 (e) of the R.I.B.A. contract, but unless there is a clause of this nature the architect would have no power to do so. It must then be assumed that the sub-contractor has knowledge of the terms of the contract and that he has provided for any extra capital required. If, of course, employer and contractor both agree to a release, such agreement forms a supplementary contract which gives the architect the necessary authority. It should be remembered that the release of the retention sum to a nominated sub-contractor relieves the general contractor of responsibility for making good any subsequent defects in the sub-contractor's work which may appear before the end of the defects liability period o the main contract, unless fraud or dishonesty can be proved. It is, therefore, better in such circumstances to request the general contractor to obtain an indemnity from the sub-contractor to cover the cost of making good any defects which may appear during the defects liability period of the main contract.

Release of Final Balance.—Under the R.I.B.A. contract, clauses 15 (4) and 30 (6), the whole of the balance of the retention sum is to be released forthwith on the issue of the certificate that making good of defects has been completed. Provision is made for adjustment later of any balance (either way) when the total of the final account is known.

Release of the final balance may be delayed because the accounts are not completed. If variations are reasonable, the final figure should be available by the end of the defects liability period.

Form of Certificate.—Certificates are usually issued in a standard form such as that published and sold in pads by the R.I.B.A.* Each certificate form in such pads is in triplicate, so that a carbon copy can be made and sent to the quantity surveyor's office. Certificates need not be in any prescribed form,

* See page 295.

but they should use the words " I (or We) certify . . .", stating
the name of the contract, names of contractor and employer,
the amount certified as due and the date, and they must bear
the signature of the architect.   It is an advantage if they are
given a serial number in the architect's records.   Provision is
made on the R.I.B.A. form for the amounts for nominated sub-
contractors to be entered.   Certificates are sent to the contractor,
who presents them to the employer for payment.

Need for Promptness.—Finance is an important factor in
the running of a contractor's business, and he naturally wants to
reduce to the minimum the capital he has tied up.   The interval
at which interim certificates will be issued is usually fixed by the
contract, and the architect should see that he gives prompt
attention to the matter at the specified intervals.   If the architect
is slow, delays his visits for valuations and does not deal with the
matter promptly on return to the office, particulars given by the
contractor quickly become obsolete, and the time-lag between
valuation and payment increases.   Whilst it may seem that the
delay of a week or two in payment of £500 or so may not be very
important, the aggregate of such outstanding amounts is substantial.   Where the contractor has no very great margin of
capital, delays in payment may cause financial difficulty from which
the employer will suffer.

14

VARIATIONS ON THE CONTRACT

Reason for Variations.—One of the peculiarities of building contracts is that, though they are usually contracts to undertake specific work for a specific price, nevertheless provision is made for variation of the work involved and for variation of the agreed price accordingly. Theoretically there should be no reason for such provision, as everything should be cut and dried beforehand. The client should know exactly what he wants and the architect should have completed his drawings and specification to convey such wants in technical form to the contractor. Everybody knowing exactly what is wanted, work can go ahead according to plan, and there is nothing to do except to see that it is done properly and duly paid for. That is, alas, only an ideal, because clients are sometimes unable to make up their minds, and architects are forced to defer completing their drawings, which makes the particulars supplied to the contractor to a greater or less extent subject to variation, and increases both the time required for the contract and its cost. Lack of thoroughness in the architect's work (e.g. an insufficient site survey, an ambiguous specification or inadequate details) may contribute its quota to the variations. Variations may also be due to site conditions or other unforeseen contingencies, delay in obtaining materials, economic reasons or "second thoughts" on the part of the client or architect. These latter should be firmly discouraged unless they are for particularly good reasons. Whilst striving for the ideal, one must face the fact that there will be variations and make provision for their definition and valuation.

Definition of Variations.—In regard to definition the R.I.B.A. contract (clauses 2 (3) (b) and 11 (1)) provides that all variations must be the subject of a written order. It is obvious that the conditions of erecting a building are such that it is not always possible to issue the written order before the work is begun. Clause 11 (4) therefore provides that they may be subsequently sanctioned by the architect in writing. A similar provision is usually made in other forms of contract. The architect must therefore be prepared to confirm in writing any decision or instruction which he gives. He must not defer his decisions, either by ignoring or forgetting letters or by giving doubtful replies, whether verbal or in writing. It is his duty to be definite. It will be seen from the R.I.B.A. contract (clause 2 (3)) that, if the contractor writes to the architect confirming alleged verbal instructions, and if the architect does not dissent in writing within seven days, such instruction is to be complied with, and, if a variation, the instruction would be sufficient authority for adjustment under clause 11.

The term "variation" is defined by clause 11 (2) of the R.I.B.A. form. It must be remembered that a variation cannot go so far as to alter the substance of the contract. To take an extreme case, one cannot say "we will not build a hospital here, we will build a school" (undoubtedly "an alteration of the design, quality or quantity of the works"), or even "we will not build a classroom block, we will build an assembly hall". Such matters would have to be negotiated with the contractor and could not be forced on him as his contract.

Variations Procedure.—The architect should adopt a systematic method for documenting all variations to the contract. In the past many architects have used standard forms for this purpose which were called "Variation Orders" (usually abbreviated to "V.O.s"). The term "Variation Order" itself does not appear in the R.I.B.A. contract, however, and its use is being discouraged. The R.I.B.A. no longer prints a standard form under this title. The corresponding form is entitled "Architect's Instruction".*

The R.I.B.A. contract requires that all variations must be the subject of "architect's instructions" which are contractually defined. A letter or memorandum signed by the architect is actually sufficient authority for an instruction, but a form has the advantage of keeping the information complete and orderly for every instruction throughout a job. It will appear distinct from other correspondence and forms, expecially if a tinted paper is used and all copies are filed separately. The following information should be on every architect's instruction:—

* See page 289.

Name of job
Name of contractor
Date of Architect's Instruction
Serial number of Architect's Instruction (each job beginning
    with 1 and being numbered in a separate series)
Subject matter of the Architect's Instruction
Architect's signature

Each instruction *must* be signed by the architect. It is useful to
indicate the distribution of all copies on the instruction. On the
architect's and quantity surveyor's copy may be put the approximate cost of the variation and, if desired, a summary of the
balance remaining from the contingency sum. It is not advisable
to put any value on the contractor's copy, as such value for an
extra will inevitably become a minimum in his eyes, and hamper
the pricing of the variation *pro rata* with the contract items.
When a contractor asks for a written architect's instruction for
a variation and says the cost will be so much it is best, in acknow-
ledging, to say that the question of price will be dealt with by
the quantity surveyor. Where the variation involves something
quite different from the contract, a definite estimate may, of
course, be obtained from the contractor and accepted as a firm
price. In such cases it is, however, advisable to consult the
quantity surveyor before acceptance: he will examine the detailed
build-up of the estimate and ensure that proper credit has been
given for balancing omissions.

When specifying the variations it is wise to mark each clearly
to show whether they are " omissions " or " additions " on the
contract. A variation can be described in one of two forms:
either:—

"For softwood door to Entrance substitute oak to detail."

or:—

" Omit softwood door to Entrance."
" Add hardwood do. to detail."

It is not advisable to quote item reference numbers from the bill
of quantities to define a variation nor to mention prices except
when a definite estimate is being accepted. The architect will
not be fully aware of what bill items other than those he quotes
might be affected. It is better to specify the variation in normal

terms and leave it to the quantity surveyor to look up his dimensions and see which items are to be adjusted.

An instruction signed by the clerk of works cannot constitute a variation within the meaning of the R.I.B.A. contract. His duty is solely that of an inspector (clause 10). The architect may delegate certain duties to him, but instructions to vary the contract must be signed by the architect personally.

Some contractors keep a " variation order book " on the site, in which the agent enters all instructions given him. He may ask the architect to sign them on his visits, giving him or sending him a copy of each. This method may appear to save the architect some office work, but should be understood by all parties only as a provisional confirmation, subject to the issue of the architect's own formal written instruction.

It should be remembered, however, that, if a contractor confirms a verbal instruction to the architect in writing, perhaps on a form headed " Confirmation of Architect's Instruction ", this constitutes a formal notification under the R.I.B.A. contract, clause 2 (3), and, unless dissented from in writing by the architect within seven days of receipt, it will take effect as an Architect's Instruction.

Some architects include the estimates of specialist sub-contractors in their formal instructions for variations, others only forward the specialist's estimate to the contractor with a letter instructing acceptance. A standard form for nomination of sub-contractors* is available from the R.I.B.A. for use when the specialist's tender itself has been obtained on the R.I.B.A. standard form of estimate.† As the estimate is usually a variation on the prime-cost sum, it is perhaps best, for the sake of completeness, to incorporate such acceptances in the series of formal instructions. However, as a prime cost sum is, from its very nature, subject to adjustment, an instruction to vary the contract is not essential.

One copy of all architect's instructions and revised or supplementary drawings should be sent, as they are issued, to the quantity surveyor, where one is employed. The instructions are his authority to measure and value any variations to the contract that they may embody. When he comes to measure he may find that

---

* *Standard form for Nomination of Sub-contractors:* R.I.B.A. See Appendix 1 page 286.

† See page 92.

there are some variations for which no written instructions have been issued.   If he feels satisfied that they are variations he will probably measure them, subject to an instruction being issued, and send a list to the architect for him to confirm.

Remeasurement.—It has been the unfortunate experience of the past that alterations made on some contracts have been so substantial that adjustment by way of omission and addition was impracticable.   It may be that improvement in contract particulars will reduce the number of such cases, but the possibility remains.   The only reasonable way in such cases is for the quantity surveyor to remeasure the whole work as it is executed. A stage comes, of course, where it is cheaper for the client in fees to do this than to measure omissions and additions.   Where the contract is of the normal type no provision is made for remeasurement in this way, and, if it is proposed, the authority of both parties should be obtained and the quantity surveyor instructed accordingly.

Valuation of Variations.—There are three ways of valuing variations :—

1. By a definite price agreed with the contractor when the order is issued.
2. By measurement and valuation by the quantity surveyor.
3. On a day-work basis, checked by the quantity surveyor.

Which method is to be followed rather depends on the nature of the variation.   If the variation is something which can be valued at contract rates or for the valuation of which contract rates can form a reasonable basis, it is best to leave the item for the quantity surveyor to deal with.   If, however, something entirely new is introduced, the contract prices would not be applicable, and the architect may like to negotiate the price in advance.   The contractor can be asked for an estimate, with its build-up, which should be referred to the quantity surveyor for examination.   On his report the estimate can be accepted, and the value of the variation will be entered in the final account accordingly.   It sometimes happens that, even when an estimate is given in this way, further variation is made before the work is carried out.   This emphasises the need for having the build-up

referred to above—not merely a lump sum without any detail—
as a basis for adjustment. Where a variation is left for the
quantity surveyor to measure, he will always, if required, give an
approximation of its value for the architect's information in
watching expenditure.

Sometimes an estimate is submitted by the general contractor
and accepted for work (covered by a prime cost sum), which it
was originally intended should be done by a specialist sub-contractor. The contractor will have added to such sum in his
tender for his profit, attendance, &c. In accepting an estimate
from him it should be made clear that it covers everything, or
he may later claim that it was only intended to match a sub-
contractor's tender and was subject to addition for profit, &c.

Day-work.—If a variation involves alteration work, pulling
down, or other work which is not of a straightforward nature, the
only fair way of valuation may be on the basis of cost. The
contractor may have quoted day-work rates, either by pricing
provisional hours of labour and quantities of material, &c., in
the bill of quantities, or he may have quoted percentages to be
added to prime cost for valuation of day-work. The R.I.B.A.
contract in clause 11 (4) (c) provides for either of these alternatives,
and in the latter case space is provided in the Appendix to the
form for insertion of the agreed percentages. This clause also
lays down that prime cost is to be determined according to rules
in a publication of the R.I.C.S.* and that vouchers specifying the
time and materials spent shall be submitted for verification to the
architect or his representative not later than the end of the week
following that on which the work is executed. Where there is a
clerk of works these vouchers will be submitted to him, as the
architect's representative, and he will sign them to certify that
the time and materials are correct. He is not concerned with
whether the item is an extra or not, nor whether day-work is the
correct method of charging: he only certifies the facts. Where
there is no clerk of works it will fall on the architect to watch
such vouchers and make any enquiry necessary on their submission.
The day-work sheets when signed will be forwarded to the
quantity surveyor, a copy being also supplied for the architect's
reference if he so requires. The quantity surveyor will examine

* *Definition of Prime Cost of Day-work carried out under a Building Contract:* R.I.C.S.

and check the pricing and agree any corrections with the contractor. If there is no quantity surveyor and the architect is dealing with the final accounts, he will undertake this duty.

Price Adjustment.—Many building contracts at the present day provide for adjustment of the price according to the fluctuation in standard rates of wages or in the market price of materials. Changes in labour rates are notified in the technical Press, and there should be little difficulty in checking whether any variation in rates has arisen.*

In the case of materials it is usual for a schedule to be prepared, before the contract is signed, of the materials on which price adjustment is to be made, and the basic price at time of tender set against each.† It is most satisfactory if the materials on this list can be limited to the principal materials required in the building. The amount resulting from adjustment of a number of small items is so little, and the time spent in preparing and checking the particulars so relatively long, that neither the builder nor the building owner will find they have much benefit, even when the difference is in their favour. What shall be subject to adjustment is, of course, a matter for agreement between the parties. Sometimes the list is already prepared when the particulars for tender are sent to the builders, and they are asked only to attach the prices. In this case the builder must in his tender make allowance for the risk of price increases on items not in the list ; if he inserts additional items, this would be unfair to other tenderers and should be taken into consideration when tenders are compared. The basic prices set out by the contractor on the schedule should be checked before the contract is signed with the estimates he has obtained ; this will normally be done by the quantity surveyor, who will report any agreed amendments.

Watching the Cost.—One of the architect's duties is to watch the expenditure of his client's money. The client has undertaken to pay a certain sum, and, though the contract may be subject to adjustment of variations, he has that sum in his mind as the amount to which he is committed. If there is likely to be any serious difference, particularly in excess, he should be kept informed. A running record of cost can be

* See page 269.   † See Appendix I, page 284.

kept by having a valuation of each variation recorded and totals of omissions and additions to the contract sum made from time to time. Prime cost sums must be adjusted against specialists' estimates as these are accepted, if formal written architect's instructions are not issued to cover them. Such a record depends largely for its accuracy on the prompt issue of written instructions. Obviously, if they are neglected, the figures will be of little value. Price adjustment on account of fluctuations must also be taken into account, where any serious changes are involved. Opportunity should be taken periodically to advise the client of the financial position, but it is, of course, important for the information to be accurate. A bombshell at the end of the contract, when the client has been lulled into a sense of security by the advice given, is worse than saying nothing at all on the subject.

Arrangements can usually be made with the quantity surveyor for the preparation of a statement monthly (or at agreed intervals) giving an appraisal of the financial position, and this is a most valuable service in the interest of cost control of the contract.

Record Drawings.—On any work of importance the client will probably want an accurate record of what has been done. There may have been variations from the contract drawings, which, if of a minor nature, could be marked on the client's copy, but if extensive (e.g. a revised drainage scheme) would require preparation of a new drawing. It should be arranged that proper records are left of electrical circuits and the runs of pipes in all but the simplest schemes, and it will usually be provided for the specialist contractor to supply these.

Claims.—The architect will from time to time have claims submitted to him by the contractor for extras on the contract, the validity of which may seem doubtful to him. There may also be differences of opinion as to the method to be adopted for valuation of variations.* The architect must remember that he has to interpret the contract fairly between the parties. He may have to make decisions on points of legal difficulty, which, but for their comparatively small value, would quite likely be submitted to arbitration or the Courts. The following thoughts are suggested as a guide to a decision on claims :—

* See R.I.B.A. Contract, clause 11; CCC/Wks/1, clause 9.

1. What did the parties contemplate on the point at the time of signing the contract? If there is specific reference to it, what does it mean?

2. Can any wording of the contract, though not specifically mentioning it, be *reasonably* applied to the point? In other words, if the parties had known of the point at the time of signing the contract, would they have reckoned that it was fairly covered by the wording?

3. If the parties did not contemplate the particular matter, what would they have agreed if they had?

4. If the claim is based on the contract, does it so alter it as to make its scope and nature different from what was contemplated by the parties signing it? Or is it such an extension of the contract as would be beyond the contemplation of the parties at the time of signing it? In either case the question arises whether the matter should not be treated as a separate contract, and a fair valuation made irrespective of any contract conditions.

5. The value of the claim in money should not affect a decision on the principle. If the claim is very small, however, whichever party is concerned might be persuaded to waive it, or it may be eliminated by a little " give and take ".

In deciding on a claim the architect should consider whether some action of the building owner is not the cause or a contributory cause, and, remembering that he is acting between the parties, impress on his client how much is the client's own fault. Some claims may be due simply to misfortune which neither party could have foreseen, and which it may be reasonable for the building owner to meet *ex gratia* to a greater or lesser extent.

A common subject of claim is extension of time for completion of the contract.* The architect must remember that his power of extension is limited by the provisions of the relative clause of the contract. In both the R.I.B.A. contract and CCC/Wks/1 there are specific reasons set out for which extension may be given, and the architect must ensure that his grant falls within one of the permitted heads. The period of extension must be based on what was a reasonable period by which completion would be delayed, not necessarily the same as the actual delay incurred which, owing to the fault of the contractor, might be unreasonable.

* R.I.B.A. Contract, clauses 23 and 33 (1)(*c*); CCC/Wks/1, clause 28.

15

PRESENTING THE ACCOUNTS

Unexpected Excess Costs.—What has often caused an architect serious concern—sometimes even been a nightmare—is the prospect of explaining the final cost to the client when the contract or other anticipated figure has been exceeded. The first step in avoiding such trouble is to keep the client informed during the progress of the work of any serious extras incurred. If he requires alterations from the agreed scheme, it must be emphasised that these will involve additional cost. On any items of importance an approximate figure can be obtained from the quantity surveyor or a specific estimate from the contractor. Such advice to the client should be in writing, or, if given verbally, should be confirmed in writing, so that there is a record. One is so apt to carry on a pleasant conversation, forgetting that the terms of that conversation may one day be the subject of investigation in the Courts. It is therefore a good rule to make that all communications of importance made verbally should be either confirmed by letter or at least recorded at the time in a diary. The evidence of such a record in a diary is the next best thing to written confirmation in a letter, and enables evidence to be given on oath on a matter which, but for the record, might have been forgotten.

There is another cause of extras which should be avoided: the temptation for the architect to spend money on his own responsibility towards the end of the contract, when he thinks that there will be savings to balance it. If the scheme has been cut and dried and properly detailed before the contract is let, there should be no necessity for such expenditure. The architect may think that a better floor finish or the addition of some particular fitting or fixture, or even ornament, will do him credit, but it is the man who pays who should decide whether he wants the improvement or not. The feeling should be resisted that the client has undertaken to spend £20,000, and that therefore it is a pity that he should be allowed to spend only £19,500. The architect is there to provide the client with what he wants. It is very difficult to gauge final cost accurately until all accounts are in, and if the architect's estimate of the position is proved wrong, he will have to justify this expenditure on " luxuries " to his client. If he is right, he is misrepresenting the position to his client and depriving him of a saving which could have been effected.

Form of the Accounts.—In the case of public authorities, who have their own technical staff, the full accounts as prepared by the quantity surveyor (or, where there is no quantity surveyor, by the builder) will have to be submitted. These will be subject to examination by the authority's staff and probably by auditors, so it may be necessary for the accounts to be accompanied by invoices of nominated sub-contractors, receipts, day-work sheets, &c. Instructions are usually issued by the authority as to their requirements.

In the case of the private client, whether an individual or a board of directors, a simple statement of the position showing the main items will be found of great value. It should be prepared in a form easily intelligible to the lay client without introducing technicalities. A suggested form is given in Appendix 1.* The summary of the variation account should be available in support and, of course, if asked for, the full variation account itself. Usually, however, if explanation can be made on a simple statement of where the money has gone, that is enough. If the client is difficult and insists on full detail, he must be given it. A private client is, of course, entitled to have the accounts examined and audited just as much as a public authority.

Architect's Examination of the Accounts.—When the accounts are submitted by the quantity surveyor, with any explanatory statement as suggested above, the architect will examine the summary and statement and ask any questions of the surveyor which he may need to elucidate any points. He should feel able to answer any queries of major importance that may be asked by the client.

In smaller contracts there will normally be no quantity surveyor and the final accounts will be submitted to the architect by the contractor. The architect will then be responsible for satisfying himself that such accounts are correct before he certifies the final payment. He should ask for the invoices of all nominated sub-contractors and suppliers and check them against the entries in the

* Page 300.

account, also checking the contract amounts allowed against them. In the case of nominated sub-contractors, he should see that all amounts certified for them have been paid. He must verify that all extra items charged are duly authorised and, if he thinks any of the prices unreasonable, ask for explanations. If there are items of price adjustment, i.e. increase or decrease in cost of labour or materials, the architect should ask for the necessary vouchers— time sheets for labour, invoices for materials. It goes without saying that the mathematics of the account and of all vouchers produced should be checked. The work involved in this examination of accounts by the architect is not normally very heavy, but clause 5.7 of the R.I.B.A. scale of charges provides for a fee where such surveyor's work is undertaken.

Audit of Accounts.—The accounts for work of public authorities will usually pass through their technical departments —architects and quantity surveyors—and on to auditors who are accountants. The architects will probably check that items are duly authorised, quantity surveyors will look at measurements and pricing. The auditors' first concern will be mathematics. It is therefore a good rule to adopt that in all documents sent forward all mathematics are checked *in the actual copy sent*. This should be done last thing before sending and independently of any previous checking, to ensure that any alterations subsequent to the original drafting or any typing errors are automatically checked. Where a quantity surveyor is employed, he will be responsible for the mathematical check. Auditors, however, look beyond this check. They may check day-work sheets, invoices for sub-contractors' accounts or vouchers for price adjustment with entries in the accounts, and may ask any questions, not infringing the authority of the architect or quantity surveyor, which they consider necessary in the interests of proper control of the expenditure. They should not interfere in technical matters. If the client is dissatisfied with the actions of architect or quantity surveyor, he may appoint another to investigate and report to him, and, of course, every facility should be given to such technical adviser.

Method of Submission of Accounts.—The final statement of account, with or without a summary or full copy of the variation account, according to circumstances, should normally be forwarded to the client by post with a formal covering letter, indicating when it is proposed to certify the balance and expressing the hope that the statement will be found in order. It is then for him to raise any points he may have, either by letter or at a meeting. The meeting may or may not be attended by the quantity surveyor. If points are raised by letter, they should, if necessary, be referred to the quantity surveyor, who will give his reply. The architect can report either by forwarding this or adapting it for a report of his own, or it may be more satisfactory for architect and quantity surveyor, now knowing the client's queries, to meet him and give the replies personally.

Accounts for Fees.—The final accounts for fees of architect, quantity surveyor and any consultants can be forwarded with the final statement of the contract accounts, or they can be deferred until the client has accepted the latter.

The legal position of an architect in regard to remuneration is discussed in Chapter 16. His account will be based on whatever terms have been agreed. The R.I.B.A. has published a set of Conditions of Engagement * to determine the minimum fees for which architects may undertake work and the kind of professional services clients should expect in return. It is advisable to explain to each client at the outset of the job how they will be calculated, their probable extent and the various stages when interim payments become due as the architect's work proceeds. Normally the scale fee is a percentage of the cost of the building. Where this does not apply the charge will be on a time basis for principals, architectural and other technical staff, but time is not charged for clerical and administrative staff. The architect must be prepared to produce details of this if the amount is questioned.

There has sometimes been difficulty owing to the client's surprise at finding a charge from the quantity surveyor at the final stage. He may think that, having paid for the bill of quantities he has finished. The importance of explaining to him the work done by the quantity surveyor and the terms of his employment has already been mentioned.† The same applies to consultants: it should be made clear to the client at the outset of each job that

---

* *Conditions of Engagement*, R.I.B.A. and also *Guide to the Conditions of Engagement*, R.I.B.A.
† Page 75.

they are being employed on his behalf and what their remuneration
will be.

Expenses.—All travelling and hotel expenses of the architect
in connection with the work will be chargeable, unless some
other arrangement has been made, also the cost of copies of drawings and other documents.   Hotel expenses charged should not
include such meals as lunch at a hotel on a day trip, but should be
limited to cases when the architect stays away for the night, and
also, of course, to *necessary* expenses (not always the same as the
total of the hotel bill).   Sometimes a fixed allowance per day or
night is agreed in lieu of actual costs.   A principal may usually
charge first-class fares for his own travelling and that of senior
architects.   In the case of public authorities their terms of employment will probably confirm this, and probably include the
highest-grade assistants.   Second-class fare only would otherwise
be chargeable for members of the architect's staff.   All office
expenses, such as postages, telephone, &c., should be regarded
as part of the architect's overhead expenses and covered by his fee,
though special circumstances—e.g. a large number of long-
distance telephone calls or parcels—might justify some special
arrangement.

16

LAW—THE ARCHITECT AND HIS CLIENT

Introductory.—It is proposed here to deal with law purely from the personal angle of the architect, considering first his legal relation to his client, and then certain legal problems he may meet in carrying out his share of the administration of the building contract or in other branches of his work. It is not for him to give legal advice to others, but it is important that he should understand, so far as possible, something of his own legal position, his rights and his duties.

The decision which will be given by the Courts is often uncertain until put to the test of an action. If it were not so, and experts in law agreed, there would be little reason for recourse to the Courts. Only salient points of common occurrence are therefore dealt with in these chapters, and they must be considered as generalisations, subject always to the particular circumstances of an individual case. They are only a warning in the hope of keeping the architect out of legal trouble ; if he finds himself so involved, he cannot hope to solve his problems by the study of text-books, but must turn to those who have a very much wider field of legal knowledge and experience.

Some of the following matter on the subject of contracts should have been covered by the reader in a study of the general law of contract, but the particular application of the principles to the case of the architect himself justifies their repetition and emphasis.

Case Law.—A number of leading cases are quoted below as being the authority for various points settled in the Courts. The technical interpretation of law reports is outside the architect's province, but it is as well that he should have some knowledge of the principal cases bearing on the work of his profession. The illustration presented by a report puts a legal rule in its proper perspective and should help in memorising it.

The architect must bear in mind, when comparing cases, that the basic circumstances which gave rise to the decision must be the same if the ruling is to hold, and he must remember to study the provisions of any written contract in the particular case, as its terms may entirely reverse the decision, so far as that contract is concerned. Many of the cases quoted are fifty to one hundred years old and even more. There were then no accepted forms of building contract, such as the R.I.B.A. form or the Government form CCC/Wks/1, already referred to, by one of which many building works are now governed. Moreover, there may be customs which can now be established as so general and well known as to have legal significance, which could not be so established at the time of the case quoted. All these varying conditions affect the interpretation and application of reported cases.

A very short précis is given of the leading cases referred to, limited to the point under consideration, and references are given to the Law Reports, which will enable the architect to look up the case more fully in the Library of his professional Institute or any Law Library.

Agreement for Appointment.—The relationship between the architect and his client is contractual ; that is, it depends on the terms of agreement made between the parties. Such an agreement must exist, otherwise the architect will have no grounds on which to sue for his fees if his client fails to pay them. Apart from the case of Public Authorities, with which he usually has a formal written contract, the architect quite often has nothing to show in the nature of a written agreement.   He has perhaps had a visit from his client, who told him what he required and discussed the subject. The client went away with the understanding that the architect would prepare drawings of a scheme. What passed at that meeting may be the only semblance of an agreement, and, as will be seen later, certain terms may be implied by the action of the parties at that meeting. In short, if any dispute arises between architect and client the test always is : what was the intention of the parties at the time of the agreement ? The parties can, of course, at any time mutually agree to vary or add to the terms already settled. If the agreement makes no reference to the point at issue, the Court will try to ascertain what the parties' intentions were and to give effect to them.

Subject to the exception dealt with later, there is no reason in law why the agreement should not be made by word of mouth, but, as human recollection is fallible, it is obviously advisable that the terms should be put into writing. It is therefore a good general rule that, where an appointment has been made verbally, the architect should confirm in writing at the earliest opportunity both the appointment and the terms of the agreement. Similarly, if he receives any letter from his client containing anything inconsistent with his own recollection of what their agreement was, he should at once write to place on record his own understanding of the matter. This should prevent any misunderstanding arising later, or, if any dispute does arise, should provide good evidence of what the agreement in fact was.

It used to be the law that a contract with a Corporation must be made under the Corporation seal to be binding upon the Corporation. The law has now been changed by the Corporate Bodies' Contracts Act, 1960. This Act in effect places Corporations in the same position as private persons for the purpose of making contracts. Accordingly, the architect need not trouble himself about taking any special precautions when dealing with a Corporation in order to ensure the validity of his contract with it.

Stamping of Agreements.—A written agreement or any writing setting out the terms of an agreement must be stamped with a 6d adhesive stamp affixed to the document and cancelled at the time of signing. It should be noted that this provision applies to correspondence relied on as constituting an agreement, in which case the letter accepting the terms should bear the stamp. A written agreement under seal requires a 10/- stamp impressed by the Inland Revenue within thirty days of execution. Failure to stamp an agreement is never fatal. Though the Court may refuse to accept a document in evidence before it is stamped, the normal procedure is to accept it on an undertaking being given that it will be stamped. The Commissioners of Inland Revenue have power to impose a penalty up to £10 in the case of late stamping, but this may be remitted or reduced, and in practice is remitted altogether in the case of a written agreement requiring a 6d stamp which is presented for stamping within fourteen days of execution. The date of execution is the date of the *first* signature to the document.

In practice, where contracts are concluded by correspondence, the letter of acceptance is hardly ever stamped. The Courts will not usually make objection because such letter is unstamped, and barristers are by their professional etiquette forbidden to raise the point of failure to stamp a document.

Extent of Architect's Work.—The extent of the work to be undertaken by the architect will depend on the terms of his contract with his client. He will normally in the first instance be instructed to prepare sketch-plans, and such instruction cannot be taken as authority to prepare working drawings and invite tenders. The sketch-plans will be submitted, and may have to be reconsidered and amended. The architect should be certain of getting clear instructions at each stage and keeping his client informed of what he is doing. He should place on record in his correspondence with his client any variations in his instructions which may be made from time to time.

Authority to Instruct Quantity Surveyor.—It is advisable to bring to the notice of the client in good time the need to appoint a quantity surveyor, any recommendation for the appointment being made at the same time. This may involve a little explanation of what the quantity surveyor does, but ensures that the building owner is aware of his existence, and will probably prevent difficulty later. The architect, being authorised accordingly, will then instruct the quantity surveyor as agent for his client, to whom in due course the quantity surveyor will render his account. The old custom of adding the quantity surveyor's charges at the end of the bill of quantities, and so including them in the tender, often without the knowledge of the client, is strongly to be deprecated, and is now generally abandoned. Direct appointment by the client, however, is not essential, as an architect, if instructed without qualification to obtain tenders, where these could not be obtained without quantities, has implied authority, as the building owner's agent, to appoint a quantity surveyor.

WAGHORN v. THE WIMBLEDON LOCAL BOARD (1877): Hudson on Building Contracts, 4th ed., ii. 52 ; "The Times", June 4th, 1877.

The Wimbledon Burial Board instructed their architect to prepare drawings and get tenders for a cemetery chapel. The plaintiff was employed by the architect to prepare quantities. Tenders were too high and no tender was accepted. Evidence was given that it was necessary for quantities to be prepared to enable builders to tender.

Held that as the Burial Board had instructed their architect to obtain tenders, and as tenders could not be made without quantities, they had impliedly authorised him to have quantities prepared.

Moon *v.* Witney Union (1837): 3 Bing. N.C. 814; 6 L.J.C.P. 305; 43 R.R. 802.

The architect to the Guardians prepared drawings and instructed the plaintiff to prepare quantities. Builders were notified that quantities could be obtained on payment of a deposit and that the successful competitor would have to defray the expenses of taking out the quantities, the charge for which was stated at the foot of the bill of quantities. A dispute arose between the architect and the Guardians, and the architect sent in his account together with that of the plaintiff. The Guardians said they had never heard of Moon. Evidence was given to prove the custom of employment of a quantity surveyor, and a verdict for the plaintiff was given by the jury.

Application was made to set aside the verdict on the ground that there was no privity of contract and that the usage had not been sufficiently proved. Tindall L.C.J., rejecting the application, said that the defendants themselves had had notification of the usage when they incorporated the architect's statement of it in their notice to builders tendering. So far as privity of contract was concerned, this was a conditional contract, one under which it was arranged that the expenses of making out the quantities should be paid by the successful competitor, if any, but if by the act of the defendants there should be no competitor, then that work which was done by their authority should be paid for by them.

The building owner may say to his architect, " Yes, you may obtain tenders, so long as it costs me nothing ". Then the architect would not have authority to appoint a quantity surveyor.

Richardson & Waghorn *v.* Beales (1867): " The Times ", June 29th, 1867.

Beales and others formed a committee to establish a Club. Their architect instructed the plaintiffs to prepare quantities. Tenders were too high and the scheme was abandoned. The architect in evidence admitted that in informing him that his design was accepted the committee had desired him to get tenders, provided he did not pledge the committee in doing so.

Held that this letter put the plaintiffs out of court, and that action should be against the architect. The plaintiffs were thereupon non-suited.

If with such limitation of his authority the architect did appoint a quantity surveyor, he would be liable himself for the quantity surveyor's charges on an action for a breach of warranty of his authority.

Remuneration.—The remuneration due to an architect will again depend on the terms of his contract with his client, and as a general rule is agreed to be in accordance with an appropriate published scale of professional charges. Failing any mention of the amount of fees, the Court will imply that the architect shall be paid a reasonable remuneration for his services. The scale fee is usually assessed as a percentage on the cost of the building work actually completed (or in the case of abandoned work on the estimated cost of the project). Though the percentage may not bear a direct relation to the work done, it is the most satisfactory way of determining the fee, so that the building owner can budget for his expense and the fee can be precisely fixed without argument. Scales of fees, incorporating these percentage rates, are issued by the various professional Institutions, and in deciding what fee is reasonable the Court will be influenced by the scales recommended by the professional Institutions, and in all probability will adopt one of those scales.* If, however, such a scale of fees is incorporated by reference in the terms of agreement between building owner and architect, it then becomes part of the contract between them and can be enforced. The advisability of incorporating such a scale in the agreed terms is obvious.

FARTHING *v.* TOMKINS (1893): 9 T.L.R. 566.

The plaintiff prepared plans for a hotel at the request of the defendant. Estimated cost was £12,000, and the scheme was abandoned.

Held that the plaintiff could not recover at the then Institute scale of 3%, but only fair charges for work actually done.

ATT.-GEN. *v.* DRAPERS' COMPANY (1869): L.R. 9. Eq. 69.

Lord Romilly in giving judgment said, " The charges of brokers on transfer of stocks and shares are paid by commission, and if a similar practice prevails with respect to surveyors' charges I shall not disturb it. It prevents disputes as to amount, and the charges fixed by the scale do not seem too high."

BURR *v.* RIDOUT: " The Times ", February 22nd, 1893.

For a building, estimated by the architect in the first instance to cost £4,000, the lowest tender (the scheme being somewhat enlarged), was nearly £8,000. The plaintiff, the architect, sued the defendant for £450, his charges. Defendant paid £110 into Court.

Coleridge L.C.J. in summing up to a special jury said that the defendant was not liable to pay the percentage claimed unless they were satisfied he had agreed to do so. If they thought the plans sent in would involve such an

* The Prices and Incomes Board issued a report on architects' fees in May 1968 (Cmnd 3653).

excess of expenditure beyond what was authorised that the defendant might repudiate them entirely, then they should find for the defendant.

The jury awarded the plaintiff £200 (including the £110 paid into Court), so the inaccuracy of the architect's estimate was evidently taken into account, though not considered sufficiently bad to justify repudiation by the defendant.

WHIPHAM v. EVERITT: "The Times", March 22nd, 1900.

The plaintiff brought an action for £169 16s for professional services and work done for the defendant in connection with the preparation of drawings and obtaining a tender for a villa at Saltburn. The amount of the tender was £5,660. The defendant considered the tender too high and abandoned the scheme.

The R.I.B.A. scale of the time allowed 2½% upon the estimated cost if drawings and specification had been prepared, and an additional ½% if tenders had been obtained. The defence alleged a verbal agreement that if the scheme was abandoned plaintiff would charge only for the time occupied in preparing the plans and obtaining the tender.

Kennedy J. in giving judgment said that there had been no such verbal agreement as was alleged by the defendant. The plaintiff was entitled to a reasonable remuneration for the work done. The rule of the Institute as to charges was not binding in law, because it was not a custom of so universal an application as to be an implied term of every contract. But in considering what was a reasonable charge it was right to take into consideration the practice adopted by the large proportion of the profession, as shown by the rules drawn up by the Council of the Institute for the guidance of the members of the profession. His Lordship thought that the plaintiff was entitled to 2½% of the estimated cost of the building. The word "estimated" gave rise to a little difficulty, but, as the plaintiff himself had admitted that the amount of the tender, £5,660, was rather high, he thought that if he gave the plaintiff 2½% on £5,000 that would be reasonable remuneration. His Lordship deducted the ½% claimed for obtaining a tender, because the plaintiff himself had not charged this in the first instance, and, further, it was doubtful whether the plaintiff had obtained a tender within the meaning of the rule. Judgment was accordingly entered for £125 and costs.

In short, whilst the Courts will not admit themselves as bound by a scale, they will probably accept it as *prima facie* evidence of a reasonable charge, particularly in view of the improved status of professional Institutions since the time of the above-quoted cases.

Financial Stability of Building Owner.—It sometimes happens that the architect thinks it necessary to enquire into the financial position of a prospective client, particularly if the scheme is a substantial one. Building is often the subject of speculation, and may be embarked on with a reliance on mortgages and insufficient capital and the intention to sell out when the building is completed (or even before then). The architect's bank will usually be able to obtain a reference from the building owner's bank, though this may be found to be couched in rather vague terms. The architect must form his own judgment and decide whether to refuse to accept the work or whether to make any special terms as to payment either in advance or by instalments. When payment is due and the building owner is found to hedge, the prompt service of a writ is the only thing to bring him to his senses and possibly save the architect before his client's bankruptcy.

A director of a limited company is not personally liable for the debts of his company, even though the company may consist of little else but himself, unless he holds himself out as being personally liable. The only remedy on obtaining judgment for a debt is to distrain on the company's assets, which may be found to be no more than a little notepaper. On the other hand, a principal in partnership is liable for his firm's debts to the full extent of his personal wealth.

Architect as Agent.—The appointment of an architect gives him a general authority as agent for his client in those matters usually entrusted to an architect. An agent warrants that he is authorised to do the acts which he purports to do for his principal, and he binds his principal accordingly. If, in fact, he has not authority he would be personally liable on an action for breach of warranty of authority. This general authority would not cover such a matter as the acceptance of a tender and entering into a building contract. These are acts for which specific authority would be necessary. The architect has not even authority to make agreements with adjoining owners without reference to his principal.

Betts v. Pickford (1906): 2 Ch. 87.

The plaintiffs sought an order requiring the defendants, who were the occupiers of adjoining land, to disconnect their building from the plaintiffs' building. The defendants argued that the plaintiffs' architect had agreed that they could connect their building to the plaintiffs' building in the way they had done.

Held that, though the plaintiffs' architect had made this agreement, it was beyond the scope of his employment, and so afforded the defendants no defence to the plaintiffs' action.

Architect as Quasi-arbitrator.—Besides being the agent of the building owner, the architect is in certain circumstances entrusted with what are called quasi-judicial duties. He is not a judge or an arbitrator in the technical sense, bound by Rules of Court or the Arbitration Acts, but he is nevertheless placed in an impartial position with a duty to exercise his judgment. In that case neither party can, in the absence of fraud, dispute his decision and recover damages.

STEVENSON v. WATSON (1879) : 4 C.P.D. 148.

The plaintiff contracted to build a hall, the plans and bills of quantities for which were prepared by the defendant. The contract provided that the architect might order additions or deductions from it, and that the value of them should be ascertained by the architect in the same manner as the quantities were prepared and at the same rates as those on which they had been priced. The contract provided that all questions or matters of dispute, which might arise during the progress of the works or in the settlement of the account, were left to the architect, whose decision should be final and binding.

The plaintiffs claimed that the architect had not used due care and skill and had not valued the variations in accordance with the terms of the contract.

Held, that the function of the architect was not merely ministerial, but required the exercise of professional judgment, opinion and skill, and he therefore occupied the position of an arbitrator, against whom, no fraud or collusion being alleged, the action would not lie.

YOUNG v. BLAKE (1887) : Hudson on Building Contracts, 4th Ed., ii, 121.

Denman J. in giving judgment said, " It puts the architect in the position of persons trusted by both parties, and if a man with his eyes open chooses to enter into such a contract giving the architect that power, he cannot turn round and by a mere allegation of negligence say ' I have discovered there was an error in the measurements, and I have asked you to act under the contract and you won't do it in your discretion, and I will now sue you because you negligently took out those quantities '. I do not think that is the relation between the parties at all. The architect is not put in that position so as to be a servant of either party in that sense, but he is in a different position altogether."

See also *Chambers* v. *Goldthorpe* * and *Roberts* v. *Hickman*.†

It is therefore necessary to distinguish acts done by the architect as agent for the building owner and those done in a quasi-judicial capacity between the parties. In the former he will be responsible to his principal for negligence ; in the latter he has the freedom of an arbitrator.

* Page 187.   † Page 187.

Negligence.—A professional man holds himself out as being qualified to do the work entrusted to him. If he fails to possess that amount of skill or experience which is usual in the profession, or if he neglects to use the skill which he in fact possesses, he will be guilty of negligence. To succeed in an action for negligence the plaintiff must establish :—

(*a*) That the defendant owed a duty to him.

(*b*) That the defendant's error was carelessly made (e.g. that he omitted to check what by the general practice of the profession he should have checked), or that, making a check, he did so carelessly.

(*c*) That the plaintiff suffered damage.

The duty in (*a*) above may be contractual, but it may also be implied by the law of tort.

DONOGHUE v. STEVENSON (1932): A.C. 562.

This appeal to the House of Lords, though not a building case, established an important principle that an action for damages for negligence may lie in tort, even though there was no contractual relation between the parties and no fraud. The particular case was one in which the plaintiff had consumed part of a bottle of ginger beer containing the decomposing remnants of a snail. She claimed against the manufacturers, who pleaded that they had sold to the distributor and therefore had no liability to her. The distributor could have no reason to suspect that the contents of an opaque bottle were other than indicated, and therefore had no liability for negligence. It was decided that the manufacturers were liable.

The application of this case to building is that an architect might be liable for negligence to a builder, even though he has no contract with him, if his act resulted in damage to life, limb or health. See also *Old Gate Estates Ltd.* v. *Toplis & others* (1939): 161 L.T. 227 and *Clayton* v. *Woodman & Son (Builders) Ltd.* (1961): 3 W.L.R. 987 and (1962): 1 W.L.R. 585 C.A.

In 1963 the House of Lords decided that a negligent though honest statement, or negligent advice, might give rise to an action for damages for financial loss.

HEDLEY BYRNE & Co. LTD. v. HELLER & PARTNERS LTD. (1964): A.C. 465.

Heller & Partners as bankers gave a favourable reference to the plaintiffs in respect of one of their customers who subsequently went into liquidation. The plaintiffs claimed damages for negligent misrepresentation.

In fact, the plaintiffs failed because the reference was specifically given "without responsibility on the part of the bank or its officials". Apart from this qualification, all five Lords of Appeal agreed on the defendant's liability in tort.

Lord Reid in his judgment said:—

" Where it was plain that the party seeking information or advice trusted the party supplying it to exercise such a degree of care as circumstances required, and it was reasonable so to trust the person supplying information, and the latter knew or ought to have known that the enquirer was relying on him, the law imposed a duty of care on the party making the statement or giving advice."

Lord Morris added:

" If a professional man such as a doctor or banker voluntarily undertook a service by giving deliberate advice he was under a duty to exercise reasonable care."

Lord Devlin put it this way:—

" A promise given without consideration could not be enforced as a contract, but if the service promised was performed and performed negligently the promisee could recover in tort."

The case is of great importance to professional men, for taken in conjunction with *Donoghue* v. *Stevenson* it means that where advice is given, even voluntarily, or to a third party with whom the professional man has no contract, the professional man may be liable for any resulting damage either through personal injury or financial loss if his advice was negligent or he made a negligent mis-statement. However, in *Bagot* v. *Stevens Scanlon* (1966): 1 Q.B. 197 Diplock L. J. appears to have stated that in spite of the decision in *Hedley Byrne* v. *Heller* an architect's liability is still contractual only, at all events where the resulting damage is purely financial. The decision gives rise to a number of difficulties, and, although it is noted here, it would not be prudent to rely on it to the exclusion of *Hedley Byrne* v. *Heller*.

The Court has to decide the question of whether there was or was not negligence on the facts of each particular case, and it is therefore imperative for the architect to take all possible precautions to maintain care and accuracy in his work. A few cases are quoted below as examples where negligence was alleged.

The importance of following correct procedure in dealing with the contractor is emphasised by the following case. Although the decision was reversed on appeal on the facts, it gives a serious warning.

CLAYTON v. WOODMAN & SON (BUILDERS) LTD. & OTHERS (1961): 3 W.L.R. 987 and 1962 1 W.L.R. 585 C.A.

A bricklayer sued his employers, a firm of builders, for damages for injury in the course of his employment. The architects were joined as defendants. A representative of the architects was alleged to have given direct instructions to the bricklayer to cut a chase in a brick wall, being of the opinion that no shoring of the wall was necessary. In fact, the wall collapsed and injured the bricklayer.

Held that the architects were liable to the bricklayer, as, following *Donoghue* v. *Stevenson* (see page 159), they owed a duty to him, since as a bricklayer he could not have reason to suppose that damage would be involved.   The architects should have realised the danger.

If the architects had given their instructions in the proper way to the builders or their foreman they would not have risked liability for the injury. The builders were held jointly liable with the architects, because of their failure in a statutory duty to shore up under the Buildings (Safety, Health and Welfare) Regulations 1948.

On appeal it was held that the architect had given no direct order for the chase, only a refusal to vary the contract.   Donovan L.J. said: " If the architect had usurped the position of the builder and given the order for the chase to be cut with no support to the wall, very different circumstances would arise."

Responsibility for supervision, except on minor matters, cannot be delegated to the clerk of works.

LEICESTER BOARD OF GUARDIANS v. TROLLOPE (1911): Hudson on Building Contracts, 4th Ed., ii, 419.

The plaintiffs entered into a contract for the erection of an infirmary and other buildings, for which the defendant was architect. The plaintiffs appointed a clerk of works. The building was completed, and some two years afterwards dry rot was discovered in the lower floor. Investigation showed that the concrete bed under the floor was not properly laid, and it appeared during the hearing of the case that there had been collusion between the clerk of works and builder.

The plaintiffs sued the defendant, their architect, claiming damages for breach of the contract to superintend the work. The defendant denied negligence and pleaded that the fault was that of the clerk of works, who was the plaintiffs' servant and whose duty it was to detect the omission and report it.

Channell J. in his judgment said :—

" It does not seem to me that it excuses the architect from seeing that his design is complied with, that he thought that the clerk of works would be sure to see that it was all right, and it seems to me that this is not a matter of detail which it was justifiable to leave to the clerk of works. . . . It is said that the clerk of works is the servant of the plaintiffs, and therefore that the defendant is excused. If a party to the contract prevents the other party from performing his contract, of course that is an answer; but it cannot possibly be put that this conduct of the clerk of works . . . amounts to the plaintiffs, through their servant, preventing the defendant from performing his contract. An employer is not liable for the fraud and misconduct of his servant if the servant does it in his own interest, and not in the supposed interest of the employer."

The measure of damages is the damage which flows from the negligence, and this, of course, may be many times larger than the architect's professional charges.   Thus in *Saunders & Collard* v. *Broadstairs Local Board* (1890) (*Hudson on Building Contracts*, 4th ed., ii. 164) damages of more than £4,600 were awarded against engineers who had been negligent. Their own fees for professional services in the matter had amounted to only £521.

An architect's estimate must be reasonably accurate, or he would be liable for negligence.

MONEYPENNY v. HARTLAND (1826): 2 C. & P. 378.

Best C.J. in his judgment said, "If a surveyor delivers an estimate greatly below the sum at which a work can be done, and thereby induces a private person to undertake what he would not otherwise do, then I think he is not entitled to recover."

If it is made a condition of the architect's appointment that the building must be erected for a given sum, it would be strong evidence of breach of this term of the contract if the tenders were all well in excess of that sum.

The two cases following refer to reports on the condition of premises. The difference between them is solely one of fact. In one case the Court found that there were in fact indications of dry rot that should have been noticed by a competent surveyor, in the second case that there were not.

HARDY v. WALMSLEY LEWIS (1967): Estates Gazette Digest 614.

The defendant surveyed a house for the plaintiff, who, on the strength of the survey, bought it for £4600. It was left entirely in the hands of the defendant to survey the property and advise the plaintiff. The defendant noticed dormant dry rot, but did not mention it in his reports and did not inspect the loft. Later, he asked the plaintiff if he would like a further report with the carpets removed and an examination of the loft. Again no mention was made of dormant dry rot. The plaintiff replied that he was satisfied with the defendant's report. Paull J. held that the defendant should have warned the plaintiff about dormant dry rot, to put him on his guard, and held that the defendant was also negligent in not discovering extensive dry rot and damp. The plaintiff had to sell the house at a loss. The measure of damages was held to be the difference between the market value at the time of (£4300) and the market value on resale (£3500), plus the solicitors' costs on resale, the agreed costs of the case and costs of levelling the floor.

KER v. ALLAN & SONS (1949), in the Scottish Court of Session (" R.I.C.S. Journal ", July 1949, p. 64).

Lord Birnam in giving judgment in favour of the defendants said he accepted it that the possibility of dry rot was a thing that ought always to be in the mind of the surveyor and he should always be on the look-out for any evidence that might to his skilled mind be suggestive of dry rot. He was unable, however, to accept the view that in the absence of any suspicious circumstances the surveyor's duty required him to cause carpets and linoleums to be lifted and to go underneath floors.

There are two things which the lay client, who asks for a report on property in contemplation of purchase, usually seems to live in fear of—viz. dry rot and bad drains. These cases emphasise the need of making it clear in a report if conditions are such as to encourage dry rot, even if none is actually visible and, if so, of including a recommendation for closer inspection. In the same way specific enquiry should be made of the client as to whether he requires a test of drains, and, if not, it should be stated in the report that drains were not tested. Even if instructed that no test is required, care is necessary that any visible defects, such as broken manhole covers, blocked gullies, &c., are noted. Another case (*Sincock* v. *Bangs* (1952): C.P.L. 562; 160 Estates Gazette 389) emphasises that, even if the client says he only wants a general survey, the architect has a responsibility to discover important defects. In that case the plaintiff, an architect, was instructed to inspect a farm. He was told not to make a detailed survey, but to give a general opinion. After the purchase had been completed, dry rot, woodworm and settlement were discovered. Barry J. held that, although the plaintiff had only been asked to give a general opinion, nevertheless he had been negligent in not discovering these defects. The purchaser of a property is so often in a hurry to secure the property by paying the deposit, that an architect must be particularly careful not to be so hurried that he cannot meet his client's requirements. If, as has been known to happen, the client takes him to the house one afternoon, walks round with him quickly and then expects an answer, he should confirm in writing that he has not had an opportunity to examine the premises in sufficient detail to ensure that there are no structural defects of importance.

The architect is responsible for his staff, and cannot avoid a charge of negligence by saying that the mistake was one made by his assistant, even though he may prove that he had taken every precaution to employ properly qualified and efficient staff.

Abandoned Work.—The work of an architect is such that instructions are generally given in stages, and it may be that a scheme is abandoned at some intermediate stage. Specific fees are set out in the R.I.B.A. scale of charges for certain stages, and it has been held that where an architect has been instructed to proceed from one stage to another, his client cannot prevent him from earning his fees on the stage on which he is engaged.

THOMAS v. HAMMERSMITH BOROUGH COUNCIL (1938): 82 S.J. 583; 3 A.E.R. 203; "The Builder", December 31st, 1937, p. 1203, June 10th, 1938, p. 1129.

The plaintiff sued the defendants for £5,000 damages, being the balance of the plaintiff's scale remuneration for work as architect in the erection of a town hall for the borough.

The plaintiff had prepared plans and estimates which he alleged were in a condition to go to the quantity surveyor when the work was abandoned, and claimed £8,000, a fee of 4% on the estimate of £200,000 in accordance with the agreed scale, of which he had received £3,000 on account. There were some allegations of incompleteness: for instance, the drawings did not show the heating and certain steelwork was not designed.

Porter J. in his judgment said the plans were only provisional, but the steelwork was quite incomplete and other matters needed amendment. It was true that there were errors and omissions in the plans, but these were partly due to changes in the plans. He found that in the circumstances the plaintiff was entitled to damages for breach of contract and he awarded him £7,000 and costs (including the £3,000 already paid).

The judgment was upheld in the Court of Appeal.

Copyright.—The Copyright Act 1956 establishes copyright "in every original artistic work which is unpublished".

An artistic work is defined by Section 1 as meaning:—

(a) the following, irrespective of artistic quality, namely paintings, sculptures, drawings, engravings and photographs.

(b) works of architecture, being either buildings or models of buildings.

(c) works of artistic craftsmanship, not falling within either of the preceding paragraphs.

The owner of copyright in a work has the exclusive right to reproduce that work in any material form. Copyright is normally vested in the author of the work, which in the case of a building would be the architect who designed it, unless he has specifically agreed to part with his rights. Section 4 of the Act makes it clear that if the work is made by the author in the course of his employment by another person under a contract of service or apprenticeship, the employer, in the absence of agreement to the contrary, is the owner of the copyright.

The period of copyright under the Act is for fifty years from the end of the calendar year in which the death of the author of the work occurs (twenty-five years in the case of photographs).

If it is made clear in correspondence that employment is in accordance with the Conditions of Engagement and Scale of Charges of the R.I.B.A. (both should be mentioned), there will be no doubt that copyright remains with the architect, as clause J of the Conditions makes specific provision for this.

In order to establish a breach of copyright in a building it would be necessary to prove that a substantial part of the artistic design has been copied.

Right to Possession of Documents.—The client, having paid the architect's charges, is entitled to possession of the drawings. Copyright, however, remains with the architect, unless there is a specific agreement to the contrary.

GIBBON v. PEASE (1905): 1 K.B. 810.

Collins M.R. in his judgment in the Court of Appeal said, " The defendant is an architect who was employed by the plaintiff on a verbal contract to do all that was necessary to be done as an architect in designing and carrying out a certain building operation on some houses belonging to the plaintiff. . . . When the work was done the building owner paid the contract price and claimed the plans. The defendant refused to give them up, contending that by the custom of the profession he was entitled to retain them. . . . In my opinion the contract in this case resulted in the making of plans the property in which passed to the building owner on payment of the remuneration provided under the contract. I find a difficulty in distinguishing this case from that of a contract to paint a picture or to design a coat of arms."

At the time of this case all copies of drawings were probably made by separate tracings. At the present day no doubt the client would have been given a set of photo-prints, and everybody would have been satisfied.

Any memoranda or notes made by the architect to help him in preparing his drawings are in a different category. They are the architect's own means to attain an end—the drawings he has contracted to provide. Unless his contract with his client provides otherwise, he is entitled to retain these notes and memoranda.

LONDON SCHOOL BOARD v. NORTHCROFT (1889): Hudson on Building Contracts, 4th ed., ii, 147.

The plaintiffs employed the defendant as quantity surveyor and brought an action against him for the surrender of certain papers containing calculations and memoranda used in the measurement.

Held that the Board had no right to the memoranda.

Death of the Architect.—Whether the liability to carry out a contract passes to the representatives of a deceased person depends on whether the contract is a personal one; i.e. one in which the other party relied on the "individual skill, competency or other personal qualification" of the deceased. This is a matter to be decided in any particular case. In the case of an architect with no partner the appointment must be regarded as personal, and the executors could not nominate an assistant to carry on the business, except in so far as the respective clients agreed. With a firm of two or more partners the appointment may be that of the firm, in which case the death of one partner would not affect existing contracts. But the appointment may be of one individual partner (e.g. as an arbitrator) where another partner in the firm could not take over, even though he may be entitled to a share of the profits earned by his partner in the arbitration.

Death of the Building Owner.—The rule referred to in the previous paragraph as to a contract being personal applies equally in the case of the death of the building owner. Here the contract is unlikely to be a personal one, and the executors of the building owner must discharge his liabilities under the building contract and for the fees of the professional men employed. The fact that the appointment of the architect was a personal one will not be material in the case of the death of the building owner.

Bankruptcy.—Again the question arises as to whether any particular contract is a personal one with the bankrupt. The trustee in bankruptcy would be responsible for the debts of the bankrupt, but, if the contract was a personal one with the bankrupt, could not continue the work in hand on his behalf. In other words, the trustee of a bankrupt builder might carry on the building contract to completion (apart, of course, from a specific clause in the contract terminating it in the event of bankruptcy), whereas the trustees of a bankrupt architect whose contract was a personal one could not continue the work.

Secret Profits.—The architect must not accept any consideration for doing or forbearing to do any act in relation to the

business of the building owner, his principal, without his knowledge.   Such acceptance by an agent would be a criminal offence.
The Prevention of Corruption Act 1906 specifies that persons in
the service of the Crown are to be regarded as agents for the
purpose of the Act.

Though the offer of a discount or commission from merchants
or sub-contractors may not be made corruptly, one cannot
emphasise too strongly the importance of refusing any such offer.
Even if made with the full knowledge of the client, it would be
inadvisable to accept.   The receipt of such a commission puts the
architect under an obligation to the firm concerned, which even
unconsciously may bias him.

The architect must disclose any pecuniary interest he may have
in any contract, as nothing of this nature which might influence
his recommendation or decision should be withheld from his
client.   Special provision in the case of officers of Local Authorities in this matter is made by the Local Government Act, 1933,
section 123, and the London Government Act, 1939, section 90,
which provide that an officer employed by a Local Authority
must give notice in writing if he has any pecuniary interest
directly or indirectly in a contract to be entered into by such
Authority, and that the holding of shares or stock in a company
(other than a public body) is deemed to be an indirect interest
within the meaning of the Act.

17

LAW (*continued*)—THE ARCHITECT AND THE BUILDING CONTRACT

Tenders.—An invitation to tender sent out to builders is not an offer which can in any way directly result in a binding contract. It is only an invitation to submit offers. A tender submitted is, however, an offer, the *unqualified* acceptance of which forms a binding contract. If the tenderer adds some condition to the form of tender sent him, that condition, in the event of unqualified acceptance, becomes part of the contract. If in accepting the architect objects to the additional condition, there is no binding contract. It is a rule of law that the parties must be *ad idem*—of one mind—before the existence of a contract can be established.

The specification or bill of quantities will usually have stated that the contractor will be required to enter into a particular form of contract, and a tender referring to those documents therefore expresses agreement to do so. The completion of the contract referred to follows as a matter of form, to which the contractor cannot object. It is, of course, essential that he should be advised before tendering how the blanks in a standard form will be filled in (e.g. percentage of value to be retained in interim payments, period of maintenance, amount of liquidated damages, &c.). If any of these have not been settled before tendering they must be mutually agreed. It obviously will save possible disagreement if such matters are clear to the contractor before tendering.

Errors in Tenders.—The importance of drawing the contractor's attention to errors in his tender, which was mentioned on page 119 above, is emphasised by a case * in which a contractor claimed damages for fraudulent representation against an architect and his principal, a Borough Corporation. The contractor alleged that the architect had noticed an error of £10,000 in the bill of quantities and had not drawn his attention to it, as the

---

* DUTTON *v.* LOUTH CORPORATION AND ANOTHER. *The Builder*, February 25th, 1955, p. 344. On appeal: *The Builder*, August 8th, 1955, p. 229.

result of which he was misled into signing the contract with the Corporation. The trial Judge gave judgment for the contractor against the architect and the Corporation. This decision was reversed by the Court of Appeal on the ground that the architect had informed the contractor in general terms that there were serious errors in his bill of quantities (though he had not specified the particular error) and was entitled to assume that the contractor would check his tender before signing the contract. Although the architect was successful in the end, the dispute might have been avoided altogether if the contractor's attention had been specifically drawn to the particular error.

Preparing the Contract.—Nearly all building contracts are in a standardised form. The best-known form for lump-sum contracts in private practice is that published by the R.I.B.A.,* which is in two parts—Articles of Agreement and Conditions of Contract with Appendix. The fact that it has developed over a long period of years, is approved by the representatives of architects and builders, and is generally well known and understood, makes its use an advantage. The duty of preparing the contract by completing the various blanks in the articles of agreement and appendix usually falls on the architect. It may be necessary to add special clauses to the Conditions for the particular job : if so they must be written in, and the insertion must be initialled by both parties at the time of signature. Any portions to be deleted must be ruled through and similarly initialled, and the articles of agreement must be properly stamped.† All other documents comprised in the contract (each drawing and the bill of quantities) should be marked for identification and signed by the parties, e.g.

This is one of the drawings
or This is the bill of quantities

referred to in the contract signed by us this   day of
19 .

In the case of the bill of quantities this identification should be on the last page, and, if thought advisable, the number of pages can be stated. If the R.I.B.A. form is used (with quanti-

* See page 57.   † See page 163.

ties) the specification is not part of the contract, and will not be signed by the parties. So much of it as affects price is incorporated in the bill of quantities, leaving only instructions as to location, &c., for the specification. Where there are no quantities the full specification is a contract document and must be signed accordingly. All the signed documents must be construed together as the contract.

CUNLIFFE v. HAMPTON WICK LOCAL BOARD (1893): 9 T.L.R. 378; Hudson on Building Contracts, 4th Ed., ii, 250.

A contract for the construction of certain sewerage works contained the following conditions :—

2. " The contractor is to provide everything necessary . . . according to the true intent and meaning of *the drawings and specification taken together*."

11. " Any defects, shrinkage and other faults which may occur within three months *from the completion of the several works* . . . are to be amended and made good by the contractor at his own cost."

A clause in the specification read :—

" The contractor will have to maintain in thorough working order and repair the whole of the works herein described for a period of three months *after the surveyor's final certificate* that the works are completed to his satisfaction."

Inter alia there was a counterclaim by the defendants for the cost of making good of defects which arose more than three months after their execution but less than three months after the final certificate. The Official Referee held that clause 11 of the conditions relieved the contractor from liability, as the maintenance period ran from the time when the work was actually carried out.

Held by a Divisional Court that the documents must be construed together, and the reference in the specification to the final certificate fixed the date from which maintenance liability ran. The judgment was upheld by the Court of Appeal.

Architects in public employment will not generally be concerned with the preparation of the contract, which would be dealt with by the Contracts Branch of a Government Department or by the Clerk to a Local Authority. They will have to advise, however, on the technical aspects of any proposed conditions.

Insurance of Employer's Risks.—The following case draws attention to the need for careful consideration of insurance requirements:

GOLD v. PATMAN & FOTHERINGHAM (1958): 2 A.E.R. 497.

A site in London was cleared for the erection of a block of offices and piling for the foundations was proceeded with. The disturbance caused by driving piles caused damage to adjoining property and a substantial claim was received by the contractors.

The R.I.B.A. form of contract (1939) was used. Clause 14 (*b*) required the contractor to indemnify the employer against such claims, *if the damage was due to the negligence of the contractor.* The bill of quantities provided, pursuant to clause 15 (*a*), that the contractor shall (amongst other things) insure adjoining properties against subsidence or collapse.

Held that, there being no negligence by the contractor, he was not liable under clause 14 (*b*) and that the requirement under clause 15 (*a*) only covered the contractor's responsibility, being contrasted with the requirement of clause 15 (*b*) (A), which specifically required covering in joint names.

The risk is considered one that the contractor cannot be expected to anticipate or assess, and the *Standard Method of Measurement* (1963), clause B 10, requires insurance of any liability of the building owner to be covered by a provisional sum in the building contract. The R.I.B.A. form (1963), 19 (2) (*a*), requires such insurance to be in the joint names of employer and contractor. The terms and extent of the insurance will be matters to be settled before signature of the contract.

Variations.—A building contract is, unless otherwise provided, an " entire contract " (i.e. an indivisible contract in which the contractor undertakes to complete the whole of the work specified for the sum agreed). Such sum is not due until he has completed, and if he does not complete, there is a breach of contract, which lays him open to an action for damages. He cannot claim *pro rata* for a proportion of the work done. But such terms are nearly always over-ridden by the written contract, which makes provision for interim payments and for variations, either of omission or addition, without vitiating the contract (R.I.B.A. form, clauses 30 (1) & 11; CCC/Wks/1, clauses 40 & 9 (1)).

The power of the architect to order extras will be defined by the building contract. The R.I.B.A. form (clause 11 (1) & (2)) gives him authority to order

" the alteration or modification of the design, quality or quantity of the Works as shown upon the Contract Drawings and described by or referred to in the Contract Bills, and includes the addition, omission or substitution of any work, the alteration of the kind or standard of any of the materials or goods used in the Works, and the removal from the site of any work, materials or goods. . . ."

Failing such a clause, the architect would have no implied authority to order variations. It must be remembered that this clause is an agreement between employer and contractor, and not between employer and architect. The architect is bound by his own contract with his client. If by his terms of employment the architect is not to order any extras without the client's authority, he would be liable to his client for such orders given without authority, though, of course, the right of the contractor against the employer is not affected if such orders are within the terms of the building contract.

Where a provisional sum is included in the contract for contingencies, such sum should be expended only on unforeseen work incidental to and required for the due completion of the contract. It should not be used by the architect to pay for extras outside the terms of the contract.

Variations must be of such a nature as could reasonably have been anticipated by the contract.

THORN v. LONDON CORPORATION (1876), 1 A.C. 120.

Lord Cairn in his judgment said, " If it is the kind of additional work contemplated by the contract, he (the contractor) must be paid for it, and will be paid for it, according to prices regulated by the contract. . . . If the additional work is so peculiar, so unexpected, and so different from what any person reckoned or calculated upon, it may not be within the contract at all, and he could either refuse to go on or claim to be paid on a *quantum meruit.*"

The architect must remember that he cannot go on adding to a contract indefinitely without regard to the nature and extent of the additional work. Of course, the contractor may agree to carry out extra work, which would otherwise be outside the contract, at the contract rates, but this would in effect be a new contract, and is a matter for negotiation.

Where, as is usual, orders for variations are required to be in writing, they should be signed. In the case of *Myers* v. *Sarl* (1860): 30 L.J.Q.B. 9, it was held that sketches and drawings made in the architect's office by his draughtsman, but not signed by him, were not written orders, where the contract required such orders to be in writing under the architect's hand.

The R.I.B.A. form of contract (clause 2 (3) (b) admits as a valid order any written confirmation given by the architect after the work has been done.   If a contract does not contain this extension, the order would have to be issued prior to execution of the work (*Lamprell* v. *Billericay Union* (1849): 18 L.J. Ex. 282).

There might be a loop-hole by which a contractor could re-cover extras without a written variation order, even though the contract makes this a condition precedent to payment for extras.   If the building owner or architect orders work, knowing or being told that it involves an extra, it might be argued that there was an implied promise to pay for the extra work, or even that it was fraud to accept the benefit of such work and not pay, just because a formal order had not been issued.

HILL v. SOUTH STAFFORDSHIRE RAILWAY (1865): 11 Jur. 192 ; 12 L.T. 63.

Turner L.J. said, " I think it would be a fraud on the part of the company to have desired by their engineer these alterations, additions and omissions to be made, to have stood by and seen the expenditure going on upon them, to have taken the benefit of that expenditure, and to refuse payment on the ground that the expenditure was incurred without proper orders having being given for the purpose."

It is important that the architect should make enquiry as to the nature of the sub-soil and make provision, if necessary, for extra cost of excavation in rock.   If rock is unlikely, but unexpectedly met with, any extra cost would be a reasonable charge against a provisional sum for contingencies, but if there is likelihood of such strata being met the quantity surveyor should be instructed to make the separate provision required by the Standard Method of Measurement, or the client may blame the architect when he is faced with an extra charge.   The usual definition of rock for this purpose is such material as cannot reasonably be removed by pick and shovel, but needs the use of compressors or blasting.   That a charge is a proper addition to the contract sum under the R.I.B.A. form of contract, where no such item was included in the bill of quantities, was confirmed in the case of *C. Bryant & Son Ltd.* v. *Birmingham Hospital Saturday Fund* (1938): 1 A.E.R. 503.

This case brings to notice two other points of importance to architects.   First, trial holes should be dug to the full depth of the proposed excavation, otherwise they are not serving their proper purpose.   For instance, if a basement is to be dug, one of the trial holes should be on the site of the basement and for the full antici-pated depth to be excavated.   Secondly, if tenders are based on one form of contract and a revised form is used for the actual contract, the changes should be examined and considered carefully by both parties, as they will be deemed to have agreed to the terms which they actually sign, as superseding those in the bill of quantities or other tender documents.

Sub-contractors' Work Omitted and Paid Direct.—A problem occasionally arises when work for which a prime cost sum appears in the bill of quantities is dealt with as a separate contract paid for direct by the employer and the prime cost sum is, therefore, omitted from the contract. If the work is carried out it is regarded as reasonable that the contractor should not be deprived of the profit which he has added in pricing the bill of quantities. Further, there may be a separate item for attendance on the sub-contractor. How far this may be omitted must depend on the extent of the services the contractor is required to provide. He may have to render just the same services as if the specialist had been the sub-contractor anticipated by the contract. What has in practice been contentious is the cash discount which the contract provides shall be allowed on the sub-contractor's account. The intention of the contract is that this discount shall pay for the financing that may be required (the contractor having to pay within fourteen days, whether he has received payment or not) and the risk which the contractor takes in being responsible for the sub-contractor's work. As, however, the usual discount is more than enough to cover this, contractors treat it as part of their profit; sometimes adding no profit to the prime cost sum at all and relying on the discount. If the work is paid for direct by the employer the discount does not come their way and they feel aggrieved. The answer is, however hard it may seem, that it is a *cash* discount and, no cash, no discount. Similar circumstances arise with nominated suppliers and, *mutatis mutandis*, the answer is the same.

Cost Variation Clauses.—A lump-sum contract is for a firm and fixed price, unless provision is made to the contrary. Since the prospect of war and consequent unsettled markets in 1939, building contracts were usually subject to adjustment for market fluctuations. Now a firm price is again more common.

If, however, there is to be adjustment, the cost-variation clause of the particular contract must be studied (R.I.B.A. form clause 31, CCC/Wks/1, clause 11). The clause in the R.I.B.A. form is to be struck out if not required, and the CCC/Wks/1 form now excludes clause 11 from the general printing: it is issued as a supplementary clause when required.

Interim Certificates—Responsibility.

—The responsibility for issuing certificates for interim payments is normally with the architect, but, either officially or unofficially, he often certifies on the advice of the quantity surveyor. Many public authorities make it part of their agreement with the quantity surveyor that he shall make valuations for interim certificates, and with private clients in contracts of any size similar valuations are made by the surveyor. Whether the architect has authority to employ a surveyor for this purpose without reference to his client is very doubtful, particularly if, as is usual, the contract provides for the architect to certify and makes no reference to a valuation of the surveyor.

Certificates—Relation of Architect to the Parties.

—The architect in issuing interim certificates is not acting in a judicial capacity but as agent of the employer to whom he would be liable for negligence (*Wisbech R.D.C.* v. *Ward* (1927): 2 K.B. 556; (1928) 2 K.B. 1). On the other hand, if the architect's certificate is made binding on both parties by the contract, the employer must not make any agreement (unknown to the builder) which might affect the architect's impartiality to the prejudice of the builder.

KIMBERLEY v. DICK (1871): L.R. 13 Eq. 1; 41 L.J. Ch. 38.

The defendant's architect, Mr. White, gave him an estimate of the probable cost of a proposed mansion, writing, " So that you may safely rely upon the £15,000 covering everything, unless you want more than I have proposed, indeed I can now promise it shall not exceed that sum." Meanwhile, the plaintiff, a builder, attended at Mr. White's office for three days, taking particulars from preliminary drawings, made up an estimate and signed a tender to perform the work for £13,690. Working drawings were prepared subsequently, and the formal contract including them was signed some two months after the tender (work having meanwhile begun). The plaintiff made no detailed examination of the documents; in fact, he was ill at the time of signing them. Before long he discovered that the building would cost considerably more than £13,690, but expecting to be paid the extra, he continued and completed at a cost of about £25,000. The building contract contained a clause which read " that all questions between the said parties touching the matters relating to this contract shall be left to the sole determination and award of the said architect . . .".

Lord Romilly M.R. in giving judgment said, " I am of the opinion that the contract or engagement between Mr. Dick and Mr. White that the total outlay should not exceed £15,000, having been concealed from, or not communicated to, the plaintiff, it completely annuls the proviso of referring all matters to the arbitration of the architect, so far as the plaintiff is concerned. In order to make it binding it was essential that before the plaintiff entered into the contract with Mr. Dick, submitting to the arbitration of Mr. White, the plaintiff should have been informed of the contract subsisting between Mr. White and Mr. Dick. . . ."

His Lordship held that, as the plaintiff's mistake in regard to the contract was due to his own negligence in not examining it before signature, or taking any steps to rectify matters when he discovered his error, he was not entitled to relief in that respect. He directed, however, that account should be taken of extra works and variations on the contract executed by the plaintiff on the direction of Mr. White.

In issuing his final certificate the architect is acting in a quasi-judicial capacity and is not liable for negligence.

CHAMBERS v. GOLDTHORPE (1901): 1 KB. 624; 70 L.J.K.B. 482; 84 L.T. 444; 49 W.R. 401; 17 T.L.R. 304.

The plaintiff, an architect, sued the defendant for his fees, and the defendant counterclaimed for negligence in the measuring up and certifying of the accounts. The contract provided that " the certificate of the architect . . . showing the final balance due is to be conclusive evidence of the works having been duly completed, and that the contractor is entitled to receive payment of the final balance ".

Held that the negligence of the architect alleged was in exercise of his functions under clauses under which he was to act impartially towards the building owner and the contractor, and that, occupying the position of an arbitrator, he was not liable to an action for negligence in the exercise of those functions.

By the R.I.B.A. form, clause 30 (1) and (6), the architect is placed in much the same position.

However, like an arbitrator he must not submit to pressure from one of the parties but must act with impartiality.

ROBERTS v. HICKMAN (1909): Hudson on Building Contracts, 4th Ed., ii, 426; 1913, A.C. 229.

The plaintiff sued the defendants for the balance due in respect of work done on a building contract of a value of £2,750. The contract contained a clause :—

" The decision of the architect relating to any matters or thing or the goodness or sufficiency of any work, or the extent or value of any extra or omitted work, shall be final, conclusive and binding on all parties."

In November 1907 the architect received and reported to his clients, the defendants, certain claims made by the plaintiff owing to the works having been suspended for several months at the instance of the defendants. In writing he said :—

" Of course, these claims will want careful investigation with the view to considerably reducing the amounts."

The plaintiff agreed to proceed without prejudice to the claims. In March 1908, when the work was nearing completion, the plaintiff applied to the architect for a certificate for £750. The defendants on hearing of this wrote to the architect :—

" I should say on no account should you issue this until we have Roberts' account."

On April 14th, 1908, the architect wrote to the defendants :—

" Unless I hear from you to the contrary I shall be giving Mr. Roberts a certificate for £600 in the course of Wednesday."

The defendants replied next day :—

" You will please understand it is no use issuing a certificate as I am sure Mr. Hickman will not sign a cheque."

The architect thereupon wrote to the plaintiff :—

" I regret I cannot enclose certificate, my clients' instructions being that the certificate I next give you is to be a final one."

On August 21st, 1908 (after the action had been brought), the architect issued his final certificate for £339 9s 4d. This was paid, and the plaintiff pursued the case for the remainder of his claim.

Hamilton J. in the King's Bench Division decided that the final certificate was conclusive, but his judgment was reversed in the Court of Appeal, and that Court's decision was upheld in the House of Lords. Loreburn L.C. in his judgment said :—

" The architect did, I think, place himself in a position which deprived his certificate of the value which otherwise it would have had. Moulton L.J. (in the Court of Appeal) after referring to what he had done says, ' He is no longer fit to be a judge, because he has been acting in the interest of one of the parties, and by their direction. That taints the whole of his acts and makes them invalid, whatever subsequent matter his decision is directed to.' I agree with that, but I should like to say this : it is not in my opinion a case in which the terms ' turpitude ' or ' fraud ' are apt. I think the real error of Mr. H. was that he mistook his position, that he meant to act as a mediator ; that he had not the firmness to recognise that his true position was that of an arbitrator, and repel unworthy communications made to him by the defendants. It is undoubted that the defendants tried in this respect to lead him astray in their own interests."

Where a quantity surveyor appointed to make a valuation for an interim certificate had not done his work properly and the contractor was aggrieved, it has been held that this was not interference or obstruction by the employer within the meaning of clause 20 (1) of the R.I.B.A. form 1939 (26 (1) (b) of the 1963 form). The certificate was the architect's responsibility, and the contractor's remedy was arbitration (*Burden* v. *Swansea Corporation* (1957): 1 W.L.R. 1167; 1957 A.E.R. 243 H.L.).

Certificates—Refusal to Certify.

—If the architect should refuse to certify or unreasonably delay his certificate, the builder can recover without, notwithstanding that the contract may make a certificate a condition precedent to payment.

KELLETT v. NEW MILLS U.D.C. (1900): Hudson on Building Contracts, 4th Ed., ii, 298.

The plaintiff sued the defendants for the balance due under a contract for sewerage works. The defendants pleaded that the engineers' certificate was a condition precedent to payment and that no certificate had been issued.

A special jury found that the engineers never addressed themselves to determine and certify that the works had been completed or what was the sum due to the plaintiff, but that they wrongfully refused or wrongfully and unreasonably delayed so to determine and certify, and that the defendants were aware of such refusal or delay and took advantage of it to refuse or unreasonably delay payment.

Phillimore J. directed entry of a verdict for the plaintiff and gave judgment accordingly.

Unfixed Materials.

—The property in unfixed materials on the building site is with the contractor, but both the R.I.B.A. Contract (clauses 14 & 30 (2)) & CCC/Wks/1 (40 (2)) make provision for including their value in interim certificates (subject to a reserve retained), on payment of which the property in the materials so included is to pass to the building owner. In the event of the bankruptcy of the contractor, such materials would not be subject to the control of the trustee, but would be at the absolute disposal of the building owner.

On the other hand, the contractor has no lien on the building he has erected as security for payment of his account. What has once been attached to the land belongs to and must pass with the land.

Removal of Improper Work.

—If the architect is given power to have improper work removed (as in R.I.B.A. form, clause 6 (4)), he must decide when he sees the work, and should not delay till the conclusion of the contract his decision that the work is defective.

ADCOCK'S TRUSTEES v. BRIDGE R.D.C. (1911): 75 J.P. 241.

Phillimore J. in his judgment said " It occurs to me that the real business-like way to construe clause 16 * is to apply it to emergencies ; to things that arise in the immediate course of building which require execution rather than judicial action. But when an architect has looked at a piece of work, on one of these visits, and has not condemned it, and the contractor has obviously treated it as finished, and taken his men from off it, and proceeded to some other piece of work, it appears to me that clause 16 ought no longer to apply. If, in fact, the work is badly done and mischief follows in consequence, the architect is not without his power, and the employer is not without his protection. The architect then uses clause 17,† and applies the retention money, and in that case is no longer acting on an emergency, he is acting judicially, and only judicially, and there is an appeal from him to the arbitrator."

There is now nothing excluded in the R.I.B.A. form from the authority of the arbitrator, so the difference between the two clauses is not so material. However, delay in ordering the removal of improper work might quite easily involve additional consequential expense, and an arbitrator would undoubtedly give weight to a complaint that the architect has not acted promptly, and so saved that expense.

The architect has a certain tolerance allowed him in interpreting the requirements of the specification. In a case which was a matter of building down to a price he was found not at fault in requiring a contractor to make good certain defects and not to renew the work (*Cotton* v. *Wallis* 1955: 1 W.L.R. 1168; 3 A.E.R. 373 C.A.). This does not mean that the terms of the specification can be ignored or that they must be interpreted in the light of the cost of the work, only that the architect has a certain latitude within his professional competence. It is obviously dangerous to put too much reliance on such latitude.

Release from Liability.—The architect's final certificate of satisfaction releases the contractor from liability for defects (except defects which a reasonable inspection could not have

---

* Of the R.I.B.A. form (1909): a special clause covering removal of defective work (quoted in Hudson on Building Contracts, 4th Ed., ii, p. 610), which was excluded from the arbitration clause (quoted *ibid.*, p. 615).

† The defects liability clause corresponding to the present R.I.B.A. form, clause 15 (quoted *ibid.*, p. 610).

revealed), but not fraud, collusion or the architect's misconduct (*Harvey* v. *Lawrence* (1867): 15 L.T. 571). The architect is not relieved from liability for breach of contract until six years from the accrual of the cause of action. Where the contract is under seal the period is twelve years. In the case of tort, for example negligence, the architect is relieved from liability after six years from the accrual of the cause of action. These are the periods prescribed by the Limitation Act 1939.* A cause of action accrues when the breach occurs, not when it is discovered.† However, where there has been fraud or mistake, the period runs from the date when the fraud or mistake was, or could reasonably have been, discovered.

Architect Preparing Bill of Quantities.—If an architect himself prepares a bill of quantities, he should ensure that his client knows of his intention and of his liability for an additional fee on that account. The architect should avoid the custom (now falling into disuse) by which the quantity surveyor's fee was added in the bill of quantities, included in the tender and paid by the contractor out of his first instalment. Such a method might conceal entirely from his client the fact that he was receiving an additional fee, and would fairly certainly cause difficulty if the scheme were abandoned or the contractor bankrupt before paying the fee.

Bankruptcy of the Contractor.—On the bankruptcy of a contractor the work will fairly certainly stop temporarily. The liability to carry out the contract, as it is not a personal one, falls on the trustee in bankruptcy, and if he does not proceed within a reasonable time the contract can be terminated. It will be seen from the R.I.B.A. form of contract, clause 25 (2), that the employer is given specific authority to terminate the contract in the event of bankruptcy, and the rights and duties of the parties thereupon are set out following.

It will be necessary to have a valuation of the work completed as at the date on which the contractor stops work, so that the necessary adjustment of moneys due can be made. This will be dealt with by the quantity surveyor, if there is one appointed for the contract.

<hr>

* Section 2.   † Section 26.

The power of the architect to certify for direct payment the balance of accounts of nominated sub-contractors depends in the case of the R.I.B.A. form on clause 27 (*c*).   He can call for receipts to show the amounts paid, and if the contractor has defaulted on any payments already certified, he can certify direct payment.   What the contractor has already received in respect of such payments and has not passed on will then count as a general payment to him.   Under the R.I.B.A. contract this direct payment can be made after bankruptcy or liquidation of the contractor.   Clause 27 (*a*) (viii) and 30 (4) (*a*) of that form state that both the employer's and general contractor's interests in retention moneys are " fiduciary as trustee ", i.e. the liquidator holds them for the benefit of the sub-contractor, not of the creditors.

It should be noted that there is no power given to the architect to certify direct payment in the case of nominated suppliers (clause 28).   They are in exactly the same position as other merchants and must rank with the ordinary creditors.

The position in regard to unfixed materials paid for in interim certificates has already been referred to.*   The employer under clause 25 (3) (*a*) retains the use of temporary buildings, plant, &c., on the site, but when no longer required they must be returned to the trustee in bankruptcy.

Extension of time.—A recent case has exposed a weakness in the R.I.B.A. form of contract.   If an architect extends time under clause 23(*g*) for delay by a sub-contractor, the building owner has no remedy for defects in design or workmanship of the sub-contractor.

J. JARVIS & SONS LTD. *v*. THE CITY OF WESTMINSTER and PETER LIND LTD. (1969): 3 A.E.R. 1025.

Peter Lind Ltd. were nominated sub-contractors for piling.   They completed the work comprised in their contract within the specified time and left the site.   Later it was found that their work was defective.   They returned and remedied the defects, but the main contractor was, in consequence, prevented from completing his work within the time limit set by the main contract.   The main contractor was delayed 21½ weeks, and liquidated damages for delay were fixed by the main contract at £1,800 per week.

Under Clause 23(*g*) of the R.I.B.A. contract form (1963) the main contractor was entitled to an extension of time for delay by a nominated sub-contractor which the main contractor could not avoid.

* Page 61.

The question for the Court was: were the main contractors entitled to extension of time under clause 23(*g*)?

The Court below said " No " and held the main contractors liable for the liquidated damages, amounting to £38,700.

The Court of Appeal said " Yes ", and consequently held the main contractors not liable. Although leading to an unjust result, the words of clause 23(*g*) were clear and entitled the main contractor to an extension of time. If the main contractor had been held liable he could have sued the sub-contractor to recover his liability to the building owner. The building owner was not able to sue the sub-contractor directly, as he had no contract with him.

Leave to appeal to The House of Lords was granted, but at the time of going to press no hearing had been reached.

To remedy this anomaly the R.I.B.A. have issued two forms of warrantry, one for the nominated sub-contractors and one for the nominated suppliers,* in which they give an independent warranty to the building owner for their design and workmanship. They are intended to be signed by the specialist and sent with the estimate.

Arbitration.—The subject of arbitration is one of too great importance to be covered adequately here. It has its own text-books, and requires separate study. The responsibility imposed on an architect by appointment as arbitrator is one not to be lightly undertaken, and he should see that he has qualified himself for the task. In certain circumstances he may need the advice of a solicitor on law or of a quantity surveyor on the value of building work.

* *Form of Warranty to be given by a Nominated Sub-contractor*—R.I.B.A.
  Form of Warranty to be given by a Nominated Supplier—R.I.B.A.

18

OFFICE ORGANISATION—POLICY, ACCOMMODATION AND EQUIPMENT

The organisation of an architect's office embraces a wide range of activities of a complex group of human beings.

A successful organisation will be one that achieves the architect's own aim of producing well-designed and well-constructed buildings which give his client good value for money and at the same time shows a reasonable profit for himself. The organisation therefore must be conducive to stimulating good design, must seek the highest technical standards and be efficient and productive into the bargain.

Because the practice of architecture is creative the personal element in an office will always be very strong. However, architects have a duty to their clients, their professional consultants and building contractors to be efficient, and good organisation as well as good design are essential to build up the kind of practice which will continue to retain the confidence of all three.

Policy.—In organising an office the architect's policy must go beyond the primary objectives of good design and organisation and must establish the best methods for achieving these in his particular circumstances. These methods will relate to the size of his office, but it is clear that at the present day there is a tremendous growth in the demand for buildings of all kinds. Even the smallest practices must be prepared to grow, and larger ones may well be required to produce more work without growing!

We are on the threshold of profound changes in the practice of architecture. Within the next few years the metric system of measurement will be introduced into this country* and with it the dimensional co-ordination of building components. The industrialisation of building and the use of system-building is transforming many of the traditional practices and procedures of our profession. The reader will appreciate that an architect must adopt a policy for his organisation which takes into account this

* See page 222.

changing complexity of architecture today. Such a policy must not only fashion the organisation of the practice he has but must also take into account the need for flexibility in adapting the organisation to rapid changes in circumstances. If, therefore, the reader feels that over-organisation is being recommended, let him bear in mind that what appears to be unnecessary or too elaborate and expensive for him today may well be quite appropriate to his practice within quite a short time.

As well as being efficient, an architect's office should also be as productive as possible, and it is essential therefore to have a policy which attempts to adopt all the aids and disciplines at our disposal. A higher output of completed work which is obtained without any lowering of standards will certainly provide an architect with more satisfaction. Another basic aspect of policy is to ensure that the practice learns from its own experience of both successful and unsuccessful work. This "feedback" of one's own experience is the best and most effective way of learning, since it is instinctive in a human being. However, it is not at all natural in an organisation, and so it must be deliberately sought after. Considerations of policy, especially such as these last, are an element of many of the items in this and the succeeding two chapters, and the reader should bear them in mind before deciding what is appropriate to his needs.

Accommodation.—One of the first problems facing the prospective practitioner will be finding an office. Having decided on the town or locality in which he wants to practise, he will have to find the floor space to use. While a position with good access to train and bus services is valuable in a large town, the practitioner in the smaller country town will probably do most of his travelling by car. Facilities for car parking or garaging at or reasonably near to the office are therefore an important consideration for callers to the office as well as for the architect and his staff. Good access to public transport services is usually important, however, for the architect's staff, who may not be so independent of them.

Occasionally clients will visit the architect at his office, and it is important that a suitable room should be available in which to receive them and have discussions in private. Whether the principal's own office is used or a special reception room provided will depend on the space available, but the atmosphere and appearance of the room will undoubtedly create some impression on a client. There is much to be said for receiving and interviewing a client in the principal's private workroom or study, where the environment will be perfectly natural and where drawings can be discussed or sketches made on the spot.

Suitable accommodation must also be provided for both the architectural and the clerical staff, and here again the environment and equipment will have a considerable effect on the occupants.

Enquiry as to offices available may be made of the local estate agents; they may be looked for in local papers, or the architect himself may advertise. It sometimes happens that somebody offers to let a share in offices, though if he contemplates expansion this may be only a short-term solution. It may suit a beginner well, as the offer may include a share in facilities, such as the telephone or clerical assistance.

It is advisable to over-estimate rather than under-estimate the space required. A small office successfully established may expand, and it may later be difficult or impossible to get further space near by, and moving can be costly and extremely disruptive to working. The beginner may, as a temporary expedient until he can see how the practice will develop, take a single room or a share in a room, but if there is confidence in the establishment of the business there should not be less than two rooms. When he employs staff he will then still have a room to himself, where he can see his clients and have his discussions with builders and others without disturbing the rest of the office. An agreement for tenancy of offices should be in writing and specify any outside services provided, such as use of lavatories, arrangements for cleaning, payment of rates, fire insurance, &c. It should make the landlord responsible for structural repairs. Decoration is a matter for arrangement, sometimes being the responsibility of landlord and sometimes tenant. Provision should be made for cesser of rent in the event of serious damage or destruction by fire. An agreement for more than three years is a lease, and must be prepared by a solicitor, if prepared for a fee.

If circumstances allow and suitable property is available the architect may buy and become his own landlord, sub-letting some of the rooms as necessary. This, however, makes a heavy demand on capital and belongs to the sphere of property investment rather than architecture.

In his roles as employer of staff, occupier of office premises or landlord the architect will also be responsible for complying with the provisions of the Offices, Shops and Railway Premises Act, 1963.* They ensure minimum standards of environment for the safety, health and welfare of people employed on the premises, but again it is as well to remember that rapid growth of the practice with a sudden increase in the number of staff and their furniture and equipment could lead to a failure to comply.

Furnishing.—The principal will require a desk with drawers in which to keep his papers, a drawing-table or trestle with drawing-board and T-square, several chairs for visitors as well as for himself, a carpet, suitable curtains, bookshelves and a plan-chest.

The architectural staff will also require suitable drawing-tables, boards, T-squares, stools, drawing-cabinets, and sufficient room to spread out drawings, catalogues, &c., and to keep out of each other's way.

The clerical staff will require desks, typewriters, storage cabinets for stationery and letter files and a safe; and separate accommodation will, no doubt, be required for reference books, samples, catalogues, the storage of all drawings and the omnipresent tea crockery.

Small Equipment.—A variety of small equipment will be necessary too, such as :—

Dumpy level, staff and other surveying equipment.
Measuring rod and tapes or chains.
Set of scales 1:5, 1:50, 1:10, 1:100, 1:20, 1:200, 1:1250, 1:2500.

> N.B. Because of the introduction of the metric system † in this country it seems likely that architects' offices will have to be equipped for the immediate future with both imperial and metric versions of the three items above.

Drawing instruments, set square and protractors.
Perforator or hole punch (for filing) and stapler.
Letter balance (with combined imperial and metric readings).
Cash box.
Set of lettering stencils.

Stationery and items which can be classified as " consumable stores " are dealt with separately below.

Telephone.—A telephone or share in one is essential. If allowed the use of somebody else's telephone, an extra entry of the user's name can be made in the telephone directory on payment of the appropriate fee. An intercommunicating extension line from the general office to the private office will be useful for speaking to the staff, as well as to enable a member of the staff to take incoming calls in the first instance. In the larger offices an independent intercommunicating system may be used, so that the principal can by pressing a button speak to any room and be answered direct. This saves an assistant's time coming in and reduces disturbance of his work.

Telephone calls must be made and answered promptly and must be kept as brief as possible. Lengthy conversations prevent outside callers from communicating with the office and, besides causing delay and annoyance, may have unfortunate consequences. A competent telephone operator is a boon to any office, and can create a good impression with outside callers. All incoming calls must be adequately dealt with, and in the absence of the principal they should be put through to the secretary or senior assistant, who should keep a record of the matters discussed, leaving it for the principal to see on his return. A daily record should be kept of all outgoing calls, together with a note of the particular jobs with which these were connected, so that a check can be made for accounting purposes.

Finally, two points of courtesy should be remembered :—

1. Never keep anyone waiting on the telephone.
2. See that the telephonist knows that when telephoning anyone of importance the caller should be put through to the other person's secretary or telephonist first, so saving the time of the person called.

Fire and Burglary Insurance.—Insurance of the building will usually be the landlord's responsibility, but the architect will need to cover the contents of his office against damage by fire and burglary. The general furniture, stationery, &c., will present no difficulty, and he should be able to fix a suitable replacement value for them. A serious consideration, however, in the event of fire is the replacement of documents in the office, particularly those referring to schemes in course of preparation. If everything is destroyed, there is nothing to be done but begin again. The client will not, of course, pay a double fee. It is therefore advisable to insure the documents in the office under a special item. It will be very difficult to assess a figure, but it should be substantial, the premium being a comparatively small matter when the contingent liability is considered. The cost of replacement (i.e. salaries and proportion of overheads) will alone be covered, unless a " Loss of Profit " policy is taken out.

Employers' Liability Insurance.—An employer is liable to pay compensation for injury caused to his employees " arising out of and in the course of their employment ". Such compensation might be very heavy in the case of serious injury, and insurance against the risk is essential. Premiums are based on the class of employee and salary paid, and are normally adjusted following a return of wages and salaries made to the insurance company each year by the employer.

Indemnity Policy.—The architect may like to protect himself against claims by his clients for negligence, error or omission in a professional capacity for which he might be sued. It should be remembered that the architect is accountable to his client whether the mistake is his own or that of an assistant. The risk may be small, but it is there, so that an appraisal of it and of the cover necessary should be carefully made and certainly reviewed annually.

In addition to this basic insurance, indemnity policies usually cover the legal costs incurred in regard to such claims of negligence, as well as other benefits, such as the legal costs in the recovery of professional fees or pursuing a claim for infringement of copyright and indemnity in an action alleging libel or slander in a professional capacity.

Other Insurances.—As the size of the practice increases, it may be necessary to consider other insurances, and the architect should consult a broker or the A.B.S. Insurance Agency Ltd., 66 Portland Place, London W.1.

A number of policies are available to cover contingencies which might arise: amongst those inviting consideration are the following:—

(a) Protection for surviving partners in the event of the death of one partner.
(b) Income during disablement or prolonged sickness.
(c) Motor cars owned by the firm.
(d) Retirement pension for principals or staff.
(e) Surgeons', specialists' and hospital charges.
(f) Travel abroad on business.

Stationery.—Headed note-paper will be a first requirement. A good design for the heading and good-quality paper are important. Name, address and telephone number must all be easily legible. If the architect knows that his address is only temporary, he will use letterpress printing, but otherwise the small cost of having a die made is well worth while, as die-stamped note-paper has a much better appearance. A letter from a stranger on poor note-paper badly printed is like a badly written examination paper: it prejudices from the start. The International "A" Series of standard paper sizes has been recommended by the R.I.B.A.* for all literature in use in the building industry. In fact, this recommendation has been widely followed by all sections of the industry, and it is true to say that by far the majority of all papers in use nowadays are A4 size (210×297 mm, $8\frac{1}{4}'' \times 11\frac{3}{8}''$). This applies to magazines, official publications, forms of building contract, trade literature and printed forms, as well as the office stationery of the professions and the contractors and manufacturers. For brief letters and documents A5 paper is used, which is half the size of A4.

Other stationery which will be required includes :—

Plain paper to match note-paper.
Thin paper for carbon copies, note-paper sizes.
Carbon paper of the same sizes.
Envelopes to suit letter paper sizes when folded.

* See Industry Note No. 1, "*A*" *Series of International Paper Sizes*: R.I.B.A., issued free.

Envelopes to suit letter paper sizes flat, and possibly one or
  two intermediate sizes.
Foolscap or A4 folders.
Architect's Instruction forms.
Clerk of works' report forms.
Time-sheets.
Certificate books.
Drawing record books.
First Site Meeting Agenda forms.
Record of Meetings forms.
Tender forms.
Etc.*

It is useful to have a memorandum form, with or without a
printed heading, on which telephone messages can be recorded.
If a paper of a bright distinctive colour is used it will catch the
eye lying on a desk, even if mixed up with other papers. It
should be large enough to be easily seen and to be filed with
correspondence. Messages should not be written on small scraps
of paper, which are likely to be mislaid, and messages about
different jobs should not be written on the same piece of paper.

A variety of small sundries is necessary in an office—paper
clips, paper fasteners of varying sizes, elastic bands, string tags,
pencils—black-lead and coloured—inks—blue and coloured—
india rubbers, &c. A useful collection can be made by going
round a large stationer's shop, or items can be left to be bought
as they are found to be required.

Diaries.—There are those who think that there is a great
difference between saying a thing and putting it in writing. The
production of a letter is certainly among the best forms of
evidence, but a diary entry of conversation made at the time
approaches it very closely. The principal should keep a diary in
which conversations of importance are recorded, though as an
alternative he may make a written memorandum dated and
initialled to go in the letter-file and also be sent to interested
parties for information or confirmation. Particularly should
notes be made of any conversation as to terms of employment,
promises of dates for delivery of drawings or bill, or similar

* A list of special forms published by the R.I.B.A. is available from the Secretary of
the Institute.

items which might later be called in question. If there is doubt it is always advisable to write a letter confirming the verbal statements made, so that the other party is quite sure of the position.

A diary will also be required by the principal to record appointments made ; probably a small pocket diary is the most convenient form, duplicated perhaps by a desk-pad to which the office staff can refer for any arrangements to be made in his absence.

The more senior members of the staff should have a diary provided for recording particulars of their meetings with contractors, &c. They could also make a fuller note in it of what they were doing each day than appears in their time record.

Information and Reference.—The extent to which the architect in practice must refer to and rely upon technical information can hardly be over-estimated. As a student he will have learnt to use text-books and reference books, information in architectural periodicals, official publications and trade literature as they were needed at each stage of a design project at his School of Architecture. While he will probably have collected a number of his own, he will also have borrowed from his school library and referred to other books and information owned by his fellow students.

Once an architect sets up in practice, however, he cannot be too strongly urged to avoid a haphazard approach. Using his student text-books as a foundation, he should make it a deliberate policy to provide himself with an efficient information and reference service. To do this he will have to set aside from the start a little time to organise it, a little space to accommodate it and a little money to equip and stock it. As the practice gets established and grows so also will this service, and it is usual in small and medium-sized practices to make it the responsibility of one of the architects; in the very large practices it is not uncommon nowadays to find a full-time technical librarian.

The most satisfactory way of accommodating the information and references is on shelves as in the library. Bound books and catalogues can be free-standing, loose leaves of information from periodicals, trade literature and other papers can be kept in free-standing files or ring binders with stiff covers.

CI/SfB Classification.—The enormous increase in technical and trade information in recent years has tended to swamp out *ad hoc* systems of classification devised by individuals for their own use.   The need for a more detailed and accurate system of indexing has been realised, and the R.I.B.A. has taken the lead in Britain by adopting and recommending to its members the SfB System.   This system originated in Sweden some years ago (the letters SfB are derived from the name of the Swedish committee concerned).   Using this system, it is possible to give any book, catalogue, official bulletin, pamphlet, etc., used by architects a classification according to its contents.   The classifying symbols are easily remembered, and frequent use will enable the architect quickly to find the material he wants.

The R.I.B.A. SfB/UDC Building Filing Manual 1961 was used to introduce the new system officially.   Recently, however, the Manual has been revised in the light of experience gained, and the *R.I.B.A. Construction Indexing Manual* 1968* is now the authoritative reference for the system.

The CI/SfB system classifies information in four main tables. Table o—Built Environment, Table 1—Elements, Table 2/3— Construction form and Materials, and Table 4—Activities and requirements.   Of the four Tables 1 and 2/3 will include the great majority of building trade literature, while the Tables o and 4 will include most technical references, text-books, official publications and regulations, &c.

With the increasing adoption of the CI/SfB system throughout the profession and the Building Industry a high proportion of technical and trade literature has a classification symbol printed on it, and this greatly facilitates the incorporation of such material into the library.

Side by side with the adoption of SfB has been the adoption of the International " A4 " paper size for literature, and this, too, is a tremendous improvement on the variety of sizes of publications used in the past.

The work required to maintain this service to the architect involves therefore the classification of a minority of incoming material before it is incorporated and the discarding of material that has become obsolete.   There is now a number of commercial undertakings which provide an information service for architects'

* See also *The Organisation of Information in the Construction Industry* and *CI/SfB Classified list of Essential References*, both from R.I.B.A.

offices, obtain trade and other literature, provide files and shelving to keep it in, give regular service to the library and an information advisory service by telephone or by post. One must remember that these firms have to operate at a profit, and some charge a fee to the firms whose trade literature they circulate, while others charge a fee to the offices receiving the service as well. In each case the trade literature supplied will not be all-embracing, as there will be firms who will rely on advertising their products directly to the professions and the industry.

Reference Books.—The foundation of a reference library will probably be the architect's text-books of his student days, and he will add to these with new published books throughout his career. The journals of his Institute, probably supplied with an annual index, should also be kept for reference, as most important events in the industry are either recorded or quoted with a reference given which can be looked up in turn. The R.I.B.A. also frequently publishes documents on technical and professional topics of importance, and the majority of these will be essential to architects at some stage of their careers.

Next in importance for reference are the various official publications often concerned with specific building types published by H.M.S.O. for Government Departments, e.g. on Housing (Ministry of Housing and Local Government), Schools, Colleges and Universities (Department of Education and Science), Hospitals and Local Authority Health Buildings (Department of Health) and so on. H.M.S.O. also publishes the many important documents on building research produced by the Building Research Station (Ministry of P.B. & Wks.) which architects need to study. Nowadays the output of these essential references is very large, and while a standing order may be given to H.M.S.O. for copies of publications referring to Building as they are published, it would be more economic for all but the largest practices to obtain the H.M.S.O.'s regular list of publications and purchase only those required for current work. Other publications of importance are British Standard Specifications and Codes of Practice, the Building Regulations, the London Building Acts and Constructional Bye-Laws (if jobs are in London) and reference copies of the various forms of contract in use.

The building regulations, together with any statutory requirements, applying to building for the locality in which jobs are being undertaken (this will include the London Building Acts if the work is in London) should be studied before completing working drawings.

An English dictionary should be in every office, available to clerical as well as architectural staff, for checking spelling. A list of useful reference books is given in Appendix 2.

Samples.—Samples can be invaluable to the architect and his assistants when preparing drawings and specifications if they are properly labelled and arranged, but if not they are merely a nuisance and get in the way. If the accommodation is available it is obviously better to set aside a special room for samples, where they can be properly arranged and displayed and can be inspected without disturbing anybody; but if accommodation is short they can be arranged on shelving or in mobile containers in one or more of the drawing-offices. It is necessary, of course, to be selective in deciding which samples to keep, the most useful ones being such things as hardware and ironmongery, electrical accessories, glass, flooring materials, sections of standard metals and wood windows and door frames, various types and colours of glazed tiling, overhead and floor springs for doors, roofing tiles and the newer materials, such as plastics, vermiculite for plasters and screeds, &c. A few facing bricks might be kept, too, but as these are usually specially selected for each job, it is better to inspect them at a merchant's showrooms or actually on a building, so that they can be seen in the mass together with their pointing.

All samples should be labelled with a reference to name and address of the suppliers, cost, &c. If possible, a separate section should be devoted to samples which have been approved for a particular job, and these should not be disturbed.

The Building Centres in London and some provincial towns,* too, provide a very useful service, for not only can a great variety of samples be seen there but the Centre can also give the names and addresses of manufacturers of almost any building material and of specialist firms, often with copies of their advertising leaflets.

Recording Experience (" Feedback ").—One of the most valuable, important and effective references an architect can use

* See page 269.

is his own past experience in practice. As it grows his memory alone will be increasingly unreliable, and sharing it with his colleagues and assistants in conversation will also be both unreliable and time-consuming. It will be found an extremely valuable policy therefore to record experience on jobs carefully and systematically in a permanent form and to add it to the reference library exactly as if it were technical information from outside. Other copies of such records may be kept separately and/or circulated to staff. In the latter case unless an architect has by coincidence an immediate interest in the matter being recorded he may be too busy to assimilate it. However, if it is in the reference library properly classified according to its contents it will be referred to with other information on the subject whenever the need arises. There are many ways of recording experience, for example, by means of " Practice Notes " which advise or warn about the use of particular materials or methods of workmanship, or by keeping copies of specifications used on a particular job which can be re-used on similar jobs, or by taking photographs of successfully built details of construction, providing they are fully referenced by job, date and detail drawing number, and so on. The architect will best be able to devise for himself the most suitable methods of recording his experience for his own practice. The important point to remember is that the record should be such as to make it as easy as possible to apply the experience to another job.

19

OFFICE ORGANISATION (*continued*)—ADMINISTRATION AND MANAGEMENT

Staff.—The size of the staff will, of course, depend entirely on the volume of work which regularly comes into the office and the number of partners in the practice. A busy single principal, giving his personal attention to every job, should be able to manage a professional staff of 15–20, but seldom more. Even to do this he will have to allocate his time very carefully between designing, correspondence, supervision, meetings and interviews, and will require a good secretary and " right-hand " man to help him. The principal is accountable to his client and must be in a position to give his personal attention to each job. His practice is a personal business and he is usually commissioned to undertake a particular job because his client has selected him in preference to someone else. He must therefore remain completely in touch with the scheme from the very early sketch design stage until the building is finally handed over. He must, of course, have assistance with the preparation of the working drawings, specifications and the incidental administration, and he cannot therefore exclude his assistants from contributing their own ideas. Nor must he be reluctant to delegate responsibility or authority. He must, however, exercise his over-riding discretion whenever this becomes necessary.

The grading of the architectural staff will vary with the size and nature of the practice. It may consist of one or two qualified assistants and two or three juniors, or it may be made up of a chief assistant or manager, senior qualified assistants and several draughtsmen. A recent trend is for the practice to be run as a " group " or co-partnership where everyone shares directly in the fortunes of the firm, the profits being distributed according to responsibility and length of membership, but subject to an agreed minimum salary being paid to the more junior members.

The organisation of the architectural staff is an arrangement which must be adapted to suit the specific requirements and temperament of the principal and his associates or staff. Two rules of paramount importance, however, should be to keep the members of the staff fully informed about the particular jobs on which they are working and to keep clear records of each job, so that in the event of illness or a change of staff the threads can be picked up quite easily by someone else.

The administrative side of the office will be organised by the secretary or manager according to the size of the office.

In the smaller office the secretary will be the confidante of the principals and the " guide, philosopher and friend " to the staff. Upon her efficiency, patience and tact will largely depend the smooth running of the practice. She will not only do the typing and filing but will also pay the bills, make out salary cheques, deal with S.E.T., P.A.Y.E. and National Insurance, keep certificate books and keep up-to-date entries in the ledgers and other account books. She will also order stationery, supplies of forms, certificate books, drawing materials, cleaning materials, stamps, &c., and keep up-to-date card indexes for filing names, addresses and other particulars of clients, staff, builders, merchants, &c. She will be responsible for distributing the incoming mail to partners and then to assistants, and in the absence of a principal will ensure that any necessary action is taken by a responsible person and see that the principal is fully informed on his return.

As the size of the office increases, so will the administration have to be strengthened. The time may come when the secretary cannot efficiently undertake by herself all the duties required of her, when she will need an assistant to help her with the typing and to whom she can delegate such duties as keeping the telephone book, post book, &c., &c.

There may be as a junior in the office a young man with an ambition to be an architect himself one day, though neither a formally articled pupil nor a trainee. He may attend a technical school in the evenings and spend his time in the office during the day in learning to draw, colouring prints, running errands, dealing with the printers and filing the drawings, posting the mail, operating the telephone, making the tea, and generally being as useful as possible.

In the larger offices of, say, thirty or more architectural staff there may be a manager with a secretarial staff to organise and control the administrative side of the practice.

The manager will be responsible to the partners for the performance of all the duties carried out by the secretary in the smaller office and in addition will:—

(a) When requested, make arrangements for meetings, the preparation of agenda and the taking of minutes.

(b) On the instruction of the partners, prepare and keep up to date the Office Manual (or guide book to the running of the office) and ensure that this is understood by all members of the staff, both old and new.

(c) Issue policy instructions to all members of the staff.

(d) Prepare financial forecasts and budgets for the partners.

(e) Effect liaison with accountants, bank managers, auditors, treasurers and solicitors.

(f) Examine and report on legal documents, such as leases, insurance policies, agreements between the firm and clients, &c.

(g) Maintain staff records and establishment data.

(h) Advertise for staff, arrange interviews and draft letters of engagement.

(i) Administer superannuation and medical insurance schemes for staff.

(j) Have charge of staff welfare.

Apart from these routine duties, in these days of rapid developments in the building industry and allied professions, he may well assist the partners to obtain and analyse data on trends, such as consortia, package deals, &c., so that they can anticipate their effect on their own practice and take the necessary action to keep abreast of, and not be overtaken by, such events.

Correspondence.—Incoming mail should be sorted out into jobs by the secretary and, if there is more than one principal in the firm, distributed to the appropriate partners, preferably in a folder or a tray. Each letter should be stamped with a date-stamp in a position under the date on the letter. The stamp should be designed to show what action has been taken on the letter—for instance, a space should be provided in which to insert the date of reply or " no action ", and another for the initials of the person making the reply, and possibly a third for the names of the assistants who must see the letter for information. Everyone who is required to note the contents of a letter (both incoming and outgoing) should add their initials after reading it. Letters with envelopes marked " private ", " personal " or

" confidential " or containing tenders for works should be handed to the principal unopened.

If a principal or partner is away and the facility is available in the office, photo-copies of incoming letters should be made before they are distributed for attention and put on his desk, so that on his return to the office he is immediately informed of the contents of such letters. Alternatively, a note of the subject matter of all incoming mail should be prepared for him.

All letters should, of course, be answered as soon as possible—on the date of receipt preferably—but any unanswered letters should be kept in a safe " pending " tray or file. Junior assistants should not be allowed to keep letters, and this " privilege " should be accorded only to the senior assistant in charge of each job. The secretary should make a daily check of unanswered correspondence (possibly against an incoming letter register in a large office) and of unfiled " out-mail " which has been circulated for information. All letters, both incoming and outgoing, should be filed as soon as possible. The file is the safest place for letters, and provides the only complete up-to-date record of the job. Nothing is more irritating (or even disastrous) than an incomplete or out-of-date file.

Wherever possible, letters should be dictated, and not written. A good shorthand typist will not only take down a letter more quickly, but probably more accurately too—unless one's handwriting is unusually legible! Letters should not be dictated piecemeal—the more that can be done at one session the better will the typist be able to arrange her work and the more quickly will it be done.

Letters which perhaps need tact in their writing or a special care in the choice of words would be written out by hand : letters, too, which are highly technical may be better written, but a special point should be made of writing any technical words or expressions quite clearly.

It is a good practice to send copies of letters giving instructions, to all the interested parties—quantity surveyors, consultants, clerks of works, &c.—for information, and the list of such persons should be noted on the letter—again for the information of all those who are interested.

Each letter should have a title and a reference. The title will be the name of the job, and should be underlined to make it stand out. It may be supplemented by a description of the particular subject-matter of the letter. The reference should be as simple as possible—merely the job number, the initials of the person dictating the letters and the initials of the person typing it. This reference when quoted in reply makes it clear to whom such a letter is to be passed. In the smaller offices it would be unnecessary.

Two more aids to administration are worth consideration:—

(a) A simple system for bringing forward reminders that a reply to a letter is overdue.

(b) A filing reference (as distinct from a job reference) on each letter. This is especially important on the larger jobs, where several consultants may be engaged, as well as contractors, sub-contractors, etc., and where the project might contain several different buildings or may be implemented in phases.

Letter-writing.—The method of dealing with correspondence having been considered, a few remarks may be added on the art of letter-writing.

The object of writing is to convey the ideas of one person to the mind of another, who is not present to be addressed verbally, and at the same time to make a permanent record of the communication. Owing to the lack of expression of the face and inflection of the voice, the writer must convey by his words alone both the emphasis he requires and the tone in which he is writing. Words and phrases must, therefore, be more carefully chosen.

Without going fully into the subject, a few suggestions may be made :—

1. Be quite sure that the points you make are clear.

2. Be as brief and simple as possible. Do not use two words where one will do. Avoid long words and periphrasis (the long word here is balanced against the less expressive alternative of several).

3. Start a new paragraph with each new point, and do not split up the point into more than one paragraph.

4. If a long letter develops, consider whether it is not better to put the matter in the form of a schedule or report, with a short covering letter only.

5. Be sure to write with your reader in mind. Do not use

H

technical terms in writing to a non-technical client, which a little thought would show you he could not understand.

6. Avoid commercial *clichés*, journalese, Americanisms and slang.

7. Avoid spelling mistakes and bad grammar. They give a poor opinion of you to an educated reader.

8. Avoid the impersonal. " It is regretted " means nothing. Regret is a personal sentiment, and, if you feel regret, say " I regret " or " We regret ". You may or may not feel you can say " the Minister, the Board or the Directors regret ".

9. Be definite. If the decision is with you, do not say " this *appears* to be correct ". If you are satisfied that it is correct, say it is.

10. Have reference books by you from which to settle any doubts on language which arise when you write.*

Some care should be taken over forms of address. Your client, whether you think he deserves the title or not, will probably be " A. B. C— Esq." on the envelope and head of the letter, though in these days of equality for all the suffix is falling into disuse and is, apparently, being gradually replaced by the plain " Mr.". The letter will open " Dear Sir " if he is a stranger, but once you have met him " Dear Mr. C—". A first reply to him, whilst he is still a stranger, would end " Yours faithfully ", but afterwards " Yours truly ", " Yours very truly " and " Yours sincerely " as acquaintanceship ripens, the further stages, if reached, being " Yours very sincerely " and " Yours ever, Bill ". Watch his endings as a guide and if he does not accept your step forward, take a smart pace back ! When dealing with a public body or Company, letters would continue to be addressed to the Secretary or other official with the opening " Dear Sir " and ending " Yours faithfully ", even though the official may become personally known.

The contractor would be addressed Mr. D. E. F— on the envelope and head of letter, even though he might in his private capacity be worthy of " Esq.". Any difficulty disappears in the case of a firm, who are addressed as Messrs. A. B. & Co. Ltd. and

* Books suggested are : *The Concise Oxford Dictionary ; Complete Plain Words* (Gowers); *Modern English Usage* (Fowler).

" Dear Sirs " (or the letter may be addressed to the Secretary or Manager individually and open " Dear Sir "). It is, perhaps, unnecessary to emphasise that Mr. and Esq. never appear together, but experience shows that nothing is impossible, and therefore the specimen letters in Appendix I * may be of use.

When it comes to forms of address for royalty, the nobility, higher Church dignitaries, &c., a suitable reference book should be consulted.†

Despatch and Filing of Correspondence.—There are three points in connection with despatch of correspondence which need emphasis :—

1. A check to see that the proper enclosures are put in. Various reminders are used, such as a marginal mark against the reference to the enclosure in the text, a footnote " 3 Encs.", or a coloured adhesive label stuck on the letter to catch the eye before inserting in an envelope.
2. A check to see that the right letter is in the right envelope (a mistake might put one in an awkward position—to say nothing of the possibility of a libel action !).
3. Care to see that over-weight letters are weighed and cor- rectly stamped.

The main classification of letters will be into the jobs in which they belong, but in the case of larger jobs they can be sub-divided into several files, e.g. client, contractor, quantity surveyor, clerk of works, sub-contractors, &c. If all letters are kept in order of date in the file belonging to the job, any letter can be turned up at once. In practice it is not uncommon either for it to have got in the wrong file, or by mistake classified under the wrong month or even year, or it may be that somebody has kept it out to refer to and never put it back. Careful filing is most important, as much time can be lost searching for a letter in such circumstances, and cases have been known where one has just had to give it up ! There are various systems of filing. The simplest is to keep letters in a pocket type folder, but it will be found more satisfactory to have them securely fastened to their container by

* Pages 283 and 285.
† E.g. *Titles and Forms of Address:* A. & C. Black.

one of the methods on the market. They can be kept horizontally in a nest of drawers or vertically in a filing cabinet to suit.

The reference on letters will simplify the business of filing.* A job register should be kept, which will provide the serial number. It will also provide a useful check on all jobs in the office, together with the date on which they were commissioned.

Job History.—It will be found very useful to keep a record of all notes and data about a job in a separate file, with a simple history sheet in front to show at a glance what stage it has reached. The various stages of the work (e.g. sketch plans, applications, approvals, &c.) should be listed and the dates on which action was taken inserted against them; the references or file numbers might be added if appropriate. This will not only save a considerable amount of hunting through files, but will also make it so much easier if it becomes necessary for someone else to take over the job. A specimen Job History Sheet is given in Appendix 1.†

The Working Party of the R.I.B.A. Professional Services Board has recently developed a comprehensive loose-leaf set of checklists, typical letters, forms and other documents which can be adapted to the requirements of any job. It is arranged in the order and stages of the Plan of Work recommended in the R.I.B.A. Handbook. It is intended to be a working aid for a specific project and it can be adapted by adding the appropriate standard forms and procedure guides that each individual architect uses and by deleting any material in the Job Book that does not apply. While in use it is both a record of what has been done on the job and a series of reminders of what still remains to be done.

Staff Time Records.—There should be a complete record of the allocation of the time of the staff. A specimen form of record is included in Appendix 1.‡ This may be required as a basis on which to build up an account for fees for services which are to be charged for on a time basis. Those to whom it is a matter of concern can also use it to build up the cost of any particular job and compare it with their fee. There is

---

* See also page 211.
† See page 302, also *Job Book* (Aqua Group): Crosby Lockwood.
‡ Page 303.

little satisfaction in this, as the fee is probably fixed and cannot be altered, and what is spent is spent. Theoretically it gives a warning for the future, but in most cases a similar job does not recur. A professional practice differs from a trade in that it is not the principal's concern to make as big a profit as he can. His first aim is to do the job properly. Each member of the staff should in his diary record not only his time on each job, but his movements, meetings and other matters concerned with his work. That the entries shall be made daily is essential, and assistants should get into the habit of entering up their diary before leaving the office. To put it off till the next day will probably mean that they have forgotten some of the detail.

Progress Checks.—Because design is a creative activity requiring imaginative effort as well as the application of more mundane techical skills, it is very difficult when practising it to adhere to a strict and detailed timetable. Nevertheless, in practice all clients will want to know with reasonable assurance when the construction of their buildings can be expected to start and finish, and these dates will inevitably commit their architects to prior dates for completing sketch designs and working drawings. The architect must recognise the programming implications when he undertakes any commission and make it his duty to ensure that the proper progress on the design (where it is under his complete control) is maintained.

There are several different techniques for planning design and other pre-contract work. The simplest way is for architect and client (together with quantity surveyor, where employed) to agree on a few target dates for the important events, e.g. approval of sketch designs, last date for quantity surveyor to receive information for billing, etc. This will be sufficient for small jobs where the individuals involved are few and can readily assess their own progress.

For medium and larger-sized jobs, with the architect employing several full-time assistants, and with perhaps several consultants to co-ordinate, the individual work of each participant must be analysed in broad detail to prepare a programme. In this case a simple bar chart can be drawn up, agreed by all participants and used for checking progress at regular meetings.

In the larger and most complex projects Network Analysis

techniques are nowadays frequently employed* for the whole
project from inception to completion.   For these the activities
of all members of the design team and of the client's organisation
are scheduled, timed and programmed in such a way that the
consequences to the whole project of any delay can be readily
appreciated.   Maintaining proper progress on very large projects is
extremely important, since so many resources are employed, and
regular progress checks are often highly formalised.

Whatever the job and whatever the technique of progress
checking, the architect must be fully aware of its implications and
of his own responsibilities.   Making up for lost time is always
difficult and costly—sometimes it is impossible.

Clerk of Works, Report Forms.—A specimen form is
reproduced in Appendix 1,† and reference has also been made to
this in Chapter 12.‡

Architect's Instruction Forms.—It is far better for record
purposes to issue all instructions under the building contract,
including variations, on an official form rather than in a letter.
A specimen standard form of Architect's Instruction on the lines
described in Chapter 14 § is reproduced in Appendix 1.||

An index should be kept of all architect's instructions issued
on each job, to ensure that they are numbered consecutively and
also to provide a convenient reference.   Copies of the architect's
instructions should be distributed to the contractor, clerk of works,
quantity surveyor, any consultants concerned, the client (if so
arranged) and a copy, of course, retained in the office file.

Certificates.—Official certificate pads may be obtained from
the R.I.B.A., and a specimen certificate is reproduced in Appendix
1. ¶ Certificates are numbered serially for each job, and show
both the amount of the present payment and the total of previous
payments.   They must be signed by the architect.

The certificate is issued to the general contractor, who will
detach the lower portion and forward it to the employer.   On
receiving payment he will prepare a formal receipt and send it

to the employer. When issuing a certificate, the architect should enclose a statement detailing how the valuation has been computed, and should send a copy of this to the client notifying him officially that the certificate has been issued. The quantity surveyor, if his own statement is used, will not require a copy, but it is important that he should be advised of the amount of the certificate issued.

A typical form of valuation statement as prepared by the quantity surveyor is shown in Appendix 1.* It will be seen that this sets out the amounts included for nominated sub-contractors, and it is important that the architect, when he issues his certificate, should set these out in the space provided, as without this formal notice the contractor may disclaim his liability to pay.†

A Certificate Index and Payments Record should be kept for all jobs.

Reports.—Reports may be required for site visits or committee meetings and interviews. These should be concise and to the point and are best drafted in a standard form such as that reproduced in Appendix 1.‡

The report should be signed by the author and dated and circulated to all parties present, and to others not present but interested, such as members of the staff working on the job, the client, &c. One copy should be filed in the Job History File.

Network Analysis Techniques.—A number of management aids to the programming of the many activities involved in any major operation of production or construction have been evolved in recent years. Such systems set out to analyse the inter-related and inter-dependent activities in a given programme, and to arrange them in a logical sequence in order to determine how best control and resources may be applied to ensure that a project timetable can be met.

Under one system known as the Critical Path Method a plan is prepared by which the various activities in a project are diagrammatically represented by a network of connected arrows, the tail representing the start of a particular activity and the head

---

* Pages 290, 292–3.   † See R.I.B.A. contract, clause 27 (b).   ‡ Page 291.

its completion, the joint of head and tail being the point in time when one activity ends and another begins. A study of the diagram will show the "critical path" to be followed and the total project time. Space does not allow of adequate treatment of the subject here, and the reader is referred to published texts.*

With such a network analysis it is possible to pin-point those activities which are having the greatest effect on the total project time and to decide where additional resources may be applied in order to shorten the critical path. Conversely, it is possible to determine which activities are not critical to the project time and to rearrange them in the programme to even out the allocation of resources.

R.I.B.A. Handbook of Architectural Practice and Management.—A copy of this Handbook should be available in every architect's office. It provides advice on professional training, registration, conduct and responsibilities; office management; project planning and cost control.

* *C.P.M. Explained* (Building Research Digests, 2nd Series, No. 53): H.M.S.O. and *Network Analysis in Construction Design* (M.P.B. & W., R. & D. Building Management Handbook No. 3): H.M.S.O.

20

OFFICE ORGANISATION (*continued*)—DRAWINGS AND SCHEDULES

Drawings.—It is important to remember that drawings are made for different purposes in the complex process which begins with obtaining the client's brief and ends with the commissioning of the completed building. Sketches are made by the architect to explore different design possibilities, and these are discussed with the client and consultants. Plans are drawn to show the circulation routes which will be used within a scheme, or the arrangement of equipment and furniture in specialised spaces so that the client's approval can be obtained. Drawings of certain kinds have to be submitted to obtain Statutory and other approvals under the Town Planning Acts, London Building Acts, the Building Regulations and so forth. And there are innumerable other purposes for which drawings are made.

But the most important types of drawings prepared by architects are " working " drawings or " contract " drawings—those used by the builder and the specialist sub-contractors and suppliers. The reason for their importance is partly because of their function and partly because they represent by far the majority of all the drawings prepared by architects. The purpose of drawings (together with the specification) is to convey to the builder all the information that is required for the erection of the building.

The drawings have to be interpreted by people who have taken no part in the original design, and it is therefore essential that they should be clear and accurate and, or course, well thought out. The importance of supplying the builder with a full set of details before he commences work has already been mentioned, and this is undoubtedly the most economical and satisfactory way to build. The time at which to make a thorough and detailed study of the building is when the drawings and specification are being prepared. It is then that the architect's whole concentration is applied to the problem, and it is better and quicker for him to solve all his problems at that stage rather than to have to come back again after the building work has commenced in order to reconsider details. Besides taking longer to pick up the threads again, he will be disturbed in his concentration on the jobs which are being currently designed in the office. For the builder, the advantages of having a full set of drawings are more obvious, as he can then plan the execution of the work with more certainty and can place orders for materials without delay.

Finally, it is more satisfactory and more economical for the client, because the bills of quantities can be prepared from the full details supplied, enabling a more accurate tender to be prepared and minimising subsequent variations on the contract which are often so costly.

Before starting the final drawings it will be found useful to prepare a schedule of all the details required, so that a drawing-office programme can be arranged. Drawings should be prepared on two or three standard-sized sheets which will simplify filing and handling.* Drawings which are on very small or over-size sheets cause a lot of extra handling, and the larger ones are easily damaged, while the small ones tend to slip behind drawers or are awkward to hang in a vertical filing cabinet.

Certain basic information must go on every drawing, and none should be issued outside the office unless this is complete. This basic information comprises the firm's name, address and telephone number, the name of the job, title of drawing, drawing number, scale, date drawn and initials of the draughtsman, and the revisions. It is relatively inexpensive to have standard sheets printed with a neat title panel in the bottom right-hand corner designed to incorporate the basic information. This panel will probably be designed by the architect himself, and if this is done well will add a distinctive and immediately recognisable character to the drawings.

Other basic information will include small key plans for very large buildings which are shaded to show the part of the building for which particular drawings apply, together with a north point so that orientation of the drawing can be quickly read. Grid lines used to position structural elements or for planning or for modular co-ordination are almost universally used, and these should be carefully referenced. It is common to use letters to designate grid lines along one axis and numbers along the other. For vertical positioning floor and roof levels are normally used as references, but modular grids are also suitable.

---

* See B.S. 1192: *Architectural Drawing Office Practice.* B.S. 3429: *Sizes of Drawing Sheets.*

These horizontal and vertical references should be used consistently on drawings and in written documents not only by the architects but also by the consultants. The users of the drawings, builders and sub-contractors will naturally do the same. This will minimise the chance of errors through ambiguous descriptions, written or spoken, such as " the wall next to the window in the Professor's office on the top floor ", as well as saving everyone time. A builder could be excused from not recognising a " Professor's office " which consisted only of bare concrete floors and walls and open to the sky at the time of discussion! Drawing and tracing paper printed with grids to various scales is readily available now. It will save time and contribute to clarity if simple symbols are used for such items as w.c.'s, lavatory basins, &c., on both small-scale plans and room elevations. Certain templates for this purpose can be bought, but may prove too expensive and too limited in range for small practices.

With the increasing production of standard components having a common dimensioned basis, it is possible, by adopting a system of modular co-ordination, to simplify the preparation of working drawings. By working off squared paper, representing the preferred structural module, figured dimensions can be either eliminated altogether or reduced to the most elementary terms. With a structural module of 300 mm, a figured dimension of 3M would mean 3×300 mm $= 900$ mm. The basic module, e.g. 100 mm (4"), would be a factor of the structural module.

It is the practice in some offices to adopt standard details for certain frequently occurring building elements, such as staircases, access panels to service ducts, internal doors and their frames, and so on. The details adopted will have been proved by experience to be thoroughly satisfactory, and this is an example of " feedback " referred to in Chapter 18.* While it will not be necessary to reproduce them every time for every job, the principle of the design, and the method of describing it through the detail drawings, can be used as the basis for each new detail devised.

Recording and Numbering of Drawings.—A record of all drawings prepared for each job should be kept in a Drawing Number Book, which should include not only the drawing number, but also the date of preparation, the initials of the person

---

* See Page 205.

who made the drawing, and a series of columns for recording the names of people to whom the drawings were issued, the dates on which they were sent out and the number of drawings sent. A specimen page of such a book is given in Appendix 1.*

Each drawing should have a number or reference designed to give the following information :—

1. Job.
2. An indication of the scale and nature of the drawing.
3. A serial number.

Various methods of recording the information can be devised, and particulars are here given of one method recommended. The job number or prefix taken from the job register will indicate the job. The nature of the drawing which will also give an idea of scale can be denoted by a " P " for preliminary or sketch plan, " E " for eighth-scale working drawings, " D " for larger scale details (from 1 : 20 scale to full size) or " SUR " for survey drawings. If drawings showing structural work or mechanical engineering services are prepared in the office, these should have their own symbols too (e.g. " S " for structural, " H " for heating, " EL " for electrical, &c.). The serial numbers should follow on consecutively, irrespective of the nature of the drawing. Adopting this method, the first sketch plans for Job No. 10 would be numbered 10/P/1, 2, 3, &c. : they would be followed by the 1 : 100 scale drawings Nos. 10/E/5, 6, 7, 8, &c., and the details numbered 10/D/15, 16, 17, &c. In a large and complicated job or a job being built by stages it may well be that Ps, Es and Ds will be mixed up, but this does not matter, as in looking through the Drawing Number Book it will be easy to pick out the drawings which are sketch-plans and those which are 1 : 100 scale or detail drawings. If a job goes on by stages, it might be as well to add a suitable suffix to the job number, e.g. 10A, 10B, &c., for each subsequent stage.

Introduction of Metric System.—The Government has announced that the whole system of imperial weights and measures used in this country will be replaced by the metric system used by the majority of countries in the world as soon as is practicable. Architects, designers and engineers will draw and calculate using

* Page 304.

metric units, bills of quantities will be compiled in metric terms, contractors will carry out work and manufacturers will supply products in metric sizes. Conversion tables, measuring instruments and reference books will be needed at an early stage, and the architect contemplating equipping an office is advised to take into account the programme of the changeover as it becomes known.

The British Standards Institution has been asked by the Government to act as the focal point for the change to the metric system in the construction industry. In May 1965 the Institution's Building Divisional Council set up the Metric Panel to investigate the implications of the change and to prepare the first draft programme for the industry. This was done in close consultation with the industry, and the resulting programme was agreed and adopted. Architects, engineers and quantity surveyors have since January 1969 begun to prepare their drawings and documents in metric terms, and the date by which eventually they should be preparing *all* their drawings and contract documents in metric terms will be about the beginning of 1972.

Changing to the metric system will be relatively straightforward as far as new construction work is concerned, but it is to be expected that the demand for maintenance, repair and alteration of buildings will almost certainly necessitate the continuing though diminishing use of imperial units in offices, on sites and in factories for a considerable time to come.

The specification angle on the subject has already been mentioned.*

Scale.—The scales normally adopted for drawings are given below, followed in parentheses by the corresponding metric scale likely to be used in future. It should be noted that the metric scales are often approximate not exact equivalents to the traditional ones.

Sketch Plans: 1:500 (1:500) outline plans for large schemes in the initial stage
$\frac{1}{32}''$ to 1$'$ (1:500) or $\frac{1}{16}''$ to 1$'$ (1:200) for anything larger than a private house which could from the first be sketched to $\frac{1}{8}''$ to 1$'$ (1:100)

* Page 103.

Block Plans: 1:2500 (1:2500) or 1:1250 (1:1250) or
                    1:500 (1:500) for a large layout, $\frac{1}{16}''$
                    to 1' (1:200) for a small layout

Working Drawings: $\frac{1}{8}''$ to 1' (1:100) or $\frac{1}{4}''$ to 1' (1:50)
                    depending on the size of the scheme

Details: $\frac{1}{4}''$ to 1' (1:50) or $\frac{1}{2}''$ to 1' (1:20) scale
                    sections and plans and room elevations
                    as necessary

                    1'' to 1' (1:10), half full size and full
                    size depending on the details to be
                    described

Surveys: Normally 1:1250 (1:1250) or 1:500
                    (1:500) for a large site, $\frac{1}{16}''$ to 1'
                    (1:200) for a small site and $\frac{1}{8}''$ to 1'
                    (1:100) for a building

It is good practice not to ink in or complete any drawings until all the details have been studied. All small-scale working drawings should, of course, be drawn mechanically, but some architects prefer to draw half full-size details freehand, as this helps to give a certain sensitivity to the design.

Figured Dimensions.—Dimensions form one of the most important items of instruction to the quantity surveyor and later to the builder, and must be clearly set out and carefully checked.

A block-plan must provide all the information for setting out the mass of the building in relation to the site, adjoining or adjacent buildings, building lines, &c.

The foundation plan must give over-all dimensions, setting-out dimensions for all foundations and walls, together with their thicknesses. If the building has a steel or reinforced-concrete frame, the setting out of the centre lines of stanchions should be shown on the foundation plan. The contours of the site should also be shown and the levels of foundation bottoms, with positions of steps indicated. The levels should be related to a specified datum.

The floor plans should show the level, detailed dimensions of rooms, corridors, thickness of walls and partitions, widths of openings, &c. The dimensions should be shown in the length as well as in the width of the building, and dimension lines and figures should be arranged clear of wall or floor lines. The dimension lines showing the setting out of window and door-openings should be arranged next to the walls and the other main dimensions built up on the outside of them. The over-all dimension lines should encompass all the detailed dimension lines. All detailed dimensions and over-all dimensions should be carefully checked to ensure that they agree. If this is not done untold confusion and errors can arise on the site. The extremities of each dimension should be shown by a clear arrow-head, cross, dot or other symbol, and care taken to ensure that they *are* all indicated and not confused with the figured dimensions. If the distance between arrow-heads is too small to allow a figured dimension to be shown clearly, it should be placed outside the dimension line. The figures themselves should be written clearly, also the stop separating metres from decimal parts.

It should be emphasised that in a new building the quantity surveyor and the builder should have no doubt as to the exact heights and dimensions between walls in both directions of *all* rooms, including all recesses, cupboards formed by partitions, passages, &c. Where working between existing walls it may be necessary to leave one dimension of a series to be verified on the site, but all others should be given. When the quantity surveyor measures he has to determine a dimension for the missing length, which might be inserted and marked as subject to verification and adjustment by the builder when setting out. If an accurate survey has been made there should be very little margin of error.

The finished floor and roof levels should be shown on the plans as well as the sections, and it should be quite clear what allowance the contractor is to make for the difference between structural and finished surfaces. All stanchions, doors and windows should be numbered so that they can be referred to in the appropriate Schedules.

It is wise to include a note on the drawings to the effect that figured dimensions are to be taken in preference to scaled measurements. This could be in the Specification, applied to all.

Sections should be drawn through portions of the building where floor or roof levels vary, at intersections of wings, through staircases and at any other points which require clarification, and the position at which such sections are taken should be clearly marked on *all* floor plans, not only on one. Floor levels and heights of rooms should be shown, and on 1:20 sections it is a good idea to incorporate a brick scale at the side of the drawing, so that the bearings of floors, lintels, wall-plates, &c., can be related to brick courses. Materials in the 1:20 (or larger) sections should be indicated by cross-hatching or other suitable method (where not coloured).

The elevations, besides indicating the external appearance of the building, the different materials used and the finished ground levels against the building, should also show the floor and basement levels dotted on and dimensioned, the levels of damp-proof courses, the opening portions of windows, external flashings and weatherings, vent pipes, rain-water pipes, and the steppings in foundations. Windows and doors can, with advantage, be numbered on the elevations as well.

Colouring of Drawings.—The days when all drawings were coloured up seem to have gone for good, though colouring of plans and sections may have some value in making the construction stand out, and so simplifying the reading of them. A wash on plans indicating floor-finishes may also be useful, as it often happens that the quantity surveyor and builder need guidance as to exactly where changes of finish are to occur. In this connection, experience shows how often such joints are incorrectly placed, the draughtsman apparently forgetting that the joint of different floor-finishes will be under a door (when shut), and that a door is normally placed in a wall on the side of the room into which it is to open.

There is, however, one case where the colouring of drawings is absolutely essential, viz. drawings of alteration work. In such cases the existing walls, &c., remaining can be hatched or filled solid in black, but all new work, jambs made good, &c., should be coloured with the appropriate conventional colours, and new floor- and wall-finishes should have a wash of colour.

Schedules.—Schedules of doors, windows, finishings and colour schemes should form part of every set of drawings. Specimens of door and finishings schedules are shown in Appendix 1.* The lay-out of the schedules can be designed in any way that the architect prefers, but it should be possible to give the following information for *each* door, window or room:—

* Pages 281 and 305.

Doors :   1. Reference number.
2. Type, related to drawing of types.
3. Position (i.e. basement, ground floor, first floor, &c.).
4. Overall size of opening.
5. Section of frame and architrave (and sill if appropriate).
6. Size of door.
7. Thickness of door.
8. Locks, latches, furniture, springs, &c., to be used.
9. If glazed, the type of glass to be used.
10. Finish (e.g. paint, stain, polish).
11. Any other remarks (e.g. whether to be of any special construction).

Windows :   1. Reference number.
2. Type, related to a drawing of types.
3. Position.
4. Overall size of opening.
5. Section of timber frame and sill (if applicable).
6. Size of window.
7. Type of fasteners, stays, hinges, &c.
8. Type of glass.
9. Whether of metal or wood.
10. Method of opening.
11. Other remarks (e.g. glazed direct to frame, pressed metal sill, &c.).

Finishings :   1. Reference (by name or number).
2. Position.
3. On floor (material and finish).
4. Skirtings (material and finish).
5. On walls (material and finish).
6. Dadoes (height, material and finish).
7. On ceilings (material and finish).
8. Cornice or picture rail (material and finish).
9. Other remarks (e.g. margin to floor, cutting in or lines to dado, &c.).

The above schedules will be required at the stage when quantities are prepared : colour schemes will probably not be settled till a later stage and so will be the subject of a separate schedule.

Schedules will also be prepared by the Structural, Mechanical and Electrical Consultants, and reference to them may have to be included in the Schedule of Finishings or the Colour Schedule. A schedule will also be required of such items as shelves over radiators, curtain pelmets, &c.

Lettering.—It is probably true to say that few architects, however brilliant they may be as draughtsmen, can print well freehand, and yet the best drawings can be ruined by poor lettering. Neatness and clarity at least should be aimed at, even if one does not possess the gift of forming perfect letters. To achieve the best results the letters should not be too large and should be evenly spaced out. For 1 : 100 drawings subtitles need not be taller than 5 mm. The lettering should be kept as simple as possible and freaks and flourishes avoided. If one's writing is better than one's printing, there is no harm in using it for notes. Sub-titles, however, should always be printed with easily read capital letters. It is not necessarily the size of a letter, but rather its boldness (depending on the thickness of the strokes), which makes it stand out clearly.

A good range of stencils is available which are worth using in a large office to secure a degree of uniformity in presentation. With practice they are quite quick to use—but they must always be cleaned before being put away !

The practical view must not be forgotten that those who pick up a drawing must be able to see *quickly* :—

(*a*) the name of the job ;
(*b*) the drawing number ;
(*c*) what the drawing is about ;
(*d*) the scale.

The architect's name comes only fifth on the list. The architect must remember that he has " grown up " with the drawings and knows his way about them. The quantity surveyor, or later the clerk of works or foreman, may have 50 or more drawings passed over to him and it will be a long time before he is familiar with them. He will probably make an index to help, but time will be wasted in finding what he wants, if drawing number and subject are not prominent on every sheet and in the same relative positions.

A recent innovation which must be referred to is the availability of various kinds of transfers which though expensive can be used to obtain virtually perfect lettering by the least skilled of draughtsmen.   Sheets of alphabets and numerals can be obtained in the widest range of type faces and in all sizes likely to be required on drawings.   The letters are of opaque plastic film and are transferred on to the drawing from the sheet of transparent plastic film, on which they are mounted when bought, by simply rubbing with a hard blunt instrument such as the end of a fountain pen.   Care must be taken not to damage or displace the transfers when the drawings are handled and a special aerosol fixative can be used to "fix" them.   Their principal use is on presentation drawings and diagrams rather than on working drawings.   Transfers of common symbols, such as arrows, trees, motor vehicles and so on, are also obtainable.

Negatives.*—Drawings are prepared on translucent material, so that several copies can be obtained for distribution.   They can be prepared on linen, tracing-paper or plastic sheets.   Drawing on linen requires a certain amount of skill and takes more time than drawing on tracing-paper.   It is usually cheaper, if a linen negative is required, to have a true-to-scale print taken on the transparent linen from a tracing-paper original.

There are various grades of tracing-paper, the thinner qualities generally being used only for sketching and scribbling.   It is well worth while using a good, stout quality of paper, as not only will it stand up to frequent handling much better, but will also allow quite a lot of erasing (either with an ink eraser or a razor blade) without falling to pieces.

Folding Drawings.—Drawings which are sent out in rolls are a nuisance to everyone !   They cannot be posted in an ordinary pillar-box, and necessitate a special journey to the post office. Unless they are well protected in a stout cardboard tube, the edges are liable to get badly damaged.   They are also unpopular with the person receiving them, as they have to be counter-rolled before they will lie flat—and even then they are apt to curl up again as

---

* The term " negative " is not used by architects in the strict photographic sense, as their drawings are positive (not looking-glassed as a photographic negative).   The word in this connection only means a drawing through which the light can pass to make a print.

soon as they are moved. If they *must* be rolled—because, for instance, they have been drawn on tracing-paper or are for exhibition purposes—they should be rolled inside out, so that when they are spread out the right way up they are not so liable to curl.

It is far better, whenever possible, to *fold* drawings which have to be sent away, as they are then so much easier to handle. They should not be " quartered ", but should be folded con-certina-wise in both directions revealing the drawing number on the outside when completely packed. They should be folded to a standard size, and in order to simplify this procedure, the folding points should be marked on the margin of the drawing. The drawings need not necessarily be of a uniform size in order to produce a standard package. The folded dimensions should be decided to suit a standard envelope, and the length and width marked out on the drawing, commencing at the corner in which the drawing number is placed. If the folds are then made by always keeping the drawing number uppermost, it will be found to be a very simple operation.

Plastic sheets are obtainable which are more expensive than paper but have a very smooth surface for drawing in ink, are more transparent than stout tracing-paper and are less affected by weather conditions.

Negatives should have their edges bound as soon as they have been completed, and should be stored in vertical filing cabinets or flat in a separate drawer. They should be used only for obtaining prints, and should never be worked on. They should never be allowed outside the office, except when they are sent to the printers. A print for office use should be taken off as soon as the negative has been finished, in order to prevent unnecessary wear and tear on the negative.

Any alterations made to a negative should be recorded on it, so that the information appears on all future prints. As it is important that the contract set of drawings should correspond with the bill of quantities, alterations should not be made to drawings issued to the quantity surveyor, except as agreed with him, before the set for the contract has been printed.

Prints.—Various types of print are available, the ones in most general use being " dye-line ", which give a brown or purple line on a white background. Blue prints are as cheap as dye-line prints, but, having a white line on a blue background, tend to be rather trying to the eyes. Curiously enough, blue prints are generally used by engineers but seldom by architects. " True-to-scale " prints are more expensive, but can be reproduced on any type of paper or linen required. Dye-line prints can also be made on opaque linen, which is usually a requirement for submission with applications for approval under the building regulations and drainage bye-laws. Photographic reproductions, either true-to-scale or to a specified scale, can be made from drawings on opaque paper, but are relatively expensive.

Storage of Drawings.*—Drawings in current use should be filed flat in plan-chests or vertically in cabinets. They should not be folded or rolled. Negatives, office-prints and specialists' drawings should, if possible, be kept separate. Rough sketches which are probably prepared on pieces of paper of various size can, however, be folded and kept in large paper envelopes or box files.

When a drawing has been revised, the out-of-date print should be clearly marked " superseded " and filed separately or else destroyed. Large paper envelopes can be procured for filing such drawings, which can, of course, be folded if necessary. All drawings, cabinets, box files or envelopes which are used for storing drawings should be marked with the appropriate job number or reference.

Drawings which are removed from the plan-chest should be returned as soon as possible, and in a large office it will be necessary to devise a form of register in which a record can be kept of any drawings which have been taken out with the names of the borrowers. In some large Local Authority and Government offices the filing and registration of drawings are undertaken by a clerk who is solely responsible for ordering prints, loaning drawings and keeping them in safe custody.

For convenience, except in a very large office, the drawing cabinets will be kept in the drawing-offices, so that quick reference can be made to drawings of current jobs. It should be part of the daily routine to put all drawings away at night; they should not be used as dust-sheets or for rough sketches.

* See B.S. 3437: *Equipment for filing drawings.*

When a job is finished the drawings should be brought up to date, removed from the drawing office and suitably filed. Unless a large amount of storage accommodation is available, only the negatives need be retained, as it will be more convenient to order new prints if they are subsequently required. Old prints can probably serve a more useful purpose as backing-sheets or scrap paper!

The filing of old negatives is probably best done in metal tubes which can be stacked in racks. A tube 6″ in diameter* will store about 200 drawings. If the space is available it will be more convenient to allocate one tube to each job, but provided that the tubes are adequately labelled, there is little objection to storing several jobs in a single tube. In such cases the drawings for each job should be secured together with a suitable tag, possibly of a distinctive colour which can also be indicated on the label.

An alternative method of storage is with large paper envelopes—the size of a " double-elephant " or " imperial " portfolio—which have the advantage of storing the drawings flat. These envelopes can be stacked vertically or clamped with wooden strips on one edge and slung from a bar rather like a coat-hanger on a rail. An index should, of course, be kept of all old drawings in store.

* Existing 6″ diameter tubes will, no doubt, remain in use for a long time, but new ones will in due course be to a metric dimension.

21

SURVEYING WORK

The Term " Surveyor ".—Many architects style themselves
" architects and surveyors " and undertake surveying work, which
is not concerned with the designing of buildings, but is a kindred
profession merging into architectural work without any definite
boundary. The term architect, which is protected by law, essen-
tially implies a designer in the artistic sense, and if registration
ever gave protection of occupation instead of only protection
of name, the definition of architect would have to be limited
accordingly. The term surveyor is not in any way protected, and
anybody can call himself a surveyor.

It may be of interest to set out the classes of surveyor into which
members of the R.I.C.S. are divided, as this will give an indication of the wide application of the term surveyor:—

General Practice
Quantity Surveyors
Land Agency and Agriculture
Land Surveyors
Minerals Division

Every corporate member of the R.I.C.S. (with minor exceptions) qualifies by examination in one or other of the above sub-
divisions, but there are a number of subjects common to two or
more subdivisions, and there is usually some overlapping in their
practice, even amongst specialists. The services described below
might all come under the term " general practice ", but it naturally
falls to some to have special experience in some particular sphere.

The Building Surveyor.—The building surveyor who is a
specialist in building construction, without claiming to be an
artist, is often employed to design and supervise minor structural
alterations or repairs. He is the nearest approach to the architect
on that indefinite boundary of the surveying profession. Much
that he does is common ground to both professions. He will
make surveys of existing buildings, decide the construction and

sizes of new beams, &c., in alterations, write a specification of the
proposed alterations or repairs, obtain estimates and supervise the
carrying out of the work. He is also often concerned with maintenance work, particularly in the case of large corporations owning
extensive property. All this work the architect should by his
training be qualified to do, and, in fact, often does. Much of the
surveying work mentioned below is also within the province of the
building surveyor and may to a greater or lesser extent be also
done by the architect.

Reports.—A common ground for architect and building
surveyor is the preparation of a report on the structural condition
of property (e.g. when purchase is contemplated). If the client
is contemplating extensions or alterations involving architectural
treatment, he will probably approach an architect from the first :
if he only wants to ensure that the drains are all right or that the
building will not fall down, he may go to a building surveyor.
If he wants advice as to the price he is paying or a mortgage valuation as well as a report, he will probably go to a surveyor with an
estate agency and valuation practice.

It is important that a report should be so prepared as to convey
the information required by the client. If an architect is asked
to report on a house, he should ascertain what the client has in
mind and his object in asking for the report. It is no use, for
instance, making a detailed schedule of the sanitary fittings and
their condition, if the client's idea is " scrap the lot ". A report
made for a client who has not seen the property will differ from
that for one who has seen it. The latter will not include information that is obvious to anybody visiting the place, but which might
help to convey a picture to one who has not seen it. A diagram-
matic plan giving the sizes of the rooms may be useful, but, if the
client's wife has already measured for carpets and curtains, may
be quite unnecessary. A report should set out information about
what the client requires, but, perhaps more important, also set
out what is not there or is defective, so far as the architect thinks
the client is likely to be or ought to be interested. In short, every
report must be made, as the saying goes, *ad hoc* (i.e. to suit the
specific purpose of the client who asks for the report), and particularly must deal with those points which a technical man
notices, but which may be overlooked by the client. On the

other hand, the report to a layman must not be couched in technical language. The reader must always be borne in mind, so that a report made, say, by a public servant to a superior technical officer would be in different wording from that made by an architect to his lay client.

Dilapidations.—The preparation and checking of schedules of dilapidations provide another service undertaken on the surveying side of an architect's practice. The usual requirement of a repairing lease is that the lessee shall keep the premises in good and substantial repair. It is almost invariably the case when a lease expires that the landlord can find certain matters in which he alleges the covenant has not been kept. He will employ a technical man, architect or surveyor, to prepare a schedule of defects under the lease, which he will serve on the lessee, usually through his solicitor. The lessee in his turn will probably need technical advice in resisting the claim or negotiating a settlement.

To practise in this branch of the profession, some knowledge is required of the law of dilapidations and fixtures, the law relating to land tenure, the measurement of builders' work and pricing. These are subjects studied by building and quantity surveyors in the normal course of their training, and, if the architect proposes to undertake this work, he should see that he is equipped with the necessary knowledge. He must remember, as explained in Chapter 16,* that if he accepts professional work he holds himself out as being capable of doing it, and will be liable for damages for negligence if he does it carelessly.

Fire Insurance Valuations.—Whilst valuation for purchase or mortgage should be avoided by the architect as outside his province, as it is outside those of building and quantity surveyor as well, valuation for fire insurance is a different matter. The former depends on market value, a very fluctuating and uncertain factor, and is safest left to the valuation surveyor or estate agent who is constantly dealing with the sale and purchase of property. Valuation for fire insurance, however, is a question of building cost, which may be based on a foot super or foot cube price, in just the same way as one would estimate approximately for a new

* Page 170.

building. It is therefore within the province of both architect and quantity surveyor.

There is one important point to consider in valuing for fire insurance. The client may think that he can save substantially in premiums by not insuring for the full value, in view of the fact that most fires do not completely destroy a building. It may be that foundations can be re-used (if they are not so old that they will not comply with modern bye-laws). However, the amount to be saved in premium in this way is comparatively small, and it is important to emphasise to the client that if he does not insure for the full cost of rebuilding he is his own insurer for the balance, and if a total loss does arise he may find he has to meet a heavy liability. Also, one must not forget the cost of removing débris.

Fire Insurance Claims.—The preparation of claims for re-instatement of fire damage to buildings needs a knowledge of quantity surveying and pricing, and the architect who is experienced in these will be able to take on such work. Otherwise, he will probably refer them to a quantity surveyor or specialist fire assessor. The valuation of damage to chattels in such cases is quite outside the scope of an architect's work.

Party Wall Awards (London).—Under the London Building Acts (Amendment) Act, 1939, sections 44–59, it is provided that if anything is to be done to a party wall as defined by the Act, notice is to be given in certain forms. If the two adjoining owners do not agree (and it is often unwise to agree in advance), each party must appoint a surveyor to whom certain powers are given by the Act to determine the difference and decide, subject to the provisions of the Act, what contribution each party is to make to the cost of the works. This statutory provision is limited to the Administrative County of London. A study of the relative sections of the Act will make the procedure clear. It should be emphasised that both building and adjoining owners have statutory rights which they can exercise under the Act,* and those rights can never be overlooked nor set aside. Printed forms for the various notices are available,† and care must be taken to

---

* Sections 45, 46.
† *Notice Forms A to G for use under the London Building Act :* R.I.B.A.

adhere to the periods of notice laid down. When acting for the building owner, the architect must, in view of the time required for notice, counter-notice and negotiation,* take early steps to set the machinery in motion, or he may find that the works are delayed awaiting settlement with the adjoining owners.

A notice setting out details of the proposed work will normally be accompanied by a drawing giving plans and sections of the party wall in question and as much of the proposed new building as may affect negotiation. The notice would be served on the adjoining owner, who would pass it either direct to a surveyor or to his solicitor to instruct a surveyor. If it is thought an advantage to give some explanation to the adjoining owner, it can be arranged to call and see him, when the proposal can be outlined, and the notice served personally. The Act † provides for the possibility of both parties agreeing on a single surveyor, but it is more usual for each party to appoint his own. It should be noted that silence does not give consent, but that in the absence of consent to a notice within fourteen days a difference is deemed to have arisen.‡ Where there are two surveyors appointed, the one acting for the adjoining owner will, on receipt of instructions, communicate with the building owner's surveyor.

The first duty of the two surveyors, before discussing the notice, is to appoint a third surveyor § in writing (the appointment must not be left until an actual difference between them arises), but the third surveyor will not be referred to except in the case of a dispute between the two surveyors. Having made this appointment, the two surveyors will then arrange to meet on the site and discuss the proposal, setting out their decisions in the form of an award, on signature of which the works can proceed. It is advisable to register an award with the Land Registry by depositing a copy, though this is not compulsory.‖

The adjoining owner's surveyor will watch his client's interests during the progress of the works, and further awards on matters arising and not settled by the first award can be made if necessary with reference, if need be, to the third surveyor. The amount of the adjoining owner's surveyor's fee is usually determined in the

---

* For instance, under section 47(2) of the Act two months' notice must be given of proposed work to a party structure (one month's in the case of a party fence wall). In case of difference, section 55 specifies periods of notice required if a party refuses to appoint a surveyor, if two surveyors appointed fail to appoint a third or if a surveyor appointed refuses to act.

† Section 55(a) (i).   ‡ Section 49.   § Section 55(a) (ii).
‖ See Land Registration Act 1925, Section 5a (1).

award, which will state that it is to be paid by the building owner (unless there is a special reason to the contrary).

Adjoining Owners (outside London).—Outside London there is no statutory control, but the normal common law rights of property owners must be respected. No use should be made of ground below the surface (except for lateral support) or of the air across the boundary of the building owner's property, unless the previous consent of the adjoining owner has been obtained. Special points to watch are the spread of wall foundations and the overhang of fascias, gutters, &c. The adjoining owner's consent must be obtained to put scaffolding on his land, and proper precautions must be taken to protect any traffic from falling debris, &c. Any possibility of collapse, settlement or other damage to the adjoining owner's property arising from the works must be guarded against, and the building owner must be prepared to make good any disturbance, including roads, paths, lawns, flower-beds, &c. Whether any permission from the adjoining owner is necessary or not, it is a courtesy to advise him of the proposed work, and it will be found that good relations established at an early stage are often of great value if unexpected difficulty should arise later.

Quantity Surveying.—It is the practice in parts of the country for architects to undertake the preparation of quantities for their work. Especially in smaller towns, this and other surveying work may help to keep a practice going where there would be no room for one with purely architectural work only. Again must be remembered the responsibility of the professional man to have a reasonable amount of skill in the work he undertakes, and if work of this nature is to be undertaken, the architect should see that he is suitably qualified, in fairness both to his client and to the builder, not to mention himself and the possible drain on his pocket of an action for damages.

Negotiations in Relation to Land.—There is a variety of matters in connection with land on which negotiation is from time to time required and usually dealt with by a surveyor, e.g.:—

Compulsory acquisition of land.
Compensation (after requisitioning, &c.).
     do   (improvements).
Easements of light and air, support, way-leaves, &c.
Certifying capital expenditure for settled estates.
Approval of plans for freeholder or other controlling authority.

Each of these, though possibly undertaken by the architect, needs specialised study to a greater or lesser extent. Some subjects involve so much specialised knowledge and experience that an architect is not likely to undertake them, e.g.

Valuation of land and buildings (for purchase or mortgage).
Valuation of fixtures and fittings or furniture.
Valuation of standing timber.

Conclusion.—In short, the architect may extend his practice beyond the design and supervision of buildings and the work necessarily ancillary thereto to such an extent as he feels he is qualified to do. To undertake something because it offers a good fee and happens to come at a slack period is likely to be disastrous, if the architect does not fit himself properly for the job.

22

PUBLIC SERVICE

Openings in Public Service.—A large proportion of the architectural profession is today employed in public service, either in Government Departments, the offices of Local Authorities, the Development Corporations of New Towns, Regional Hospital Boards or the Boards of the several Nationalised Industries. They are employed in an advisory as well as in an executive capacity, and in the Ministries of Health, Education, Housing & Local Government and Public Building & Works there are special Development Sections that undertake research into and the development of new ideas in planning and forms of construction.

The number of architects employed by Local Authorities varies with their size and the nature of their statutory duties. County Councils and County Borough Councils, who have planning as well as building powers, will usually have quite large architectural departments with quantity surveyors and clerks of works, whereas the small Borough or Urban District Council may employ only one or two architects, without a separate architectural department. The staffs of Local Authorities are employed on conditions of service which are much the same as those in the Civil Service, except that it is much more common for Local Government officials to transfer to other Authorities as a means of gaining promotion.

In all public services the staff is divided into various recognised grades, each with a maximum and minimum salary and regular, annual increments. Entry is usually in one of the lower grades, and promotion to higher grades is based on seniority as well as technical and administrative ability. There are clearly defined conditions of service which govern the officials' employment, and these determine such matters as holidays, sick leave, superannuation, notice to be given in case of resignation or dismissal, retiring age and pensions. An official in public service is often precluded from practising privately in order to supplement his salary, but by way of compensation he can almost certainly count on security of employment and a pension on retirement, so long as he behaves himself properly.

Architects in salaried employment of Government Departments, Local Authorities, National Health Service and various Nationalised Industries or Public Boards are invariably covered by statutory pension schemes. These vary in detail and, subject to certain conditions, transfer from one pension scheme to another is usually possible without loss of pension rights. Contributions vary between 5% and 6% of salary, except in the case of Civil Servants whose scheme is a non-contributory one, though they must make a contribution of $1\frac{1}{4}\%$ of salary towards widows' pensions. Contributions are usually repaid on leaving the particular service before any benefits become payable and where there are no rights of transfer to another pension scheme.

Benefits become payable on retirement, normally at varying ages between 60 and 65 or on premature retirement due to permanent ill-health, or on death before retirement. Most schemes require that 10 years' service shall have been completed to qualify for a pension, the amount depending on length of service. In addition, a lump sum retirement grant is payable based on average earnings. The widow of a pensioner is entitled to one-third of her husband's pension, and in the case of his death before retirement a death grant is payable in addition.

Full details should be obtained of any scheme in which the reader is interested.

In both the Civil Service and Local Government there is a distinction between established (or permanent) staff and temporary staff, even though the temporary men may have had many years' service. Temporary appointments usually apply to workmen or junior clerical staff, but they may also be made in the case of technical staff for some special purpose, such as a particular building project or programme, in cases of temporary pressure of work, or otherwise to supplement the authorised permanent staff.

A temporary officer is not entitled to the full benefits which are enjoyed by the " established " staff under their conditions of service. Under certain conditions a person holding a temporary appointment may qualify for a pension under a superannuation scheme.

Both Government Departments and Local Authorities, although employing substantial staffs, nevertheless also employ private practitioners—in some cases regularly, in others only when extreme pressure prevents their own staff from coping with the work themselves. The formation of a panel of private practitioners gives elasticity to the organisation, and takes advantage of all the best professional skill available.

Duties.—The work of an architect in public service is technically the same as that of the architect in private practice. His client will be the Ministry, Board or Committee by which he is employed, and he will act on their instructions and satisfy their requirements in exactly the same way as the private practitioner, subject to compliance with rigid Standing Orders drawn up by the Department or Council. He will undertake all the duties of preparing drawings and specifications, arranging contracts and sub-contracts, supervising the execution of the work and certifying payments.

He will have the added advantage of being able readily to consult the Authority's other officers on any technical, legal or administrative matters, or he will be able, with the approval of the Authority, to appoint a private Consultant. In a large Department, the Chief Architect will probably employ on his staff a number of assistants with special technical qualifications, who will be able to undertake the preparation of drawings and specifications for the mechanical and electrical engineering services, structural engineering work and other specialised items. Having all these specialists at his disposal is obviously a tremendous asset when large and complicated projects are involved and only limited time is available in which to complete them.

Where a Government Department is responsible for laying down standards of accommodation and cost—such as the Department of Education and Science for Schools and Colleges for Further Education and the Ministry of Housing & Local Government for Housing—official architects are employed to check submissions made by Authorities, to satisfy themselves that such projects comply with the appropriate Ministry's building regulations and requirements for accommodation, etc., and are consistent with the programmed cost figures. This must be done before making a recommendation for loan sanction or otherwise authorising the work to proceed within an agreed budget cost. Their checking function is, however, strictly limited and in no way supplants the duty of the submitting Authority's architect in this respect. Further, since the introduction of the Town &

Country Planning Acts, all Local Planning Authorities are required to appoint their own Planning Officers and Staff to prepare and implement the Structure Plans for their areas and to advise their Committees on all matters relating to the architectural quality of projects submitted to them for approval. These officers are generally required to be corporate members of the Town Planning Institute, and a large proportion are qualified architects. Some Planning Authorities combine the offices of Chief Architect and Planning Officer, even though the Departments may be separately organised.

Official architects today, whether in Local or Central Government Departments, are therefore exercising an increasing influence on the social as well as the architectural progress and development of our towns and villages.

" Public " Clients.—The great difference between the private client and the " public " client is that in the latter case there is no single individual who can give instructions for the erection of buildings or authority for the expenditure of public money. Whereas the private client may be an individual or a board of directors who are free to make their own decisions concerning the scope of the development proposed, " public " clients must act through Committees or by direct instructions from Parliament, their powers and functions being limited and defined by Standing Orders or Acts of Parliament. All proposals or decisions made by committees, sub-committees or Government Departments must be authorised or subsequently confirmed by a higher authority which is ultimately responsible to the electorate. The expenditure of public money is subject to elaborate financial control which is quite divorced from any profit motive, as the primary objective of spending public money is to render some public service. To do this a variety of interests must be satisfied, and this necessarily demands that a rigid procedure shall be followed before any final decisions can be given. There can be no latitude for " give-and-take " methods and no departure can be made from the strict legal interpretation of any orders given or contracts made. Where the expenditure of public money is concerned there can be no deviations on individual responsibility from the strict path of statutory authority. Both the legality and the accuracy of accounts in public service are subject to minute

I

scrutiny by an auditor, and any official or committee member who cannot satisfy him on both these points may be surcharged for any sum of money which may have been mis-spent or improperly applied.

Local Authority Consortia.—Over the past decade Local Authority building consortia have developed from small beginnings to the present position where they cover most of England and Wales. In the field of educational building there are now eight consortia committed to the continuing development of industrialised systems or rationalised systems of building. In addition, there are a number of consortia concerned with housing programmes with somewhat similar aims and organisation.

A consortium is a voluntary association of Local Authorities for the pursuit of common aims—usually a desire to build more speedily and more efficiently. An Authority which is a member of a consortium does not forfeit its individuality or its freedom to manage its own affairs. It does, however, agree to co-operate with other member Authorities in the carrying out of a common programme of development work and in organising large-scale building programmes which the members themselves have drawn up.

In the early post-war years the Hertfordshire County Architect's Department and others pioneered new developments in building schools, but the origins of the consortium idea applied to building came with the formation of CLASP in 1957 and SCOLA in 1961.* Subsequently SEAC, CMB, CLAW, ASC, ONWARD and MACE † have been formed to deal primarily with the very pressing needs for educational buildings, usually up to four storeys, and to a certain extent with other related building types. Thus, in the educational field the consortium groups cover nearly all County and Borough Authorities in England and Wales. One of the consortia methods has in recent years been specially adapted for University development, for example at York and Bath. The total value of building programmes using

---

* Consortium of Local Authorities Special Programme.
　Second Consortium of Local Authorities.
† South Eastern Architects' Collaboration.
　Consortia of Method Building.
　Consortium of Local Authorities, Wales.
　Anglian Standing Conference.
　Organisation of North West Authorities for Rationalised Design.
　Metropolitan Architectural Consortium for Education.

consortia methods is now approaching £80 million–£100 million per annum.

Most consortia hold an Annual General Meeting of members to co-ordinate policy, but the direction of technical development is controlled by a Board of Chief Architects. The Department of Education and Science has a co-ordinating function for the educational consortia, and quarterly meetings are held under the aegis of that Department on technical development. Most consortia have set up a Central Development Group of architects, quantity surveyors and other professions to carry out the detailed technical development and to maintain close control, but the application of the building methods is by the Architect's Departments of the member Authorities.

Structural methods vary: though most consortia use a light steel frame, some have the option of a reinforced-concrete frame and some rely on advanced forms of traditional construction. All rely on the adoption of common dimensional modules, so that there is inherent the possibility of interchange of major components, which enhances the benefits of large-scale production.

The variety of design and aesthetic expression offered by the eight educational consortia gives the individual job architect considerable scope to choose from a wide range of dimensionally related components, and a considerable variety of external and internal finishes is possible.

Local Authority consortia act as a forum for the exchange of ideas and the carrying out of a continuous programme of research specifically related to the needs of the building client. The collective effort of consortia has produced significant advances in building techniques, particularly for school building and, more recently, for housing. Britain leads the world in these developments, and the ideas and methods have been adapted and used successfully in other European countries and have inspired the SCSD * educational programmes in the United States.

Building Contracts.—A difference will be found in the forms of building contract used in public service and private practice. In public—particularly Government—service conditions of contract are apt to be more elaborated in the hope of covering as many unforeseen circumstances as possible, and so removing

* School Construction Systems Development.

the need for the use of individual discretion in decisions. The more that is left to the individual's judgment, the more differences there will be between decisions, and dissatisfaction will be felt among those who are differently treated. However much the conditions of contract are elaborated, there will always be problems, such as those which were raised by the introduction of Holidays with Pay, and later the coming into force of the National Insurance Act. With an individual client one can go to him and say that, whatever the legal position may be, he is morally bound to meet such unexpected increases, and an honest and conscientious client will probably agree. Although in the public service the interpretation of the contract is the main issue, the Departments are sometimes willing to consider making *ex gratia* payments in hard cases, subject to the safeguards necessary in the public interest.

The R.I.B.A. form of contract as specifically adapted for the use of Local Authorities is now widely used, but some Authorities add supplementary clauses to comply with certain requirements of their Standing Orders.

Summary.—To sum up, the architect in public service has not the worry of running a private practice—of finding capital and offices, ensuring a flow of work and avoiding losses. His appointment is normally secure, and he can look forward to a steady income and a well-earned pension on retirement. On the other hand, he is not so much his own master, his hours are more rigid and he may be liable, or may find it necessary in order to secure promotion, to transfer to another locality—even abroad—which may upset his domestic life at very short notice. He has great responsibility in the expenditure of the money placed at the disposal of his Committee or Department by people—the general public—who, unlike private clients, are quite unknown to him.

23

FINANCE

Capital.—Until that day comes when all earnings are paid in advance, capital will always be necessary. Even the builder's labourer must be a capitalist in a small way to finance himself till the end of the week's work, although in these days he often draws " subs "—i.e. payments on account—before his wages are due. As salaries are paid weekly or monthly, and fees are not paid till the relative work is finished (and sometimes many months after that), there is a need to be provided with ready cash to pay the salaries, rent and other expenses, as well as to draw something from which to pay the butcher and baker at home. An architect starting in business must find that capital somehow, either from his own cash, by mortgage of his house or securities, the assistance of relations with cash or guarantee or the good offices of his bank manager, who will normally readily acquiesce if security is available (as part of his business is to lend money for profit), but who may otherwise not present the same smiling countenance. If a suggestion on the last matter may be made, it is that boldness and confidence, when backed by honesty, will pay.

In a properly run business, capital is, of course, always represented by assets. The money is not borrowed to spend, but to use. Starting with, say, £2,500 capital, after six months there may be only £400 in the bank, the position being as follows :—

Disposal of Cash.	£	Income and Assets.	£
Furniture. . . .	400	Fees received . . .	700
Salaries	500	,, due	900
Drawings . . .	800	Work in hand—proportion of	
Rent and other expenses .	400	fees due. . . .	900
	——	Value of furniture . .	400
	2,100		——
In bank . . .	400		2,900
	——		
	2,500		

In other words, the original £2,500 has increased to about £2,900 (subject to depreciation of furniture, which will be dealt with later), and some income has been drawn meanwhile as well. As fees are paid, the bank balance will be increased, but further payment of salaries, &c., will drain it again. The case is rather like the problems that used to be set in arithmetic examinations about a bath being filled at so many gallons and being emptied at so many gallons per hour. The architect must for his own comfort see that there is plenty of water in the bath, and that it doesn't run away when he isn't looking.

The amount of capital required must, of course, depend on the prospective volume of work and consequent size of staff. It will be several months before any fees are received, although a considerable amount of preliminary work will have to be financed. Under the R.I.B.A. Scale of Professional Charges a portion of the full fee may be drawn at certain stages of the work, but as these stages now take very much longer to complete, and overhead costs are considerably higher than they were before the war, the need for adequate capital is obvious.

The Normal Service which the architect gives to his client is defined in the R.I.B.A. Conditions of Engagement and Scale of Fees. The Normal Service is divided into five stages which mark the progress of the architect's work. For the first stage, " Inception ", when the architect advises his client on the architectural and consulting services he needs, receives an initial statement of requirements and outlines possible courses of action, the architect may charge on a time basis.* However, this charge would only be made if the project proceeded no further or if the engagement were properly terminated. On the completion of the second stage, " Preliminary Design ", which consists of preparing, describing and illustrating outline proposals, including an approximation of cost, the fee earned is one-sixth of the full percentage fee based on the estimated cost of the works.† A further one-sixth of the full percentage fee is earned on completing the " Final Design " of the scheme with drawings, outline specification, cost estimate and timetable for the project for the client's approval.‡ Completing the " Detail Design " entails the preparation of full working-drawings (or " production drawings " as they are described in the R.I.B.A. document), specification where necessary, information necessary for the bills of quantities, incorporating design work done by consultants and nominated sub-contractors, obtaining estimates from nominated sub-contractors and

---

* Part 2.1 and Table A.   † Part 2.2 and Table A.   ‡ Part 2.3 and Table A.

suppliers and carrying out cost checks. When this is complete a further five-twelfths of the full fee is payable by the client.* " From Tender Action to Completion " is the fifth and final stage of the normal service, at the end of which the remaining one-quarter of the full fee is payable.†

In the current R.I.B.A. Scale of Charges the duty of making and negotiating applications for Town Planning consents and for Building Regulations and Building Act approvals is not specifi-cally included in any particular stage, but it is, of course, an essential part of the Normal Service. (In Scotland, however, the submission of applications is not part of the architect's responsi-bility, but only the preparation of necessary drawings and technical information.)

Most Local Authorities and Government Departments are prepared to enter into agreements with private architects on these terms, but there are special conditions applicable to repetitive housing work.‡

Except on the larger commissions or in the event of delay in proceeding with the work, it is not usual for an architect to send in an account until the contract stage has been reached, and if he can afford to do this it is more satisfactory, because a definite contract figure is then known and his client can, at last, see something definite for his money. It may, however, take from nine to twelve months, or even considerably longer, to reach this stage by the time all the statutory consents have been obtained, bills of quantities prepared and time allowed for tendering and analysing and reporting on tenders. However, starting from scratch, £2,500 should be enough to start a small business if care is taken to build up capital and not to draw extravagantly.

Purchase of a Practice.—A problem often arises on the death of an architect as to the disposal of his practice. Subject to what is said later of the establishment of goodwill by partner-ship, there is normally very little goodwill attached to an archi-tect's business. In other words, the architect's business is a per-sonal one, unlike a button factory, where a successor can simply take over the order-book, keep the name and be assured of a continuation of orders, provided he gives satisfaction. The architect's clients may have a second string to whom they will

* Part 2.4 and Table A. † Part 2.5 and Table A. ‡ Part 3.3.

turn, taking no notice of the nominee of executors. It is therefore impossible to fix a fair price for the acquisition of a practice. There is one equitable solution ; viz. for the architect acquiring the business to say, " I cannot agree to pay a lump sum ; the prospect is too uncertain. If, however, any of Mr. X's clients come to me I will pay you 10% of the gross fees received for their work within three years (or whatever period may be agreed)." Such an arrangement should be satisfactory, as giving a fair return to both parties according to results ; it would, of course, be quite apart from any payment for assets acquired, such as furniture, stationery, lease of offices, &c. The debts due to the deceased would be collected by the executors, who would also pay out liabilities incurred. A suitable arrangement would have to be made for the division of work in hand.

Whether on taking over a business the name should be continued is a matter for decision in each case. There are many firms of Messrs. A & B or C & D where there is no A, B, C or D (and in some cases has not been for many years). Owing to the personal nature of the architect's business, the retention of an old name is not generally of great importance.

Salaries.—It is difficult to be very definite on the subject of salaries, as so much depends on the ability and experience of the individual. As a rough guide a fully qualified assistant architect with little previous practical experience might expect to earn £1,200 a year as a start, but one who has had a year or two's experience might be offered £1,400 a year. Salaries will increase with experience, as greater experience saves time—the work is done more quickly and accurately and other people's time is not taken up in answering questions. The experienced assistant, who can take complete charge and help in the management of a job, will earn £2,000 a year or more.

Deductions from Salaries.—There are two deductions which it is compulsory for the employer to make, where applicable, viz. National Insurance Contributions and Income Tax. The former is made by stamping cards weekly with a stamp representing the appropriate contribution, a fixed part of which must be deducted from the salary of the employee. A further contribution, graduated according to salary, is payable monthly through the Collector of Income Tax by all those with salaries over £9 per week (or £36 per month), the amount being entered week by week on the P.A.Y.E. income tax cards. When remitting, the employer adds an equal contribution from himself. Full instructions are obtainable from the local office of the Ministry of National Insurance.

Deduction of income tax is made in accordance with code numbers allotted to each individual when the Tax Office has ascertained the allowances due to him. Tables are issued to the employer setting out for each code number and each week of the year how much of the salary is free of tax and what tax instalment is payable on the balance in each week. Tables on a similar basis are also available for salaries paid monthly. Tax deducted is remitted to the collector monthly. The cards are finally totalled at the end of the financial year, a certificate given in the prescribed form to each employee showing how much tax he has paid through his employer, and any further adjustment is a matter between the employee and the Inspector of Taxes.

Each member of the staff should with his pay be given a statement showing how it is made up (a specimen is given in Appendix 1*). This may be either on a pay envelope or on a separate sheet, and will correspond with the entries in the Salaries Book.

Selective Employment Tax.—This tax is imposed on all employers and charged for every employee. All employers must pay, but firms classified as "manufacturers" are able to recover the tax paid (hence the selectivity). It is paid by a stamp on National Insurance cards merged with the insurance contributions. At the time of going to press the weekly stamp for an adult male employee is 81s. 7d., being 48s. S.E.T., 16s. 8d. employee's insurance contribution and 16s. 11d. employer's insurance contribution.

Fees.—The fees payable for the services of an architect are fairly well defined by the official scales of the R.I.B.A. and other professional Institutions. More closely graduated scales are in use in some cases of Government Departments and Public Authorities, where the services required may be rather different from

* Page 305.

those in the case of private clients, because some of the administrative work is done by the Department's own staff.

For some services—e.g. in connection with litigation or arbitration, preparation of schedules, reports, surveys, &c.—fees are based on the time spent, and the R.I.B.A. Scale lays down a minimum charge per hour for principal's and assistants' time for each category of work.* For assistants the rate is calculated from the " gross annual salary ", and it is fairly generally recognised that the cost of actual salaries of architectural and other technical staff employed, plus 125% is reasonable. Where the principal does part of the technical work (as distinct from supervision), his time doing this is charged in the prime cost as that of a senior assistant.

A typical example of an account for fees is given in Appendix 1.†

Expenses.—Most scales of fees provide for the recovery of certain expenses of the architect. These may be specifically referred to as travelling and subsistence expenses, lithography, copies of documents, &c., or the general term " out-of-pocket expenses " may be used.

The duplicating of copies of specifications, &c., is recognised as an expense not covered by the normal fees. The architect will add this cost in his own account, charging it net without any profit or without taking any discount. On the other hand, in the case of a report, schedule of dilapidations, &c., the fair copy of the document is expected to be covered by the fee, in just the same way as is the typing of a letter. If several copies were asked for, there would be justification in charging for typing.

All fares paid in travelling in connection with a job are normally chargeable to the client. First-class railway fares are admissible for a principal or very senior assistant. It is quite common practice not to charge small local bus fares, &c., but these must, of course, be reimbursed to assistants, even though not charged to the client.

Subsistence expenses are chargeable by the architect if he is away for a night on business in connection with a job. These may be either a fixed rate per night, as is the case in the scales of Government Departments, or the architect may charge his

* Part 6.   † Page 301.

hotel bill, excluding such items as his conscience will tell him are his personal liability. Subsistence expenses are not usually chargeable when the architect is away only for the day, but he should be prepared to meet expenses of his staff, e.g. on lunches in excess of their normal limits, which may be made necessary by their travels on business.

Postages, telephone bills and other office expenses are normally part of the architect's overheads and not chargeable to the client, but exception may be required by special circumstances, if, for instance, an excessive number of long-distance telephone calls was required.

Keeping the Books.—It is essential that the architect in private practice should have some knowledge of book-keeping, so that he can keep the books of his business properly. The subject is not an abstruse one, and if not in the curriculum of his training, a short course in a technical school or by correspondence may be recommended, and will soon enable him to grasp the essentials. The R.I.B.A. has recently published a manual, *Management Accounting for the Architect*, which has instructions, worked examples and blank forms related to a system suitable for typical architectural practices.

In a small office the books will be kept by the principal, though in larger offices the keeping of the personal ledger could be delegated to a secretary or administrator, with slips recording each entry to be made in the private ledger passed to the principal keeping the books, to ensure the double entry being made. There are some practices sufficiently large to give full-time work to an accountant. Every entry will not be made immediately it arises, but time will be set aside once a week or once a fortnight to bring the books up to date. The following procedure is suggested:—

(*a*) Bring cash-book up to date from cheque-book and paying-in book counterfoils. Then go through these entries in the cash-book and make the second entry and reference it. If a rule is made to reference as the second entry is made, it will reduce the possibility of the second entry being forgotten altogether.

(*b*) Go through expenses-book and enter all expenses to Personal Expenses account, making the second entry in the same way.

(c) Go through unentered invoices, petty-cash vouchers, &c., and enter these. In the case of petty cash, only one entry is required, the entry already made in the petty-cash book being the other. The petty-cash voucher should be marked with the folio reference and returned for entry of the reference in the petty-cash book.

(d) Go through the list of jobs in hand and enter any fees settled in the fees-book, making the second entry in the client's ledger account.

(e) Exceptional transactions.—A note will have been made of any unusual transaction at the time of its occurrence and a slip put in the " pending " folder until books are next written up. For instance, a letter may come in as a result of which it is agreed that an overcharge has been made. The relative record slip now coming forward, the amount would be credited to the client's account and debited to fees (if the error was on the fee).

Making-up Annual Accounts.—Once a year accounts must be totalled up and balanced and a profit and loss account and balance sheet must be prepared. It will probably be found that the final statement does not balance, but a search for the error might be a prolonged affair. It is best, therefore, to leave such error to be found on audit, when the whole of the entries made are followed through and mathematics are checked. A slip in a cast or omission to make the second part of a double entry, or other cause of the error, will then be found.

One of the subjects to be considered in making up annual accounts is depreciation. An architect starting in practice may spend £300 on furniture, which appears in his accounts as an asset at that figure. He should aim to bring his assets as soon as possible from purchase price to market selling values to make a true representation of his financial position, and he will therefore credit " Furniture and Equipment " account with a sum for depreciation and debit a special depreciation account, the balance of which will be an expense charged to the profit and loss account. Though depreciation may not be allowed in this form for income-tax purposes, it is advisable to show it year by year so that the balance sheet may reflect the true position of the business.

Audit.—It is advisable to have accounts audited by a qualified accountant. Accounts so certified carry more weight with the Inspector of Taxes, who will have to make assessment of tax payable, than the mere statement of the principal. The accountant is also available for advice if in difficulty with the income-tax authorities and, if necessary, to carry on negotiations with them. Moreover, in the case of partnership the accountant is somebody impartial who can be entrusted with interpretation of the financial terms of the agreement.

24

PARTNERSHIP

Meaning of Partnership.—Partnership is defined by the Partnership Act 1890 as " the relationship which subsists between two or more persons carrying on business in common with a view to profit ". The mere sharing of offices or staff on financial terms agreed is not " carrying on business in common ", which means that the whole business is a joint concern and the whole of the profits or losses are shared.

Where two or more persons enter into partnership they are jointly and severally responsible for the acts of the partnership. Further, they are each liable to the full extent of their personal wealth for the debts of the business. There is no limit to their liability, as in the case of directors of a limited company, to whom failure may only mean loss of their shares in the company, perhaps a very small matter. Each partner binds all his other partners by his acts done in the course of business. He does not, of course, bind them to responsibility for his private transactions. If he goes to a stationer's shop and orders note-paper, his order binds his firm to pay, but if he goes to a florist and orders flowers for his wife, the florist cannot claim payment from his firm or from the other partners individually (unless, of course, they were dealers in flowers).

When Does a Partnership Exist ?—Partnership is usually established by a written partnership agreement, about which something will be said later, but evidence of existence of an agreement is not necessary to convey the existence of the partnership to third parties. This can be seen from the firm's note-paper, bearing the name of the firm and probably the names of the individual partners. A limited company must have " Ltd." affixed to its title, and the names on its note-paper will be referred to as " Directors ". Owing to the personal nature of a professional business, such businesses are not incorporated as limited companies. In many cases, however, a partnership is evidenced merely by one of the partners holding himself out as such. If he says, " I am Mr. Tooth of Tooth & Bond, architects," he holds himself out as being a partner and legally accepts the responsibility of partnership.

Reasons for Partnership.—Why, one may say, should an individual agree to be responsible for the acts of somebody else ? What compensating advantages are there?

1. If a business expands, there comes a time when the principal cannot have a full and proper knowledge of every job, nor be able to give it that supervision by an experienced man which is necessary. He is faced with a choice. Either he must have a senior salaried assistant able to take the supervision out of his hands, or he must find another man to share the ownership and management of the business with him on terms not necessarily equal but satisfactory to both parties. There have been, of course, many large businesses run by a single man, but bearing in mind that the architect is expected to apply his own technical experience and give his personal attention to his clients, and not be merely the head of an administrative machine, the architect's office cannot be run like a button factory. The addition of a partner divides the responsibility for management, and as the business increases further partners can be added. Partnership can, of course, be combined with the employment of a responsible manager or senior assistant, who can relieve the partners of a good deal of the work. Such a man can, in fact, be a partner in all but name, taking a share in profits by way of bonus, at the partners' discretion instead of under agreement, but not having the responsibility of a principal.

2. Economy in expenditure can be effected by the pooling of accommodation, equipment or staff by partners. Whereas one principal might not have enough work to employ three assistants, two jointly might be able to do so. The two partners and staff of three might be accommodated in two rooms, whereas as separate businesses they would need four. Of course, both staff and accommodation can be shared without any partnership existing. Each principal would have his own work, the time of staff being recorded and their salaries allocated accordingly.

3. The search for capital may lead to a search for a partner, but to take a partner solely or principally for this purpose is likely to be dangerous. There is no truer saying than that " the man who pays the piper calls the tune ", and one can only say " Beware ! "

4. A partner may be able to introduce more work to a business which is short of it.

5. The taking of a partner establishes a goodwill value in a business. As has been explained, an architect in practice alone has hardly any goodwill attached to his business. If, however, he takes a new and younger partner, in the event of death or retirement current contracts with the firm will be automatically continued by the remaining partner. It can usually be arranged for long-term agreements to be made with both partners, and therefore a certain amount of the business will continue with the firm. Moreover, the younger partner will have been introduced in the deceased's lifetime to the clients, who may make him their " second string " and naturally carry on with the surviving partner. This preparation for continuation of the business may have some financial value for the retiring partner or deceased-to-be.

A young person seeking a partnership may be prepared to pay for the assurance of future business when he enters the partnership, either in cash or by accepting a reduced income for a period, or he may agree to make a lump-sum payment to the elder partner or his estate on the latter's retirement or death, such payment being commensurate with the benefit which he derives from the business.

Selection of a Partner.—It is obviously an advantage for partners to have similar views on the professional side, and it is essential for them to have complete confidence in each other in every way. It is therefore most common for a firm to take in its junior partners from its own staff, whose capabilities and suitability can have been judged during their period of service as assistants. To advertise for a partner has obvious dangers—one might be lucky, but the risk is considerable. A period of trial in such a case is essential, though a few months' experiment cannot give the same knowledge of each other as several years of working in the same office.

If the new partner is introduced to facilitate continuation of the business, his age must naturally be such that he can continue active work for some time after retirement of his senior. A (aged fifty) might take a partner of, say, thirty-five. In ten or fifteen years' time A perhaps retires, and B looks for a younger successor, and so on. Where the new partner is taken merely on account of expansion of business, the age difference has not the same importance.

Terms of Partnership.—The architect who has built up his own business and takes a partner naturally expects some return for his efforts, the result of which he is sharing. He may get an immediate return through the new partner buying a share in the business—i.e. making a payment for goodwill—or he may get a deferred return through some arrangement for lump-sum payment or pension on retirement. Apart from this he will probably take more than a half-share of the profits. The proportion in which profits are divided will depend on the income of the business, and should be so arranged that the new partner receives substantially more than the senior assistant and has a prospect of further improving his income on expansion of the business.

Salaried Partners.—Some firms, as an attraction to senior members of their staff, and, perhaps, as a step to full partnership, have what are known as "salaried partners". Such partners are paid a fixed salary, with or without some share in profits, and have the full responsibilities of partnership. The advantage to them is that, though they have a fixed salary, to the outside world they have the same authority as full partners. Their name appears on the note-paper (though some firms seem to print a short rule to separate the sheep from the goats!). They may or may not have capital in the business. If such partners were given a share in the profits they would have access to the accounts, but otherwise this would not be necessary, though it might be advisable. A salaried partner's rights and liabilities will usually be different from those of a full partner and will be defined in the partnership deed. The advantage to the full partners is that valuable members of the staff come under agreement for a specified period instead of being free to leave at a month's notice. This tie may, on the other hand, deter an assistant from accepting such a partnership, unless he sees a better prospect than he can find elsewhere.

Associates.—Some offices give a reference on their note-paper to " Associates ". This term implies that the persons in question have the status of principals but not of partners. Possibly they are senior assistants to whom the principals want to give some credit for their share in the work of the office (this is particularly applicable to architects, where design is very much an individual matter). Not being partners, they have not the responsibility of partners and quite possibly are paid by salary.

Consultants.—Also on the note-paper may appear names designated as " Consultants ". Their position is very similar to that of Associates, but they are, so to speak, " above the line " (perhaps retired partners) instead of " below ". Such consultants would probably be paid by a kind of retaining fee with some share in the profits.

Group Practice.—A recent development is the increased formation of " group practices " when independent firms of architects associate themselves for mutual benefit without sharing their profits or having joint responsibility to their clients. They may share staff and offices, telephone and other overheads, dividing these expenses on an agreed basis. They may be in different streets or even different localities, forming a " pool " to get work done. Such cooperation may help to ease times of pressure by " spreading the load ".

Professional Consortium.—Mention was made * of a combination of contractors working together as one unit and offering their combined services to the client for one lump sum. A similar consortium can be formed of professional firms: architect, consultants and quantity surveyor. The members of such a group may, of course, be normal partners; they may, however, be independent firms with agreed terms for sharing the combined fee, but each with their own responsibility to the building owner, not all responsible for the work of all, as partners would be. The

* See page 72.

architect would naturally be the leader and co-ordinator. The
exact relationship, whatever it might be, should be made clear
to the client.

The Partnership Agreement.—The partnership agreement
should be drawn up by a solicitor, but the main terms will be
settled between the partners, who should consider the following
points :—

1. Name of the firm.
2. Place of business.
3. Bankers to the firm.
4. Accountant to the firm.
5. Period of the partnership (i.e. a fixed period or indefinite).
6. Capital to be provided by each partner.
7. Division of profits.
8. Drawings (probably a fixed monthly amount).
9. Any terms as to consideration to be paid to the senior
   partner(s).

There are various standard clauses on such matters as limitation
of private work, provisions in the case of personal bankruptcy,
arbitration, &c., which will be inserted by the solicitor, but
should be carefully examined to see that their content is understood and agreed.

In fixing the amount of drawings it must be remembered that
the firm is assessed for and charged with income-tax on its profits,
which must be apportioned as partners' drawings. The periodical
cash drawings of the partners must therefore allow for this. The
senior partners would be well advised to consult their accountant
on the proposed terms.

The terms of the partnership are entirely a matter for mutual
agreement between the partners. A partnership for an indefinite
period (in the absence of any particular provision as to the length
of notice required) may be terminated by any partner at any time
by notice to the others.* If the partnership is for a fixed period,
it will be terminated at the end of that period, though there may
be particular provisions for its earlier termination upon notice
of a specified period being given. All partnerships are terminated
by death, and can be terminated by mutual consent. Where

* Partnership Act 1890, Sections 26 and 32.

there is ground for dissolution (e.g. where one partner has committed a serious breach of the partnership agreement) the partnership can be determined by recourse to Law.

Certificate of Registration.—It should be noted that if the firm's name does not consist of the names of all the partners it is necessary to comply with the requirements of the Registration of Business Names Act 1916. A certificate of registration must be obtained and exhibited in a conspicuous position in the principal place of business, and the names of all the partners must appear on all business letters on which the name of the firm appears. Application forms for the certificate can be obtained from the Registrar of Business Names.*

Acts of the Partnership.—The acts of the partnership will be expressed in just the same way as those of an individual. Where an individual's verbal agreement is binding, so will be that of any one of the partners. Formal written agreements will probably be made with the partners jointly and severally, the agreement being signed by each of the partners. Ordinary correspondence, however, will have only one signature. This can either be the name of the firm (e.g. " Smith, Brown & Jones ") written in manuscript in the hand of one of the partners, or the individual signature of one of the partners over the name of the firm. The latter gives, perhaps, a more personal character to the letter, at the same time indicating which partner is dealing with the matter. Routine letters can be signed in the absence of a partner in the same way with the signature or even the initials of an assistant or secretary, instead of that of one of the partners, but the office copy should be left for initialling by the partner concerned at the first opportunity.

It is, of course, important that exact instructions are given to the firm's bank as to the signature or signatures which will appear on cheques, as they will only pay cheques drawn in accordance with the instructions given them.

* At Companies House, 55 City Road, London, E.C.1, from whom *Notes for Guidance* can be obtained.

STRUCTURE OF THE BUILDING INDUSTRY

Composition of the Industry.—The Building Industry is a complex organisation centred on the building contractor, who is responsible for the actual erection of the building work. Contracting firms vary very much in their size and capabilities. Many are small firms whose limit may vary from one or two houses in the smaller cases to individual contracts of, perhaps, £50,000 or so in value. However, the bulk in value of building work is in the hands of a comparatively small number of larger firms, often with several branches, and many also carrying out work in other parts of the world.

Before a building can be erected, however, the preliminary work of design is necessary, and this is normally in the sphere of the architect. According to the size and complexity of the work, he may need to form a team of specialists to advise him on particular aspects of the design, such as structural, mechanical and electrical engineers, or to guide him on the costing, which is a role of the quantity surveyor. On appointment of the contractor, or even sometimes before,* specialist sub-contractors may be nominated to carry out work outside the scope of the general contractor himself, and merchants may be selected to supply special materials which will be specified. A clerk of works may be appointed to assist the architect with the day-to-day supervision on the site. These have all been dealt with in previous chapters.

Organisation of the Contractor.—It is evident from the above that no "typical" organisation of a contractor's administration can be given. That considered here is mainly of a medium- or larger-sized firm. Obviously for the world-wide contractor this would have to be expanded and for the man on his own or with a small staff somewhat contracted.

* See page 91.

The Problem

1. Workmen must be engaged and each individual's time recorded in detail on his time-sheet and then allocated to the various jobs. This must then be

   (*a*) converted into money payment due, and the money must be drawn and paid out;
   (*b*) charged to the cost account which is kept to record as accurately as possible the prime cost of each job.

B. Materials and plant required must be—

   (*a*) ordered;
   (*b*) paid for, either immediately or through a credit account;
   (*c*) charged to the cost accounts referred to above (or in the case of plant to " overheads ").

C. Work must be tendered for either on quantities supplied or by taking particulars from drawings or site, the job in progress must be watched, interim payments applied for, variations adjusted and final accounts agreed.

D. The work on the site must be planned and programmed, so that materials and adequate resources are brought together at the right time to ensure continuous and economical working by the various members of the construction team. Depending on the size and complexity of the job, this programming may be undertaken with simple rule-of-thumb methods or highly sophisticated management aids.

General Management

At the top is the managing director, or in a private business perhaps a sole principal, though even small businesses may be limited-liability companies. Where there are several directors, some may specialise in a particular branch of the business and others may be appointed on a part-time basis for their outside contacts, special knowledge or financial expertise. Under the directors will come the heads of the various departments, each responsible to the board or to the particular director for the smooth running and profitability of their sections.

Secretariat

The secretary may range from the builder's wife in a one-man business to a highly qualified secretary in a large organisation. The secretary will be responsible for the business side of the organisation and possibly the non-technical accountancy, including wages, although in the office of a large contractor this may be a department of its own. All correspondence, filing and general office duties fall to the secretary's department, and members of the secretarial staff may be allocated to serve the heads of other departments, so that each head has his own secretary, and his deputy has at least a share in one. Estimators would require help from the secretary's department for working calculating machines and may have such staff permanently attached. In fact, in the secretary's department a contractor's office differs little from any other commercial office.

The payment of wages may in itself involve quite a substantial staff. The men's individual time sheets must be collected, checked and the material information transferred to the pay sheets. Income-tax cards must be brought up to date, and adjustments from these, together with National Insurance contributions, must be entered on the pay sheets. If there are incentive payments * these, too, must be entered on the pay sheets. Pay sheets must be made up, the detail of each man's pay set out on a slip or pay envelope for him and a note made of the total cash required with the form in which it is to be drawn. The cash received must be made up into envelopes for paying out.

Estimating Department

The chief estimator will be in charge of this department. His main function is to get orders for work, either by negotiation or by competitive tendering, in such a way that the firm may pursue its business as profitably as possible. Under him will come buyers, cost clerks and site checkers.

The buyer is a man in contact with merchants and the industry generally and is expected to buy materials in the best market to the best advantage of his firm.

Cost clerks deal with invoices received, check them with delivery notes and estimates, enter them in the cost account and pass them for payment.

Site checkers are responsible for checking the materials

* See page 273.

delivered to the site and satisfying themselves that the goods delivered tally with the delivery notes.

Contracts Management

The contracts manager runs the construction side of the project, and under him come the agents or general foremen responsible for individual sites. Under the general foremen may come trade foremen. Other operatives on a site will probably mainly be casual labour hired locally for the particular contract, though the firm may have a number of tradesmen and certain key men, such as gangers, in their permanent employment. The small firm doing only local work is fairly certain to have one or two tradesmen, bricklayers, carpenters, etc., in regular employment. The contracts manager would be responsible for liaison with the architect (and in negotiated contracts perhaps also with the building owner), the professional consultants and the quantity surveyor, and would deal with sub-contracts.

The department of the surveyor may be under the contracts manager, or it may be entirely independent. The duties of the surveyor include co-operation with the quantity surveyor on applications for interim payments and preparation of the final account, for the checking of which he would be responsible. He would during the period of the contract watch progress, with a view to ensuring that the profit margin envisaged at the tender stage is maintained and, if possible, improved on. Alternatively, he would take steps to rectify any setback to the running of the contract.

Where incentive payments are to be made, a bonus clerk would have to take the necessary particulars. Though these may be in the nature of measurement, the information will be for the department dealing with the payment of wages.

On very large contracts, particularly in remote country districts, the contracts manager may be faced with the need for a camp for workpeople, with sleeping and feeding accommodation and supervising, catering and maintenance staff.

It might even be that the whole office organisation of the job is transferred to the site office, so that the contract is run almost as an independent unit.

Works Departments

Some contractors specialise in some branch of their business, which others would sub-let. Joinery works are, perhaps, the most common. They would be under a joinery works manager and would contain the necessary machinery and skilled staff for making the firm's own joinery, and possibly accepting orders from other contractors. Storage space for timber would adjoin the works. The works manager would do his own ordering of timber and check the accounts.

Plumbing work is now largely sub-let, but there may be contractors with their own department. A mason's yard is not unknown, and a firm may have its own electrical department. Sometimes it will be found that the department doing such specialised work is constituted as a separate company.

Plant Department

This department would be under the control of the plant manager, who may be just a storekeeper in a small business or the director of a subsidiary company in the largest firms. There will be a " yard " in which plant is stored and issued to the various sites as required. Plant will vary from scaffolding, ladders, etc., necessary for the smallest contracts to hoists, mechanical excavators, etc., required for the larger.

This department will also be responsible for transport, varying from a van or truck to a fleet of lorries.

Builders' Federations.—The principal building firms of the country are organised into Regional Federations affiliated to the National Federation of Building Trades Employers with headquarters in London. These Federations do for the builders what the Professional Institutions do for architects. They provide a representative negotiating body which can look after the members' interests, keep their members informed of developments in the Industry and help them with advice when necessary.

Most of the specialist firms which are normally sub-contractors on building contracts have their own federations.

Operatives' Trade Unions.—The main representative body of the operatives' side of the building trade is the National Federation of Building Trades Operatives. To this organisation are affiliated the various individual trade unions of bricklayers, plasterers, plumbers, &c. The National Federation and the various individual unions, through their representation on the National Joint Council of the Building Industry, maintain contact with the employers. The duty of the trades unions is to watch the interests of their members in such matters as wages, working conditions, &c. On large contracts a "shop steward" will be appointed by each trade union, and usually there is a Federation steward, through whom complaints are made and negotiations take place. Smaller contracts will be visited when necessary by full-time union officers. Regular contributions are paid by workmen to their union, but this is, of course, done direct, and not through the medium of the employer's pay-sheet. As in the case of the employers, the operatives have regional organisations, which hold regular meetings and maintain closer contact with the men than would be possible from a central organisation.

Manufacturers' Trade Associations.—There are a number of associations representing manufacturers from whom useful information and advice can be obtained as to the use of the material which their members manufacture or use. Amongst these may be mentioned—

Aluminium Federation
British Constructional Steelwork Association
British Precast Concrete Federation
British Woodwork Manufacturers' Association
Cement and Concrete Association
Copper Development Association
Federation of Coated Macadam Industries
Floor Quarry Association
Gypsum Plaster Board Development Association
Lead Development Association
Natural Asphalte Mine Owners' and Manufacturers' Council
National Federation of Clay Industries
National Salt Glazed Pipe Manufacturers' Association
Pitch Fibre Pipe Association of Great Britain
Sandlime Brick Manufacturers' Association
Timber Research and Development Association
Zinc Development Association.

In fact, nearly all manufacturers have some sort of publicity organisation for their particular Trade.

The Building Centre, Ltd.—Mention should be made of this organisation, which is backed by the manufacturers of building materials and maintains a showroom in London* where samples of many materials can be seen.   It is an agency from which names and addresses and often leaflets of manufacturers can be obtained, particularly useful sometimes as a source of information when one only knows the branded name of the material.   Enquiries can be made by telephone, or, for those some distance from London, post-paid enquiry cards can be obtained from the Director.

There are similar Building Centres in Belfast, Birmingham, Bristol, Cambridge, Dublin, Glasgow, Liverpool, Manchester, Nottingham and Southampton.   There are also Building Information Centres at Coventry and Stoke on Trent.

The National Joint Council for the Building Industry.† —However true it may be that " unity is strength ", if there are two " unities " there will be two " strengths ", and unless there is some machinery for bringing opposing or diverging parties together, there is little hope of efficiency.   The National Joint Council is composed of equal numbers of representatives from the employers and operatives, appointed by the employer and operative organisations adherent to the Council, and covering some of the specialist or individual trades, as well as the general Industry. There are Regional Joint Committees and Area Joint Committees as connecting links between the Council and individual members. The Council has done much to stabilise and improve working conditions in the Industry.   Mention is made below of the principal matters dealt with by the Council, as the architect may meet them in checking prime cost accounts or in making adjustments under the price variation clause of lump sum contracts.

Determination of Wages.—One of the principal functions of the National Joint Council for the Building Industry is the determination of rates of wages in the Industry.   The rates of wages vary with the district, and the whole country is graded by districts into several categories.   The basic category is Grade A. London and Liverpool have craftsmen's rates $1\frac{1}{2}$d per hour above those in Grade A localities.   Labourers' rates are fixed at rates below the standard craftsmen's rate.

---

* 26 Store Street, London, W.C.1.
† *Constitution, Rules and Regulations :* The National Joint Council for the Building Industry.

Watchmen are paid by the shift, and the rate per shift is also subject to annual review at the statutory meeting of the N.J.C.B.I. and adjustment according to the retail price index.

The rates of apprentices are fixed at a percentage of the craftsman's rate, varying according to age from 25% at 15 to $87\frac{1}{2}$% at 20. Young male labourers similarly get a percentage of the labourer's rate, from $33\frac{1}{3}$% at age 15 to 100% at age 18.

There is also an agreed scale of rates for female operatives, both those engaged on craft processes and those who are not.

Certain tradesmen are entitled to receive a tool allowance varying from 1s to 3s per week (National Working Rule 3 E), provided they equip themselves with tools, in some cases in accordance with an approved list appended to the Working Rules.

An extra rate of 4d per hour above the standard rate for craftsmen is payable to charge hands appointed as such. There are also national " differential rates " for qualified bar benders and qualified tubular scaffolders, under certain conditions, of 2d per hour below the standard rate for craftsmen, the differences being " national differential margins ". A special rate may also be fixed or altered by application to the Council for a section of the industry in a defined district, and the difference between that rate and the corresponding standard rate is a localised differential margin.

Workmen are entitled to various extra payments under headings which are classified as being for

> Discomfort, Inconvenience or Risk (e.g. work at heights, in water or in foul conditions).
> Continuous Extra Skill (e.g. timbermen, whole-time scaffolders, drivers and operators of mechanical plant).
> Intermittent Responsibility (e.g. scaffolders working as such part time).
> Large-scale Demolition.

Full particulars will be found in Working Rules 3 A-D.

Working Rules.—The National Joint Council is responsible for the framing and revision of the National Working Rules* which cover the following sub-heads:—

* *National Working Rules for the Building Industry* : The National Joint Council for the Building Industry. Branch Federations issue their own local editions of the Rules with some additional clauses.

Rule 1   Wage Rates.
  ,,   2   Working Hours.
  ,,   2A Guaranteed Time.
  ,,   2B Termination of Employment.
  ,,   3   Extra Payments.
  ,,   4   Overtime and Holidays.
  ,,   5   Night Gangs.
  ,,   5A Regular Night Work.
  ,,   6A Daily Travelling.
  ,,   6B Travelling (not daily) and Lodging.
  ,,   7   Recognition of Union representatives.
  ,,   8   Sub-contracting for labour only.
  ,,   9   Payment for absence due to sickness or injury.

Regional Conciliation Panels are set up to hear complaints of breaches of the Working Rules and the Council has established a National Conciliation Panel to hear appeals from the Regions.

Supplementary Rules and Memoranda.—The following are included as supplements with the published National Working Rules:—

Supplementary Rules for Woodworking Factories and Shops
Operation of Paint-spraying Machines
Code of Welfare Conditions for the Building Industry
Industrialisation of Building Processes
General Principles concerning Incentive Schemes
National Joint Apprenticeship Scheme
Safety Equipment.

Apprenticeship.—The National Joint Council has instituted a scheme for encouraging and promoting apprenticeship in the Industry. Very briefly, the apprentice is indentured on leaving school at the age of fifteen or sixteen for a period of four years (reduced for those who have attended approved full-time day technical courses). He is required, until the end of the school year in which he reaches the age of 18, to attend Day Technical Classes, when available, for the equivalent of one day a week, for which period the employer must give leave of absence and must pay him. He must also attend Evening Technical Classes on such evenings each week as may reasonably be required for the whole period of his apprenticeship. The employer pays the fees for all the classes.   The apprentice starts at one-quarter to one-third the craftsman's rate of pay, according to age, progressing by stages to seven-eighths of the rate.   Apprentices under eighteen must not work overtime, and in any case overtime must not interfere with attendance at technical classes.   The apprenticeship is under the supervision of the Local or Regional Joint Apprenticeship Committee constituted by the National Joint Council, and that Committee is a party to the apprenticeship deed.   The National Joint Apprenticeship and Industrial Training Commission exercises general supervision.

Holidays-with-Pay Schemes.—There are two schemes, one covering general or " annual holidays " and the other " public or statutory holidays ".   They are based on agreements between the employers' and operatives' organisations in the Building Industry and the corresponding bodies in the Civil Engineering Industry.   The schemes are administered by a non-profit making company limited by guarantee and are covered by Working Rule 1 (*i*) & (*j*).*

The principle of the general holiday scheme is that the operative is entitled to two weeks holiday in the year.   He is not entitled to an additional day if a public holiday should come in the selected six days.   The employer contributes 13s od per week (9s 6d in the case of female operatives and those under eighteen) to provide pay for this holiday by buying special stamps from the above-mentioned company and stamping a card for each man.   The employer in whose employ the workman is at the date of the annual holiday pays out the total value of the stamps on the card (less a fixed administrative charge) to the workman, and on forwarding the card to the company is reimbursed.

The Public-Holidays-with-Pay Scheme is similar.   The operative is normally entitled to holiday on Easter Monday, Whit Monday, August Bank Holiday and Boxing Day (other days when locally recognised public holidays differ).   The weekly contribution of the employer is 7s 9d per week (5s 6d in the case of female operatives and those under eighteen) and on the pay-day before each holiday the operative is entitled to be paid the value of the stamps accrued on his card.

* The Building and Civil Engineering Holidays Scheme Management, Ltd., Manor Royal, Crawley, Sussex.

Welfare Code.—The National Joint Council, in view of its charge by the constituent bodies to concern itself with welfare conditions, has issued a Code of Welfare.* This covers such subjects as shelter, accommodation, provision of meals and drinking water, sanitary conveniences, washing facilities, first aid and site conditions. It has the authority of a Working Rule. Contractors must, of course, comply with the requirements of the Factory Acts affecting building work and the specific requirements of The Building (Safety, Health & Welfare) Regulations.†

Combined Regulations for the Building and Civil Engineering Industries have been prepared‡ which revoke the relative portions of the 1948 Regulations above-mentioned. Regulations are also in force governing the use of woodworking machinery,§ lead paints ‖ and electricity,¶ also on such special subjects as work in compressed air and diving operations. The Offices, Shops and Railway Premises Act 1963 applies to construction sites occupied for six months or more.

Incentives.—In November 1947 permission was given for an experimental period of two years for employers to initiate incentive schemes for bonus payments proportionate to output. The framing of the scheme was left to employers, with certain limitations, with the intention of reviewing the results at the end of the period. It was agreed, as a result of the experiment, that it was undesirable at that stage to lay down a detailed scheme on a national basis. Machinery was, however, set up in the form of Regional Joint Advisory Panels to give guidance in the working of schemes, and a Joint Committee of the National Executives to review progress and receive submissions on matters of general principles or policy. A statement of general principles concerning incentive schemes has recently been published by the National Joint Council.

---

* *Code of Welfare Conditions for the Building Industry* (published with the Working Rules): The National Joint Council for the Building Industry.
† S.I. 1948, No. 1145: H.M.S.O.
‡ *Construction (General Provisions) Regulations* 1961 (S.I. 1961 No. 1580): *Construction (Lifting Operations) Regulations* 1961 (S.I. 1961 No. 1581): *Construction (Health & Welfare) Regulations* 1966 (S.I. 1966 No. 95): *Construction (Working Places) Regulations* 1966 (S.I. 1966 No. 94): H.M.S.O. A useful guide to these is *Guide to the Construction Regulations:* N.F.B.T.E.
§ S.R. & Os. 1922 No. 1196 and 1945 No. 1227.
‖ S.R. & O. 1927 No. 847.
¶ S.R. & Os. 1908 No. 1312 and 1944 No. 739.

Co-operation of Contractors and the Professional Side.
—The various professional Institutions and trade Federations
have their liaison committees for co-operation, but, apart from
these, there are several joint bodies which do valuable work in a
particular sphere.

(a) *The National Consultative Council of the Building and Civil
Engineering Industries.*—This Council is an advisory body
appointed by the Minister of Public Building and Works
to advise him on matters concerning the Industry. It is
able to convey to him the views of the Industry as a
whole as distinct from the advice which he can obtain
from his own technical staff.

(b) *Joint Contracts Tribunal.*—This body composed of representatives of the R.I.B.A., R.I.C.S. and N.F.B.T.E., as
well as of several Associations of Local Authorities, is
responsible for the R.I.B.A. form of contract referred to
above and its periodic revision. They also consider
points on interpretation of the contract and from time to
time issue "Practice Notes", which are, of course,
advice not legal rulings.

(c) *The Standard Method of Measurement Joint Committee.*—The
Committee is composed of equal numbers of quantity
surveyors and builders nominated respectively by the
R.I.C.S. and the N.F.B.T.E. The original Committee
produced in 1922 the first Standard Method of Measurement, and this has been succeeded by revised editions to
meet new suggestions and changed conditions. This
Committee is responsible to the two parent bodies for
publication of the document as well as for the Code of
Measurement for Small Dwelling-houses. The Committee occupies itself in the interim between revisions in
watching developments and noting suggestions for improvement.

(d) *Joint Consultative Committees.*—There is a National Joint
Consultative Committee of Architects, Quantity Sur-
veyors and Builders for liaison between these branches of
the Industry and study of subjects of mutual interest.
They have produced the Code of Practice for Selective
Tendering * and have issued various procedure notes.

* See page 115.

A table prepared by this Committee showing the consultative machinery of the Building Industry is in a pocket in the back cover. In addition to this National Committee there are similar Regional Committees.

(e) *The British Standards Institution.*—This Institution has a scope much wider than that of the Building Industry. A study of the list of Standards will reveal such differing subjects as women's dresses, rubber rings for preserving jars and castor oil. However, there are a large number of Standards established for building materials, and the Committees responsible for framing these have representatives of builders, architects and surveyors as well as experts in the manufacture of the material concerned. The Institution also publishes the Codes of Practice referred to above.*

(f) *The National House-builders' Registration Council.*—This Council, whose members represent all branches of the Industry and other interested parties, registers house-builders who undertake to build to a minimum specification laid down by the Council. The Council, whose representatives inspect the house at several stages of progress, issues a certificate for a small fee that the house is erected in accordance with the prescribed standards. This gives some confidence to purchasers of new houses, and it is contended that the " pedigree " established will help an owner to convince a prospective purchaser that the house is well built.

Civil Engineering Work.—The main professional organisations associated with civil engineering work are the Institution of Civil Engineers and the Association of Consulting Engineers. The national employers' organisation is the Federation of Civil Engineering Contractors. The various specialised branches of the industry, e.g. plant hirers, demolition contractors, road surfacing contractors, &c., have their own trade associations. The wage negotiating body is the Civil Engineering Construction Conciliation Board for Great Britain, which issues working rules and procedure for the settlement of disputes. The Federation of Civil Engineering Contractors constitutes the Employers' side,

* Page 109.

K

and the Operatives' side consists of representatives of the Labour Unions of Transport and General Workers and General and Municipal Workers, and also representatives of Craft Unions, notably those of the Bricklayers and Carpenters.

A distinction between the Civil Engineering and the Building Industry is that the former, being often concerned with large-scale works, comprises a comparatively small number of large firms with one central federation, whereas the latter includes a very large number of small firms with the federation organisation largely decentralised.

Structural Engineering Work.—The professional institutions mentioned under " Civil Engineering Work " are also concerned with this branch of engineering, as also is the Institution of Structural Engineers. The employers are organised into the Engineering and Allied Employers' National Federation, which publishes the working rules. The British Constructional Steelwork Association deals with the Employers' side on such matters as prices, methods of measurement, &c.

The Building Research Station.—This establishment at Watford, a branch of the M.P.B. & W., carries out research on building materials and is prepared to advise on difficulties within its sphere. It has a number of publications, a list of which is obtainable from H.M.S.O.

The Forest Products Research Station.—This station at Princes Risborough, a branch of the Ministry of Technology, is not confined to building matters, but has a wider outlook. It is engaged in research into such things as the seasoning of timber, the cause of and remedies for dry rot and similar troubles, and has several publications on these subjects, issued by H.M.S.O.

The National Building Agency.—This body was established by the Government in 1964 to tackle the problem of increasing the output of the building industry to meet the heavy demands of the present day. It is managed by a Board of Directors appointed by the Government, and although it is attached to the Ministry of Housing and Local Government, it is independent of direct Government control. It functions as a company limited by guarantee and financed partly from a Government grant-in-aid and partly by fees charged for its services, though it is non-profit-making and must apply all its income solely for the promotion of the objects for which it was constituted. The Agency also operates from its Scottish office in Edinburgh and regional offices in Manchester and Newcastle.

The Agency offers consultative services and organisational facilities to promote increased efficiency, productivity and improved techniques in the building industry. These include the co-ordination of building contracts on the sites of conveniently grouped clients; the co-ordination of bulk-purchasing of selected building components; the evaluation of building systems and the issue of detailed appraisal certificates for them; and consultative and advisory services both to the industry, to public authorities and to private clients. At present its work is concentrated on housing of all kinds, but it is not limited exclusively to this type of work.

FORMS AND PRECEDENTS

1. PRELIMINARY CLAUSES FOR A SPECIFICATION (where there is no bill of quantities)

The following list of subjects for Preliminary Clauses is not exhaustive, but contains the main items which should be considered on each occasion. It is not necessary to repeat in the Specification anything which appears in the Conditions of Contract. In preparation of this list use of the R.I.B.A. Form of Contract has been assumed, and its contents have not been repeated: if a different form is used, it should be ensured that the R.I.B.A. clauses are all covered.

1. A general description of the works and list of drawings supplied.
2. Location of site and any instructions as to access. This may, if preferred, be included in the covering letter sent out with the specification.
3. Any subdivision of the works or of the estimate for them into sections.
4. The Form and Conditions of Contract to be used, and how any blanks will be filled in.
5. Any amplification of the Conditions of Contract (which must not override, modify or affect the Conditions); e.g. explanation of procedure to be followed in complying with the Conditions.
6. Insurances required under clause 19, (1) (b) and (2). Fire is covered by 20. Injuries under clause 18 are the contractor's liability, but he is required under 19 (1) (a) to insure against injury to persons. National Insurance is a statutory liability of his which he cannot disclaim.
7. Any restrictions on the site or existing buildings, e.g. means of access for men and materials, portions reserved for the employer's use, etc.
8. Materials and workmanship generally, samples, etc.
9. Plant, tools, scaffolding.
10. Any tests required of materials or finished work, with provisional sum to cover cost of tests which are satisfactory.
11. Sheds, offices, messrooms, etc.
12. Latrines.
13. Clerk of Works' office and attendance.
14. Telephone on the works.
15. Watching and protective lighting.
16. Protection of the works from weather, etc.
17. Artificial lighting for the works.
18. Water for the works and temporary plumbing.
19. Appliances and fuel for drying the building.
20. General attendance.
21. Service to be given to sub-contractors.
22. Coins, antiquities and articles of value found (in the case of the R.I.B.A. contract these are covered by clause 34).

23. General cleaning up, removal of rubbish, etc.

24. Provisional sum for contingencies.

Note.—The above are exclusive of actual temporary work which may be required owing to the nature of the particular job (e.g. dust-proof screens, diversion of services, etc.).

2. INDEX TO SPECIFICATION

INDEX

Note.—If preferred, references can be to clause numbers of the specification instead of to pages.

3. SCHEDULE OF FINISHINGS IN THE SPECIFICATION*

SCHEDULE OF FINISHINGS

Note: s.w. = softwood.

Room	Ceiling	Walls	Floor	Dado or frieze	Skirting
First Floor.					
Bedrooms	Plaster & dist.	Plaster & dist.	1″ (25 mm) s.w. boards	—	6″ × 1″ (150 × 25 mm) square s.w.
Bathroom	″ ″	Plaster & flat paint	1″ (25 mm) s.w. boards and rubber tile	6″ × 6″ (150 × 150 mm) col. glazed 1·2 m high	—
W.C.	″ ″	″ ″	″ ″	—	3″ × ½″ (75 × 13 mm) rounded teak
Landing	″ ″	Plaster & dist.	1″ (25 mm) s.w. boards	—	6″ × 1″ (150 × 25 mm) square s.w.
Ground Floor.					
Dining Room	Plaster & dist.	Plaster & flat paint	1″ (25 mm) oak block	—	6″ × 1″ (150 × 25 mm) oak moulded
Sitting Room	″ ″	Plaster & flat paint (including frieze)	″ ″	3″ × 1″ (75 × 25 mm) s.w. frieze rail	″ ″
Hall	″ ″	Plaster & flat paint	6″ × 6″ (150 × 150 mm) quarry tile	—	Quarry tile 3″ (75 mm) high
Kitchen	″ ″	Plaster & gloss paint	″ ″	—	″ ″
Larder, etc.	″ ″	Plaster & dist.	″ ″	—	″ ″

* Where room data sheets are not provided.

4. TENDER INVITATIONS AND FORM (N.J.C.C. CODE)

A. Preliminary enquiry for invitation to tender

Dear Sirs,

Heading

I am/We are authorised to prepare a preliminary list of tenderers for the construction of the works described below.

Will you please indicate whether you wish to be invited to submit a tender for these works. Your acceptance will imply your agreement to submit a wholly *bona fide* tender in accordance with the principles laid down in the 'Code of Procedure for Selective Tendering 1969' [1] and not to divulge your tender price to any person or body before the time for submission of tenders. Once the contract has been let, I/we undertake to supply all tenderers with a list of the firms who tendered, and lists of the tender prices.

You are requested to reply by ... Your inability to accept will in no way prejudice your opportunities for tendering for further work under my/our direction: neither will your inclusion in the preliminary list at this stage guarantee that you will subsequently receive a formal invitation to tender for these works.

Yours faithfully ...

a Job...
b Building owner...
c Architect...
d Quantity surveyor...
e Consultants with supervisory duties...
f Location of site ... (site plan enclosed)
g General description of works...
h Approximate cost range £... to £...
i Form of Contract... Clause 23(j) of the RIBA Conditions of Contract will/will not [3] apply. Clause 31 A/B [3] will apply.
j Anticipated date for possession...
k Period for completion of works...
l Approximate date for dispatch of all tender documents...
m Tender period ... weeks

B. Formal invitation to tender

Dear Sirs,

Heading

Following your acceptance of the invitation to tender for the above, I/we now have pleasure in enclosing the following:

a two copies of the bill(s) of quantities;
b general arrangement drawings indicating the general character and shape and disposition of the works;
c two copies of the form of tender;
d an addressed envelope for the return of the tender, and instructions relating thereto.

Will you please also note:

1 working drawings and details may be inspected at ...
2 the site may be inspected by arrangement with the owner/architect [2]
3 tendering procedure will be in accordance with the principles of the 'Code of Procedure for Selective Tendering 1969' [1]
4 examination and correction of priced bill(s) (Section 9 of the Code), Alternative 1/Alternative 2 [2] will apply.

The completed form of tender is to be sealed in the endorsed envelope provided and delivered or sent by post to reach ... not later than ... hours on ... the ... day of ... 19 ...

Will you please acknowledge receipt of this letter and enclosures and confirm that you are able to submit a tender in accordance with these instructions.

Yours faithfully,

Architect/Quantity Surveyor...

C. Form of tender

Tender for... (description of Works)

To... (Building Owner)

Sir/s,

I/We having read the conditions of contract and bill(s) of quantities delivered to me/us and having examined the drawings referred to therein do hereby offer to execute and complete the whole of the works described for the sum of ... £... and within ... [4] weeks from date of possession and I/we undertake in the event of your acceptance to execute with you a form of contract embodying all the conditions and terms contained in this offer.

I/We agree that should obvious errors in pricing or errors in arithmetic be discovered before acceptance of this offer in the priced bill(s) of quantities submitted by me/us these errors be corrected in accordance with Alternative 1/Alternative 2 [2] contained in Section 9 of the 'Code of Procedure for Selective Tendering 1969'. [1]

This tender remains open for consideration for ... weeks. [5]

Dated this ... day of ... 19 ...
Name ...
Address ...

References

Published by RIBA Publications Ltd for the National Joint Consultative Committee of Architects, Quantity Surveyors and Builders. It is obtainable from the RIBA, RICS and NFBTE. Delete as appropriate.

[3] Delete either A or B.
[4] To be completed before Form of Tender is sent out.
[5] Delete if not required.

5. LETTER ASKING FOR PRICED BILL OF QUANTITIES FOR EXAMINATION

March 7th, 1969.

By Hand

Messrs. R. & S., Ltd.,
Contractors,
48, High Street,
Westborough.

DEAR SIRS,

Extension to Messrs. X. & Co.'s Factory

Your tender for the above is under consideration for acceptance and
* {we should be glad if you would send your priced bill of quantities }
{we enclose a blank copy of the bill of quantities and should be glad if you}
will complete it with your prices and forward
to the quantity surveyors for examination, together with supporting estimates
for any materials which you have entered in the Schedule of Basic Prices.

Yours faithfully,

(*Signed*) L. M. & N.

Note.—The quantity surveyors may quite possibly write this letter themselves
on instructions by telephone from the architect to do so.

* Alternatives according to the procedure adopted.

6. SCHEDULE OF BASIC PRICES FOR MATERIALS

SCHEDULE OF BASIC PRICES FOR MATERIALS

No adjustment of the contract sum under the provisions of clause 31 of the Conditions of Contract will be made in respect of materials and goods required for the Works, other than those included in this Schedule.

No adjustment of the contract sum under the provisions of clause 31 of the Conditions of Contract will be made in respect of fuel, haulage or mechanical plant.

Materials and Goods	Basic price delivered	
	Unit	£ s. d.

7. LETTER OF ACCEPTANCE TO CONTRACTOR

March 25th, 1969.

Messrs. R. & S., Ltd.,
Contractors,
48, High Street,
Westborough.

DEAR SIRS,

Extension to Messrs. X. & Co.'s Factory

We are instructed by Messrs. X. & Co. to accept your tender dated February 6th, 1969 in the sum of £10,346 for the above and we enclose for your information a copy of the amounts of the other tenders received.

We are advised by the quantity surveyors that there were only minor clerical errors in your priced bill and that they will send you a note of these.

Our clients are anxious for work to be started as soon as possible and we should be glad if you would telephone and arrange an appointment here to discuss a starting date and progress schedule. We will at the same time hand you two sets of drawings and give you our instructions for starting this work.

We will write to you tomorrow with instructions for the acceptance of estimates of those nominated sub-contractors whose work is urgent.

Yours faithfully,

(*Signed*) L. M. & N.

8. APPOINTMENT OF A NOMINATED SUB-CONTRACTOR

Standard Form for Nomination of Sub-Contractors

For use in connection with the RIBA Standard Forms of [main] Contract 1963 Edition

To [main contractor]

Job title and ref.

Prime cost or
provisional sum

on page number
of the bill or specification

Name of nominated
sub-contractor

Address and tel. no.

Amount of estimate

£   :   :

An estimate for the work to which the above-mentioned prime cost or provisional sum relates has been obtained on the Standard Form of Estimate for Nominated Sub-Contractors.

The firm named above is hereby nominated as a sub-contractor under the main contract to execute this work.

A completed copy of this estimate on the Standard Form is enclosed together with copies of the drawings, specifications and/or bills of quantities, upon which the estimate is based, as are listed below.

Unless you have any reasonable objection under the terms of Clause 27(a) of the contract, you should enter into a sub-contract with this firm before the expiration of the period mentioned in the last paragraph of their estimate incorporating, inter alia, the conditions of this completed Standard Form of Estimate.

A Standard Form of Sub-Contract [issued under the sanction of and approved by the National Federation of Building Trades Employers, 82 New Cavendish St, W1, and the Federation of Associations of Specialists and Sub-Contractors, 14 Bryanston St, London W1 and also approved by The Committee of Associations of Specialist Engineering Contractors, 172 Buckingham Palace Rd, London SW1] is available for use in this connection.

Architect   ....

Address and tel. no.   ....

....

....

Signature and date   ....196..........

List of drawings,
bills of quantities
specifications
attached   ....

....

....

Circulation of this document and all enclosures to:	Main Contractor ☐ ☐	Quantity Surveyor ☐ ☐	Nominated Sub-Contractor ☐ ☐	Clerk of Works ☐	Consulting Engineer [s] ☐ ☐	Architect's File ☐ ☐

9. AGENDA FOR FIRST SITE MEETING

Architect's name
and address

Agenda for first site meeting

Job _____

Date and place of meeting _____

_____

1 Introductions _____

_____

_____

_____

2 Programme of work
a Sequence of work and phasing
b Variations to scope of the contract
c Contract period
d Draft progress chart
e Progress photographs

3 Administration
a Issue of drawings and documents
  - i Architects
  - ii Structural consultants
  - iii Mechanical and electrical consultants
  - iv Quantity surveyors
  - v Specialist drawings
  - vi Additional copies of drawings

b Contract documents
c Variation orders
d Daywork sheets
e Interim valuations
  - i Payments to sub-contractors
  - ii Receipts for payments

f Site meetings and minutes
g Correspondence
h Insurance
i Notice to local authority. Statutory consents
j Defects liability period

4 Site organization
a Contractors' huts and lavatories
b Access to site and notice boards
c Dumping of topsoil and spoil
d Site protection
e Temporary services
f Liaison with employer
g Control of noise and disturbance

5 Supply and approval of materials
a Architects
b Structural consultants
c Mechanical and electrical consultants
d Materials reserved or already on order

6 P.C. and provisional sums
a Orders to be placed or confirmed now
b Sub-contracts to be made now
c Further sub-contracts and orders
d Contractors responsibility for co-ordination

7 Engineering services
a Mechanical
b Electrical
c Co-ordination by general contractor

8 Other business

9 Next meeting

10. CLERK OF WORKS' REPORT FORM

No...............

....

....

CLERK OF WORKS' REPORT for the week ending.....................19......

X, Y, & Z, Architects.

State of Works

Drawings received		Drawings required		Men employed on Works	
				Excavators	. .
				Bricklayers	. .
				Labourers	. .
				Carpenters	. .
				Labourers	. .
				Masons	.
				Labourers	. .
				Plasterers	. .
Visitors		Weather		Labourers	. .
				Tilers .	. .
				Labourers	. .
	Mon.			Slaters	. .
				Labourers	.
	Tues.			Plumbers	. .
				Mates	. .
	Wed.			Smiths	. .
				Labourers	.
	Thurs.			Electricians	. .
				Engineers	. .
	Fri.			Painters	. .
	Sat.			Total number	.

....

Clerk of Works.

Additional Notes Overleaf.

11. FORM OF ARCHITECT'S INSTRUCTION

Architect's name
and address

**Architect's
Instruction**

Works

situate at

To contractor   Instruction no.

Under the terms of the **Contract**   Date

dated

I/We issue the following instructions. Where applicable the contract sum
will be adjusted in accordance with the terms of the relevant Condition.

For office use: Approx costs

Instructions   £ omit   £ add

Office reference   **Signed**

Architect/Supervising officer

Notes   Amount of contract sum £

± Approximate value of previous instructions £

£

± Approximate value of this instruction £

Approximate adjusted total £

To Contractor ☐   Copies to Employer ☐   Quantity surveyor ☐   Clerk of works ☐   Structural consultant ☐

Heating consultant ☐   Electrical consultant ☐ .   ☐   ☐   Architect's file ☐

12. VALUATION FOR CERTIFICATE*

SOUTHDOWN SCHOOL

Approximate Statement for Certificate No. 5.

August 15th, 1969.

		£
Approximate value of work done . . .		13,430
Unfixed materials on site		1,500
		14,930
Less retention 10%		1,493
		13,437
Price Adjustment—Labour: add . . .		113
		13,550
By previous certificates		9,500
Balance.		£4,050

† Net Amounts included in the above for Nominated Sub-contractors, subject to Cash Discount.

Firm	Service	Previous	Present	Total
		£	£	£
Messrs. G. H. & Co.	R.C. Construction	3,800	1,200	5,000
,, I. J. & Co.	Felt Roofing	—	500	500
,, K. L. & Son	Metal Windows	—	1,000	1,000

* If prepared by a quantity surveyor, the R.I.C.S. form reproduced on pages 292 and 293 may have been used.

† Note that Nominated *Suppliers* are not required by the R.I.B.A. contract to be mentioned.

13. RECORD OF MEETING

record of meeting

Architect's name
and address

number

job

location of meeting

date held

present	representing	present	representing

The following items summarise the discussion. Please take the appropriate action by the agreed date

no.	item	action by	agreed date
	Distribution of this record: copies to	Architects	

date   signed

L

4. VALUATION FOR CERTIFICATE

Valuation

Quantity Surveyor	R.S. & T. Chartered Quantity Surveyors Bank House, Northtown.
Architect/S&O.	L.M.N. Esq. FRIBA Chartered Architect 21 High Street, Southtown

My/Your current valuation under the Contract

dated the 23rd day of May 19 69 for

indicates that a(n) interim *balance is due

the works known as situate at	Southtown Church of England Primary School Newfields, Southtown
from the employer of	Blankchester Diocesan Board of Finance Church House Blankchester
to the contractor of	X Y Z Ltd 55 High Street, Blankchester

Contract sum £ 45,500

Valuation no.	5
Date	19th Nov 1969
Date on site	18th Nov 1969
For certificate no.	5
†Gross valuation £	15,043
Net retention stated below £	1,493
Net valuation £	13,550
Previously certified £	9,500
£	4,050

Balance Indicated (in words)	Four Thousand and fifty pounds

Statement of Retention

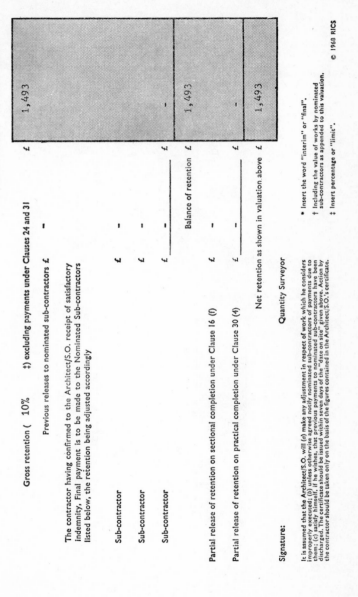

Gross retention (10% ‡) excluding payments under Clauses 24 and 31   £   1,493

Previous releases to nominated sub-contractors £   —

The contractor having confirmed to the Architect/S.O. receipt of satisfactory Indemnity, Final payment is to be made to the Nominated Sub-contractors listed below, the retention being adjusted accordingly

Sub-contractor   £   —

Sub-contractor   £   —

Sub-contractor   £   —

Balance of retention   £   1,493

Partial release of retention on sectional completion under Clause 16 (f)   £   —

Partial release of retention on practical completion under Clause 30 (4)   £   —

Net retention as shown in valuation above   £   1,493

Signature: Quantity Surveyor

It is assumed that the Architect/S.O. will (a) make any adjustment in respect of work which he considers improperly executed; (b) unless otherwise agreed notify nominated sub-contractors of payments due to them; (c) satisfy himself, if he wishes, that previous payments to nominated sub-contractors have been discharged. The certificate should be issued within seven days of the "date on site" given above. Action by the contractor should be taken only on the basis of the figures contained in the Architect/S.O.'s certificate.

* Insert the word "interim" or "final".

† Including the value of works by nominated sub-contractors as appended to this valuation.

‡ Insert percentage or "limit".

© 1968 RICS

15. STATEMENT OF NOMINATED SUB-CONTRACTORS' AMOUNTS

This form is A4 size and the last line appearing here is at the bottom of the form.

Quantity Surveyor

Statement of amounts included in respect of

Nominated Sub-contractors

| Works known as | Southtown Church of England Primary School |
| situate at | Newfields, Southtown |

Valuation no.	5
Date	19th Nov 1969
Date on site	18th Nov 1969
For certificate no.	5

The following amounts have been included in the calculation of this valuation in respect of work materials or goods, executed or supplied by the nominated sub-contractor(s) listed below.

The sums stated are the gross amounts due to the named nominated sub-contractor(s). No account has been taken of any retentions which the contractor might withhold under the terms of the sub-contract(s), or of any discounts for cash to which the contractor might be entitled if settling the accounts within 14 days of the receipt of the architect's certificate or of a duplicate copy.

Payment of nominated suppliers is not conditional upon the issue of a certificate

Nominated sub-contractor		Gross total to date £	Certified previously £	Balance £
G.H. & Co. Ltd	R.C. construction	5,000	3,800	1,200
I.J. & Co. Ltd.	Felt Roofing	500	-	500
K.L. & Son Ltd.	Metal Windows	1,000	1,000	-

Signature   Quantity Surveyor

16. FORM OF ARCHITECT'S CERTIFICATE

Architect's name
and address

Certificate

* I/We certify that under the terms of the Contract

To be presented to the
employer for payment

dated   day of   19   for the

works known as   Serial no. **2GB   0199**

situate at   Date of issue

*   payment as detailed below is due   Date of valuation

from the employer   Instalment no.

of

to the contractor

of

† Gross amount £

Net retention stated below £

Contract sum £   Net amount £

Previously certified £

Amount due
for payment   £
(in words)

Signed

Architect/Supervising officer

* Insert word 'Interim' or 'Final'
† Including the value of works by nominated sub-contractors as
detailed on the direction relating to this certificate

Statement of Retention

Gross retention under the terms of the Contract £

Previous releases to nominated sub-contractors £
The contractor having confirmed receipt of satisfactory indemnity,
final payment is to be made to the nominated sub-contractors listed below
the retention being adjusted accordingly

Sub-contractor   £

Sub-contractor   £

Sub-contractor   £   £

Balance of retention £

Partial release of retention £

Net retention as shown
in certificate above £

© 1967 RIBA

17. DIRECTION ON CERTIFYING

Architect's name
and address

· I/We direct that under the terms of the Contract for the

Direction

works known as

of amounts included
for nominated sub-contractors
in certificate

situate at

the following amounts have been included in the calculation of the certificate to
which this direction relates, in respect of work, materials or goods, executed or
supplied by the nominated sub-contractor(s) listed below.

Serial no.

Date of issue

The sums stated are the GROSS amounts due to the named nominated sub-
contractor(s). No account has been taken of any retentions which the contractor
might withold under the terms of the sub-contract(s), or of any discounts for cash
to which the contractor might be entitled if settling the accounts within 14 days of the
receipt of the architect's certificate or of a duplicate copy thereof.

Date of valuation

Instalment no.

Nominated sub-contractor	Gross total to date	Certified previously	Balance included in certificate

Signed

Architect/Supervising officer

18. NOTIFICATION TO NOMINATED SUB-CONTRACTORS

Notification

to nominated sub-contractor
concerning amount included
in certificate

Architect's name
and address

to nominated
sub-contractor

I/We inform you that under the terms of the Contract for the

Serial no.

Date of issue

works known as

situate at

Date of valuation

a certificate has been issued for presentation to the employer

The contractor

Instalment no.

of

has been directed that in the said certificate an amount is due to you as follows

Gross total to date	Certified previously	Balance included in certificate
£	£	£

Signed

Architect/Supervising officer.

The sum stated is the gross amount due. No account has been taken of any retentions which the contractor might withhold under the terms of the sub-contract or of any discounts for cash to which the contractor might be entitled if settling the account within 14 days of the receipt of the architect's certificate or of a duplicate copy thereof.

© 1967 RIBA

19. CERTIFICATE OF PRACTICAL COMPLETION

Architect's name and address:

**RIBA Certificate of
Practical Completion**

Job title and no.:

Serial no.:

To   [main contractor]:

In accordance with Clause 15(1) of the RIBA Standard Form of Contract, I/we certify that subject to the making good of any
outstanding items, or of any defects, shrinkages and other faults which appear during the defects liability period,

[delete a or b as necessary]

a   the works were completed to my/our satisfaction and taken into possession on:

and that the said defects liability period will end on:

b   a part or section of the works, namely:

the approximate value of which I estimate to be: £

was completed to my/our satisfaction and taken into possession on:

and that in relation to the said part or section of the works,
the said defects liability period will end on:

I/we declare that one moiety of the retention moneys deducted under previous certificates in respect of the said works or sections
thereof is to be released.

Signature: Chartered architect   Date:

Original to: Main contractor ☐   Copies to: Client ☐   Quantity surveyor ☐   Clerk of works ☐   Architect's file ☐

Structural consultant ☐   Heating consultant ☐   Electrical consultant ☐   ☐

Copyright by R.I.B.A.

20. CERTIFICATE OF MAKING GOOD DEFECTS

Architect's name and address:

**RIBA Certificate of
Making Good Defects**

Job title and no.:

Serial no.:

To [main contractor]:

In accordance with Clause 15(4) of the RIBA Standard Form of Contract, I/we certify that all outstanding items and all defects, shrinkages and other faults which appeared during the defects liability period in respect of:

[delete a or b as necessary]

a   the works were completed and/or made good to my/our satisfaction on:

and I/we declare that the residue of the retention moneys deducted under previous certificates is to be released.

b   the part or section of the works referred to in my/our Certificate
                                        of Practical Completion dated:

were completed to my/our satisfaction on:

and I/we declare that the residue of the retention moneys deducted under previous certificates in respect of such part or section of the works is to be released.

Signature: Chartered architect   Date:

Original to: Main contractor ☐   Copies to: Client ☐   Quantity surveyor ☐   Clerk of works ☐   Architect's file ☐

Structural consultant ☐   Heating consultant ☐   Electrical consultant ☐   ☐

Copyright by R.I.B.A.

21. FORM OF FINAL STATEMENT OF ACCOUNT

HOUSE IN STATION ROAD, SOUTHTOWN

Statement of Final Cost

March 14th, 1969.

		£	s.	d.
Amount of contract		2,573	0	0

Additional Works.

	£	s.	d.			
1. Additional lavatory basin in Bedroom 3 .	25	3	6			
2. Painted walls to Kitchen in lieu of distemper	8	7	6			
3. Oak block floor to Dining Room in lieu of beech	7	1	3			
4. Two additional shelves to Larder . .	2	7	8			
5. Stone paving to path in lieu of gravel .	12	3	7			
				55	3	6
				£2,628	3	6

Less Omissions.

	£	s.	d.			
1. Wardrobe in Bedroom 4 . . .	17	2	9			
2. Dwarf wall in lieu of fence to boundary .	6	9	1			
3. * Net omission from adjustment of provisional sums and sundry small items .	19	1	1			
				42	12	11
				£2,585	10	7

Add.

		£	s.	d.
Increased cost of wages and materials . .		19	9	3
		£2,604	19	10

Note. Both additions and omissions can be extended *ad lib.* with suitable items.

---

* This item is the difference remaining after all items detailed have been added or deducted. If it can be on the omission side, all the better. It is arrived at by working backwards from the final total.

22. ACCOUNT FOR FEES (on the architect's headed note-paper)

To Messrs. C. D. & E., Ltd. February 28th, 1969.

STATEMENT NO. 3 (FINAL)

To X, Y & Son.

Name of the job

From 1st May, 1966 to 21st February, 1969	To Professional Services :			
	Taking instructions and advising at Inception			
	Preparing Preliminary and Final Designs and approximate estimate of cost			
	Preparing Design Details and Production Drawings and specification			
	Selecting and instructing consultants			
	Instructing Quantity Surveyors			
	Obtaining statutory consents			
	Inviting competitive tenders and advising thereon			
	Preparing contract documents			
	Instructing contractors and supplying two sets of drawings and specification			
	Supervising work during progress and certifying completion			
	Certifying payments and passing final account			
	Final account as agreed with Messrs. A.B. & Co. . £83,268. 13. 4			
	R.I.B.A. Scale of Charges, Part 2 and Table A. Abatement of Fee for Engineering Services (b) as agreed.	£	s.	d.
	(a) Building Work £62,158. 17. 6 @ 6%	3,729	10	8
	(b) Engineering Services £21,109. 15. 10 @ 4%	844	7	10
	(c) Survey of site . .	75	0	0
		£4,648	18	6
	Less received on account: Statement No. 1 £2500			
	,, ,, £1000			
		3,500	0	0
		£1,148	18	6
	Plus expenses 1st April 1968 to date: £ s. d.			
	Drawings . 24 6 0			
	Travelling . 45 7 6			
	Hotel . 22 0 0			
	Trunk calls . 5 4 6			
	(as agreed)	96	18	0
	Balance due . .	£1,245	16	6

DY/ABC *With compliments.*

23. JOB HISTORY SHEET

Job .... Job No...............

Address...

Client ....

Address.................................... Tel. No. ....

Sponsoring Authorities...........................(Officer...........................)

.... (Officer...........................)

Local Authority...

Adjoining Owner(s) ....

....

Party Wall Surveyors..

Date of Instructions...........................

Final design approved .... Estimated cost ....

Production Drawings commenced .... completed ....

Application for Planning Consent...

Approval received........................... Reference ....

Application for Building Regs. Approval.....................................

Approval received .... Reference ....

Application for Approval of Means of Escape....................................

Approval received .... Reference ....

Quantity Surveyors...Tel. No.....................

Consultants...Tel. No.....................

....Tel. No.....................

....Tel. No.....................

Bills of Quantities commenced ....completed....................

Tenders invited ....Tenders received..........

Successful contractor ....Tel. No....................

Address...

Contract amount........................... Date of contract...........................

Nominated Sub-contractors and Suppliers

.... | ....

.... | ....

.... | ....

.... | ....

General Foreman...Tel. No.....................

Clerk of Works ....Tel. No....................

Starting Date ....Completion Date.......................

Defects Liability Period commences .... expires.......................

Final Account certified...............................Amount.......................

24. STAFF TIME RECORDS

(Monthly sheet for each member of the staff.)

J. G. JONES.

Salary....................................   July, 1968.

	Southtown School	N.W. Hospital	London Bakery	Westborough Housing I	Westborough Housing II					
1										
2	7½									
3	7½									
4	6½	1								
5	7½									
6			7½							
7										
8										
9	7½									
10	3			4½						
11	3+2*			4½						
12	7½									
13	7½+1									
14										
15										
16	7½+2									
17	6				1½					
18					7½					
19	7½									
20	7½									
21	+3									
22										
23		7½								]Away
24										ill.
25										
26	7½									
27	3				4½					
28										
29										
30					7½+2					
31					7½+2					
	96½+8	8½	7½	9	28½+4 =	150+12				

* 2 hours' overtime is indicated by +2. The sheet total will show the total overtime to be paid for.

25. PAGE OF DRAWING RECORD BOOK

Job............................　　　　　　　　Job No........................

Drawing		Scale	Date	Drawn by	Subject	Issued to			
Prefix	Number					Client	Local Authy.	Q.S.	Contractor
P	1 A/B/	*1/16″	20.1.69	E.J.K.	Grd. Floor Plan	(1)† 21/1/69 A/(1) 3/2/69 B/(2) 20/2/69		B/(1) 20/2/69	
P	2 A/	1/16″	20.1.69	E.J.K.	1st Floor Plan				
P	3	1/16″	20.1.69	E.J.K.	Elevations				
E	4	⅛″	15.5.69	L.M.N.	Grd. Floor Plan				

Note.—This example is of one left-hand page. It would be continued on the right-hand page with further columns for issue of drawings, e.g. to Consultants, Clerk of Works, etc.

　* Or metric scale if used.
　† The number in brackets indicates the number of copies issued.

26. SALARY STATEMENT

Week Ending February 14th, 1969.

C. W. Reynolds.

	£	s.	d.
Salary	10	0	0
Overtime 3 hrs. @ 7/–	1	1	0
	£11	1	0

	£	s.	d.			
Income Tax	1	19	0			
National Insurance		16	8			
				2	15	8
				£8	5	4
Expenses				—	—	—
				£8	5	4

27. SCHEDULE OF DOORS   In pocket on back cover

28. ROOM DATA SHEET

Folders between pages 306 and 307

29. PROGRESS SCHEDULE

APPENDIX 2

BIBLIOGRAPHY

Note. Books on Design or General Building Construction are not included. Prices are, of course, subject to alteration.

Specification

B.S. Handbook No. 3	B.S.I.	£6. 10. 0
Sectional List of British Standards—Building	,,	—
Sectional List of B.S. Codes of Practice for Buildings	,,	—
British Standards (as required)	,,	varying
Codes of Practice (as required)	,,	,,
Specification (annually)	Architectural Press	55/-
The Building Regulations 1965	H.M.S.O.	13/-
The Building (First Amendment) Regulations 1965	,,	6d
The Building Regulations Explained and Illustrated for Residential Buildings (Powell Smith & Whyte)	Crosby Lockwood	35/-
Guide to the Building Regulations 1965	H.M.S.O.	1/6
The Building Regulations 1965 Technical Memoranda—Fire—Stairs—Space and General Index	,,	4/-
The Building Standards (Scotland) Regulations 1963–1964	,,	13/-
Explanatory Memoranda to Building Standards (Scotland) Regulations	,,	24/6
* Ministry of Public Building & Works Advisory Leaflets	,,	5d each
* National Building Studies: Bulletins; Reports; Research Papers	,,	varying
* Post-War Building Studies	,,	,,
Building Research Station Digests (monthly)	,,	6/6 per annum
* Forest Products Research Bulletins: No. 1. Dry Rot in Wood	,,	4/-

* For details see *Government Publications: Sectional List No. 61 (Building)*: H.M.S.O.

Specification (*continued*)—

* Road Research Board Bulletins	H.M.S.O.	varying
Preambles for Bills of Quantities	G.L.C.	70/– unbound 80/– bound
Constructional Byelaws with Explanatory Memorandum (for London practice)	G.L.C.	5/3
Specification Writing (Willis)	Crosby Lockwood	20/–

Approvals and Controls

Local Government in England and Wales (Jackson)	Penguin	3/6
Local Government (Mapstone)	Estates Gazette	27/6

General Surveying Practice (*see also* **Law**)

Land Surveying (Jenkins)	Estates Gazette	21/-
Practical Surveying (Usill)	Technical Press	30/-
Report Writing and Proofs of Evidence (Wilks)	Estates Gazette	25/-

Quantities

†The Standard Method of Measurement of Building Works	R.I.C.S.		25/-
†Code for the Measurement of Building Work in Small Dwelling Houses	,,		7/6
Elements of Quantity Surveying (metric) (Willis)	Crosby Lockwood		35/-
An Example in Quantity Surveying (Willis)	,,	,,	40/-
More Advanced Quantity Surveying (Willis)	,,	,,	66/-
Ditto. Supplement: Two metric examples	,,	,,	15/-
Junior Principles of Quantity Surveying (Wood)	Estates Gazette		60/-
Principles of Quantity Surveying (Wood)	,,	,,	116/-

Estimating and Pricing

The Architects' Journal (in an issue about the end of each quarter)	Architectural Press	2/-
Building	The Builder	1/6
Spon's Architects' and Builders' Price Book	Spon	45/-

* For details see *Government Publications: Sectional List No. 61 (Building)*: H.M.S.O.
† Separate imperial and metric measure editions, each at the same price.

Estimating and Pricing (*continued*)—

Laxton's Builders' Price Book	Kelly's Directories	50/-
Definition of Prime Cost of Daywork under a Building Contract	R.I.C.S. ,,	1/6
Do. of Daywork of a Jobbing or Maintenance Nature	,,	1/6
Do. of Daywork for Heating &c. Contracts	,,	1/6
Do. of Daywork for Electrical Contracts	,,	1/6
Schedule of Basic Plant Charges	,,	10/-
The Cost of Building—Variations from 1914 to date	The Builder	2/6
Dept. of Education Building Bulletin No. 4 (Cost Study)	H.M.S.O.	under revision
Cost Planning of Buildings (Ferry)	Crosby Lockwood	25/-

Building Contracts

Standard Form of Building Contract for use with Quantities, Private Edition	R.I.B.A.	⎫
Ditto. without Quantities, ditto		⎬ 10/- each
Ditto. with Quantities, Local Authorities' edition		
Ditto. without Quantities, ditto	,,	⎭
Fixed Fee Form of Prime Cost Contract	,,	15/-
Agreement for Minor Building Works	,,	3/-
A Code of Procedure for Selective Tendering (revised 1969)	N.J.C.C.	2/-
Selective Tendering for Local Authorities (M.P.B.W. Management Handbook 2)	,,	2/-
Standard Forms of Estimate and Nomination for Nominated Sub-contractors	R.I.B.A.	45/- (3 pads)
Form of Tender for use by Nominated Suppliers	R.I.B.A. & R.I.C.S.	3d
Form of Warranty to be given by a Nominated Sub-contractor	R.I.B.A.	20/- per 100
Form of Warranty to be given by a Nominated Supplier	,,	20/- per 100
The Placing and Management of Contracts for Building and Civil Engineering Work (Banwell Report)	H.M.S.O.	4/-
General Conditions of Government Contracts for Building and Civil Engineering Works (Form CCC/Wks/1)	,,	8d

Building Contracts (*continued*)—

Apprenticeship Scheme Contract (Form MOW/AT/4)	H.M.S.O.	3d
Standard Form of Sub-contract	N.F.B.T.E.	3/–
The Evolution of the R.I.B.A. Form of Contract (Close)	N.F.T.B.E.	1/6
Civil Engineering Procedure	Institution of Civil Engineers	10/–
I.C.E. Conditions of Contract	,,	2/6
Handbook (annually)—incorporates I.C.E. Contract, Working Rule Agreement and Schedule of Dayworks	Federation of Civil Engineering Contractors	15/–
Hudson on Building Contracts (Rimmer & Wallace)	Sweet & Maxwell	£8
Law and Practice of Building Contracts (Keating)	,, ,,	105/–
Emden & Gill's Building Contracts and Practice	Butterworth	72/–
The Standard Form of Building Contract (Walker-Smith and Close)	Knight	55/-
Contract Administration (Aqua Group)	Crosby Lockwood	18/–

Law (*see also* **Building Contracts**)

John Citizen and The Law (Rubinstein)	Penguin	7/6
Elements of English Law (Geldart)	Oxford U.P.	7/6
The Book of English Law (Jenks)	Murray	35/–
Principles of the English Law of Contract (Anson)	Oxford U.P.	55/-
General Principles of the Law of Torts (James)	Butterworth	40/–
Phipson's Manual of Evidence (Elliott)	Sweet & Maxwell	25/- (paper)
The Law relating to the Architect (Rimmer)	Stevens & Sons	47/6
Architects' Registration Act, 1931	H.M.S.O.	1/-
Ditto. 1938	,,	1/-
London Building Acts (Amendment) Act, 1939 (for London practice)	,,	9/-
Public Health Act, 1936 (for Practice outside London)	,,	17/6
Public Health Act, 1961 (Ditto)	,,	5/6
War Damage Act, 1964	,,	1/–
Town and Country Planning Act, 1947	,,	12/6
Town and Country Planning Act, 1953	,,	4d

Law (*see also* **Building Contracts**) (*continued*)—

Town and Country Planning Act, 1954	H.M.S.O.	5/-
Town and Country Planning Act 1959	,,	4/6
Town and Country Planning Act 1962	,,	20/-
Town and Country Planning Act 1963	,,	8d
Town and Country Planning Act 1968	,,	12/6
Housing Act 1936	,,	4/6
Housing Act 1949	,,	4/-
Housing Act 1957	,,	4/6
Offices, Shops & Railway Premises Act 1963	,,	5/6
Ditto. A General Guide	,,	2/6
Arbitration Act, 1950	,,	2/-
The Architect as Arbitrator	R.I.B.A.	10/–
The Public Health Acts (4 vols.)	Knight	£16/16/0
The Law of Dilapidations (Adkin)	Estates Gazette	37/6
The Law of Fixtures (Adkin & Bowen)	,, ,,	21/6
Arbitrations and Awards (Soper)	,, ,,	47/6
Cheshire's Modern Law of Real Property	Butterworth	75/-
Outline of Planning Law (Heap)	Sweet & Maxwell	32/6

General

R.I.B.A. Directory	R.I.B.A.	£8/8/- (free to members and students)
The Charter and Bye-Laws of the R.I.B.A.	,,	—
Code of Professional Conduct	,,	—
Regulations made by the Council in pursuance of the Architects (Registration) Act, 1931	A.R.C.U.K.	1/-
Conditions of Engagement	R.I.B.A.	2/6
Guide to the Conditions of Engagement	,,	—
Management Accounting for the Architect	,,	£6/10/0
Job Book	,,	£5 (2 vols.)
Journal of the Town Planning Institute (subscription 42/- per annum)	Town Planning Institute	5/-
Schedule of Professional Charges	,, ,,	1/-
Town Planning Institute Year Book	,, ,,	7/6
Royal Institution of Chartered Surveyors —List of Members	R.I.C.S.	42/- (members 10/6)
The Services of the Chartered Quantity Surveyor	,,	—

General (*continued*)—

Notice Forms A to G for use under the London Building Act (for London practice)	R.I.B.A.	7d each
S.I. 1948, No. 1145. The Building (Safety, Health and Welfare) Regulations 1948	H.M.S.O.	3/-
S.I. 1961, No. 1580. Construction (General Provisions) Regulations	,,	1/9
S.I. 1961, No. 1581. Ditto. (Lifting Operations)	,,	2/-
Guide to the Construction Regulations	N.F.B.T.E.	4/-
Constitution, Rules and Regulations	National Joint Council for the Building Industry	—
National Working Rules for the Building Industry	,, ,,	3/6
Holidays-with-Pay Scheme	Building & Civil Engineering Holidays Scheme Management, Ltd.	—
National Agreement as to Working Rules and Conditions in the Heating Ventilating and Domestic Engineering Industry	Joint Conciliation Committee of the Industry	1/-
Year Book of the Heating and Ventilating Industry	Heating & Ventilating Contractors' Assocn.	£2/15/0
Industrial Agreements and National Working Rules	National Federated Electrical Association	5/-
The Electrical Contractors' Year Book	Electrical Contractors' Assocn.	42/6
Government Publications: Sectional List No. 30 (Ministry of Works)	H.M.S.O.	—
Ditto. Sectional List No. 61 (Publications on Building)	,,	—
The Concise Oxford Dictionary	Oxford U.P.	25/-
Complete Plain Words (Gowers)	H.M.S.O.	8/6
Modern English Usage (Fowler)	Oxford U.P.	28/-
A Concise Building Encyclopaedia (Corkhill)	Pitman	21/-
Titles and Forms of Address	Black	15/-

General (*continued*)—

The Use of the Metric System in the Construction Industry (PD 6031)	B.S.I.	8/–
Building Drawing Practice (metric units) (B.S. 1192)	,,	7/6
Drawing Office Organization	British Institute of Management	15/-
Handbook of Architectural Practice and Management	R.I.B.A.	£9/5/0
Pre-contract Practice (Aqua Group)	Crosby Lock-wood	20/-
Specification Notes (Aqua Group)	,, ,,	6/–
Contract Administration (Aqua Group)	,, ,,	18/–
Job Book (Aqua Group)	,, ,,	9/6
Building Administration (Warland)	University of London Press	18/-
Building by Local Authorities (Layton)	Allen & Unwin	40/–
Programme and Progress	H.M.S.O.	3/6
Building Research and Information Services	,,	3/6
Preparing to Build (M.P.B.W. Management Handbook 1)	,,	3/6
Building Project Management	N.J.C.C.	1/–
The Critical Path Method Explained B.R.S. Digest No. 53	H.M.S.O.	4d
Communications in the Building Industry: The Report of a Pilot Study	Tavistock Publications	25/–
The Coordinating of Dimensions for Building	R.I.B.A.	35/–
The Industrialisation of Building	,,	15/–

INDEX

Note.—The names of publications are given in italics and those of law cases in capitals. Titles in the Bibliography Appendix are not indexed, unless mentioned on text pages.